Water and the |||||||||||||||||

To M

Happy Birthday

Iain

As a vital human need water has been absolutely critical to decisions as to where cities originate, how much they grow and the standard of living of the inhabitants. The relationship is complex, however; we need both continual availability and protection from its potential impacts: either too much or too little can have devastating consequences.

Yet over recent decades flooding and scarcity episodes have become commonplace in even the most advanced countries. Moreover, future projections of changing climates, burgeoning populations and escalating urbanization has created an intense need for intervention measures that are appropriate to this uncertain context. A gradual recognition of the difficulties in managing these risks has turned the focus towards people and places; key tenets of spatial planning. Indeed, flooding and scarcity events cannot be disassociated from the socio-economic context within which they occur; being directly related to how we live, where we live and how we govern.

Iain White's book initially draws together information on a host of connected subjects from population growth to water scarcity to the relationship between humanity and nature before demonstrating how utilizing notions of risk and resilience could help improve the relationship between the city and its most precious resource. Part of the hugely successful Natural and Built Environment series, this book combines discussions of risk, water and spatial planning to provide an invaluable text for planning, geography and urban studies students in how to address urban water problems within a rapidly changing world.

Iain White is a qualified town planner, a chartered member of the Royal Town Planning Institute and a Lecturer in Spatial Planning at the University of Manchester. His main research interest lies in exploring issues surrounding water and the built environment.

The Natural and Built Environment Series

Editor: Professor John Glasson
Oxford Brookes University

A tarred road, she shoots every drop o' water into a valley same's a slate roof. Tisn't as 'twas in the old days, when the waters soaked in and soaked out in the way o' nature. It rooshes off they tarred roads all of a lump, and naturally every drop is bound to descend into the valley.

(Rudyard Kipling, Friendly Brook, 1914)

Water and the City

Risk, resilience and planning for a sustainable future

Iain White

Routledge
Taylor & Francis Group

LONDON AND NEW YORK

First published 2010
by Routledge
2 Park Square, Milton Park, Abingdon, Oxon, OX14 4RN

Simultaneously published in the USA and Canada
by Routledge
270 Madison Avenue, New York, NY 10016

Routledge is an imprint of the Taylor & Francis Group, an informa business

Typeset in Stone Serif and Akzidenz Grotesk by
Pindar NZ, Auckland, New Zealand
Printed and bound in Great Britain by
TJ International Ltd, Padstow, Cornwall

British Library Cataloguing in Publication Data
A catalogue record for this book is available from the British Library

Library of Congress Cataloging-in-Publication Data
White, Iain.
Water and the city: risk, resilience, and planning for a sustainable future / Iain White.
    p. cm.—(The natural and built environment series)
  Includes bibliographical references and index.
  1. Municipal water supply. 2. Sewerage. I. Title.
  TC405.W5835 2010
711'.8—dc22   2009053694

ISBN13: 978-0-415-55332-2 (hbk)
ISBN13: 978-0-415-55333-9 (pbk)
ISBN13: 978-0-203-84831-9 (ebk)

Contents

· ·

Illustrations

· ·

Figures

Boxes

Table

Preface

· ·

Each and every day there are an estimated 193,107 new urban dwellers (UN-Habitat 2009). This is equivalent to a city larger than the size of Dallas every week, the population of Rio de Janeiro just over every month or a new Russia every two years. Across the globe the city has been overwhelmingly selected as the habitat of choice for humanity and has consequently become the nexus for an array of physical, economic, social, political and cultural capital. One drawback of this concentration of people and resources has been that threats to urban citizens are amplified, and whilst cities are commonly seen as places of safety, incongruously they are also the hub of modern risks. As the populations and value of cities rise, so has the need for urban areas to continuously identify and adapt to potentially detrimental influences. This has proved challenging however; despite living in an age of unparalleled knowledge and expertise we currently have the highest ever exposure and vulnerability to natural hazards.

At the forefront of these risks are concerns over water. As a vital human need water has been absolutely critical to decisions as to where cities originate, how much they grow and the standard of living of the inhabitants. The relationship is complex however, and in developed nations it is easy to forget how vital the effective management of the resource is to humanity's survival. We both need continual availability and protection from its potential impacts: either too much or too little can have devastating consequences. Given this importance you would expect that the relationship between cities and water would be a sophisticated exchange characterized by a desire to simultaneously secure safe fresh water supplies and an urban environment protected from flooding. Yet, over recent decades flooding and scarcity episodes have become commonplace: although the intention may be simple, achieving this aspiration in practice has proven difficult.

Changing climates, burgeoning populations, escalating urbanization and a mounting reliance on the economic value of cities associated with modernity has created an intense need for effective intervention measures. Water has traditionally been managed by a technocentric paradigm, but hard experience has taught even the most advanced nations that flood defences or water supplies may not be reliable; technology can intervene, but nature can occasionally provide catastrophic evidence of its inherent limitations. As the frequency, scale and impacts of natural disasters challenge the hegemony of engineered orthodoxy the debate has increasingly turned to people and places; key tenets of spatial planning. Indeed, these events cannot be disassociated from the socio-economic context within which they occur; being directly related to how we live, where we live and how we govern.

As the need for more effective managerial intervention has become apparent, so has an engagement with related concepts such as risk, vulnerability and resilience. But despite their emerging value within planning, the way that these natural science concepts have been articulated and applied by social scientists has still to reach maturity. The spatial exposure to water risks is becoming well understood, but practices which increase the scope and strength of the hazard or the relative vulnerability of people and communities are not yet influencing decision making. The book as a whole contends that the risk of flooding and water scarcity is partly the result of historical development paths and governance processes, and that our exposure and vulnerability to these threats during the twenty first century will depend upon how we act now and in the near future.

Initially, this study is, in some ways, a work of synthesis; collating and analysing information on a host of connected subjects from population growth to water scarcity to the relationship between humanity and nature, and considering these in relation to the management of water. Later chapters then unpack and discuss notions of risk and resilience before relating these to spatial planning. The final section of the book develops and demonstrates how a risk based conceptual framework can assist in making cities more resilient to water hazards. A core aim is to stimulate debate in some small way by investigating the potential for spatial planning to assist the development of a more resilient city, with particular regard to the ability to manage water more effectively on a city scale. This strategic dimension is critical: without it we cannot progress from a resilient building towards a resilient city.

Acknowledgements

· ·

Thanks to a number of readers and commentators. In no particular order: Professor John Handley; Dr Paul O'Hare; Dr Andy Price; Dr Neil Smith and Lisa White.

A number of images in the book are also generously supplied by a number of people, and thanks must go to: EM-DAT: the OFDA/CRED International Disaster Database, Université Catholique de Louvain, Brussels, Belgium; the Environment Agency; Dr Susannah Gill; David Hodcroft; Nigel Lawson; Tony Price; NASA/Goddard Space Flight Center Scientific Visualization Studio; Michael Timmins and UNEP/GRID-Arendal Maps and Graphics Library. Thanks also to Nick Scarle from the University of Manchester for his help in preparing figures for publication.

Part I

The past, present and future context

···

1 Nature, climate and hazard

··

And on the pedestal these words appear:
'My name is Ozymandias, king of kings:
Look on my works, ye Mighty, and despair!'
(Percy Bysshe Shelley, 'Ozymandias', 1818)

The inspiration for Shelley's 'Ozymandias' is reputed to be the discovery of a colossal bust of Ramesses II by the Italian engineer and explorer Giovanni Belzoni a few years previously. Despite its enormous size, the statue was only a fragment of a larger sculpture created to provide a physical representation of the supreme power of the Pharaoh in the second millennium BC. The subsequent dilapidated condition offered Shelley a differing interpretation however and the overriding message of the poem is hubris, designed to accentuate the transience of civilization when compared to time and the dominance of nature. The symbolism conjured by the sonnet compellingly warns against the arrogance of humanity and emphasizes that although power and knowledge may imbue a sense of greatness, in reality this is illusory: the built environment and human activity are temporal and constrained by external factors, most notably local environmental risks. The poem has wider resonance as historical records indicate that one of the key drivers for the success of settlements is how they adapt to their physical and climatic context. The metaphor is clear: although humanity can survive in extreme environments; to grow and prosper normally requires a more beneficial relationship with the land, water and climate.

The Vikings provide an example of this process in practice. When the Norse initially settled in Greenland around the tenth century, the Earth was experiencing a relative global warm period and evidence shows these communities were subsequently abandoned as the temperature cooled. In addition to climatic changes, the role of water as fundamental to life has also been pivotal. Many ancient civilizations managed water as an overriding priority, the Egyptians for example successfully exploited the resources of the Nile enabling relatively high population densities (Pearce 2006a). In the third century BC the Sinhalese began the tradition of constructing complex irrigation systems greatly boosting the development of Sri Lanka. A subsequent ruler, King Parakramabahu the Great

(1123–86), made his view of the value of water to his country clear with the provident epigram: 'not even a little water that comes from the rain must flow into the ocean without being made useful to man' (Hennayake 2006: 51).

Conversely to societies prospering via informed water management, long lasting multiple episodes of drought have also been identified as one of the causes of both the collapse of Mayan culture in the ninth century and Native American peoples in the twelfth century (Diamond 2005). Conflicts, combined with these examples of the constraints of geography and ecology, continued throughout the second millennium and it is estimated that a total of 42 cities were abandoned between 1100 and 1800 (Vale and Campanella 2005). But the Doomsday scenario of societies suffering a total collapse is only the most extreme possible example of failed strategic planning and management. The relationship between cities and climate is, after all, not a simple deterministic one, where urban areas fail if changes occur. More commonplace, is an insidious gradual impact of environmental constraints, which can be endured, but effectively curtail the ability to confer a better quality of life upon citizens. In a globalized world, cities are competitive and disadvantaged areas will inevitably struggle. Although modern technology, international trade and other advances since the Industrial Revolution has limited the historic tendency for abandonment, it arguably perpetuates inequality and inefficiency by enabling cities to decline, yet continue, albeit at a lower standard of living.

Adapting to urban risk

The nature of the specific threats and the available technology and knowledge may alter the mitigation strategies, but successful settlements have always attempted to adapt to risks by altering urban form and function. In antiquity, invasion by hostile forces was the major threat and settlements became fortified, located in defensible areas and contained their own supplies of water and food to combat sieges. The design of these towns and cities was also surprisingly flexible to changes in risks, such as by the development of the star-shaped city during the Renaissance, which was resistant to the newly invented cannons and bombards. Cities inhabitants have also adopted more active interventionist strategies in response to emerging risks. For example, in 413 BC Archimedes is said to have protected the Greek city of Syracuse by using mirrors to direct sunlight and burn the sails of 200 besieging Roman ships, whilst on a more contemporary note, the Thames Barrier in London or earthquake resistant buildings in Japan, also facilitate the proactive protection of cities, but in a more technologically advanced fashion.

Successful settlements have always had a sophisticated response to quantifiable risks and design has responded in a flexible manner to the variable nature of the threats. Concomitantly, the logical desire to examine urban form and function with a view to simply facilitating a more advantageously designed city also has a well defined history. The consideration of quality of life as a key driver is not just a modern concern: in *Politics* for example, Aristotle discusses the nature of an ideal city with regard to aspects such as its site and construction. More recently in the early twentieth century, Ebenezer Howard adopted a more conventional intervention strategy based on a similar premise of improving the quality of life of residents, but in response to the different risks of health and deprivation. The 1930s and 1940s also instigated a wider view of the potential positive benefits that the proactive planning of society could provide and brought the notion of 'amenity', which aimed to shape planning along the lines of 'beauty, health and convenience' to further improve cities and the quality of life of citizens (Abercrombie 1933). More modern movements, such as New Urbanism or Smart Growth, have also questioned development paradigms and highlighted the need to think more strategically and long term to create successful settlements.

Although contemporary concerns may differ from those of antiquity, history demonstrates that the development of design led solutions and proactive intervention strategies to manage risks and improve standards of living have always had a symbiotic relationship with cities. We need to ask ourselves however why, in an age of unparalleled knowledge and expertise, do we arguably have the highest ever exposure and vulnerability to hazards, especially those of an environmental nature (Munich Re 2008)? In a competitive, globalized world, cities are increasingly being marketed as places: an area to invest in, a commodity to consume or a desirable place to live. Yet, in many areas there has been a lack of strategic thinking concerning the potential long term consequences of patterns in urban development and the consequent exposure of people and places to present and future environmental risks.

The overriding emphasis has been on defence via a technocentric methodology, but this has received criticism as the power and variability of climate challenges design parameters. Whilst protecting areas is a viable approach to enable development and growth to continue, it does embed risk in a city, and raises the new anthropogenic driven threat of infrastructure failure. As absolute protection cannot be guaranteed, managing environmental risks via hard engineering could therefore have a long term detrimental effect on the ability of cities to compete in the modern age and subsequently reduce the quality of life of citizens. So although cities may not be abandoned as in the past, an exposure to extreme natural events may mean it is more difficult to prosper in an interconnected world. It is clear that although altering city design can mitigate risks and improve standards, it can also prove an exacerbating force or inhibit the ability to successfully intervene. Therefore, the nature and development of urban form should be a key consideration in designing sustainable and prosperous cities for the long term.

The development of urban form

Cities have unquestionably become the principal habitat of humanity. This is a surprisingly recent development however. The transition from nomadic hunter gathering to agrarian societies and eventually to modern city living has not been a smooth and gradual ascent; rather, a long evolution over thousands of years before an explosive urban conversion over the last two centuries. Although there are examples of relatively highly developed and advanced cities emerging in the distant past from areas such as Mesopotamia, the Indus Valley, China and Central America, the wide scale establishment of the city took time to be realized. Theories concerning the driving forces for the more extensive development of cities include a wide variety of agents from warfare, astronomy, mathematics, writing and the domestication of animals, to the invention of the plough and the potter's wheel (Mumford 1961; Reader 2005). More contentious hypotheses include the view that water was a central driver and cities were developed as 'hydraulic civilizations', essentially a mechanism devised to create the bureaucratic structures necessary to control people and therefore enable the wide scale exploitation of water resources (Wittfogel 1957). It is clear that the original motivations and inspirations for large ancient urban environments are both contested and extensive, influenced by localized knowledge, needs and a broad array of external factors. However, what is less debatable is that cities are usually very slow to change and historic development decisions can have lasting effects into the far distant future. As Girardet (1999: 13) explained:

> Cities, as structures that are fossilised upon the landscape, tend to exist for a long time. But they should be built with long time scales in mind and the lifestyles of their inhabitants should not be defined by reckless transience.

The composition and structure of towns have been subject to a differing array of influences, but there are broad recurring themes, in particular the pursuit of resources and security, that hold enduring value. In simple terms, from a land use and risk perspective what we now recognize as cities grew organically from a desire to settle in an advantageous area, safe from natural hazards and near vital resources or trade routes. Over time these settlements expanded and haphazard urban extensions were created, providing new inhabitants with access to the resources and various capital of the city. Prior to the large scale exploitation of energy and resources over the last two centuries, urban areas were constrained by the limits of building space, arable land and the water supply. For example, cities in Ancient Greece displayed an unwillingness to encourage excessive growth and would send out colonies around the Mediterranean before they suffered overcrowding (Mumford 1961). Mumford further highlights the dismissive response by Alexander the Great after his chief architect proposed to build him the largest city of all time, with the cutting remark: 'impossible to provision' (1961: 131).

There was a realization during the Hellenic period that the success of cities was tied to the ability to secure resources from its hinterland and beyond, and that any growth should be managed to prevent a parasitical decline. An example of an urban area that did not follow this approach was Ur, a city in ancient Sumer, reputed to be the largest city in the world around 2000 BC (Chandler 1987). The city experienced huge unplanned growth and suffered catastrophic consequences as a result, as amongst other factors huge deforestation and the incremental salination of agricultural land due to expanding irrigation needs, eventually contributed towards the ultimate sentence: its abandonment around 500 BC.

In addition to attaining a sustainable supply of vital energy, food and water resources, an appreciation of the quality of land available for development was also important in creating a safe and secure built environment. Cities worldwide have been increasingly subject to sprawl, partly due to the overwhelming view that urban living is a route to individual prosperity and the ability of cities to command power and resources. Although sprawl is synonymous with unplanned development and the rise in mobility, it has also been pursued as a goal of various countries, especially where there is a large supply of land – the low-density expansion of the US during the twentieth century being a prime example.

The example of Greek society in controlling growth by developing new towns was not typical therefore and the gradual, largely unplanned expansion of cities may have helped to bequest a lasting exposure to natural risks, as the more desirable land has already been utilized. Gloucester, sited on the River Severn in England, provides a simple illustration of this process occurring in practice. Originally a Roman town, the historic core was designed to be elevated, defensible and safe from the frequently flooding River Severn, which has had a recorded history of inundation for around two thousand years (Doe 2006). Recently, significant and damaging flood events in 2000 and 2007 have caused huge damage to the town, and whilst the historic Roman core remains largely safe, it is the urban extensions, some of which are relatively modern, which have been most exposed and vulnerable. Decisions on the use of land can therefore exert an enduring influence on the management of risk.

Tewkesbury, a town in Gloucestershire, England, provides an excellent visual example of this lingering influence in practice. The abbey was built on a slight hill to provide protection against flooding, and, as figure 1.1 demonstrates, during a flood event in 2007 the decisions of the builders almost a thousand years ago look to be very astute.

In addition to a gradual increased exposure to risk associated with the expansion of settlements, an emphasis on technology as a tool to both control nature and manage risks also changes the relationship with the natural world. For example, the design of the old London Bridge made the Thames flow much more slowly than the present day and contributed to the habitual freezing over of the river, which was estimated to have occurred 23 times between 1620 and the last recorded event in 1814. However, changes to land use are not always so passive and can create a legacy of exposure and vulnerability. Hard experience

Figure 1.1

Tewkesbury in Gloucestershire, England, during the 2007 floods
Source: Image courtesy of Getty Images

has taught society that flood defences may fail or that water supplies are subject to the vagaries of the weather; technology can intervene, but risk cannot
be completely designed out of a system and nature can occasionally provide
catastrophic evidence of this limitation. The frequency, scale and impacts of
natural disasters challenges the hegemony of engineered orthodoxy within
planning and management, as the inability to consistently protect society from
flooding and water scarcity events is inextricably linked with development,
urbanization and people. A greater awareness of the uncertainty inherent in
a predominately technocentric approach to water management has heralded
a change in narrative to a more pragmatic, natural discourse more familiar to
our ancestors, where in England for example, the government suggest that we
need to 'make space for water' (Defra 2004).

However, it should be noted that there is considerable inertia in the built
environment, with the lifetime of a typical building estimated to be between
20 to 100 years (Graves and Phillipson 2000). Perhaps more pertinent is the
relative torpor of the built form within a city. For example, although figures are
hard to find on this subject, between 1995 and 1998 in England approximately
8,100 hectares of urban land was changed from one land use type to another,
which only represents a change of around 0.7 per cent over the 3-year period
(ODPM 2002). Land use decisions therefore have the potential to bequeath a

hazardous inheritance far into the future, as the potential of the city to alter its form is limited.

As both cities and climates evolve slowly over time an urban area can alter its relationship with the natural environment and subsequent exposure to risks; a process that can happen very swiftly in response to economic restructuring or driven more slowly by aspects such as short term income generation, property development or job creation. Arguably this incremental, predominately socio-economic process lacks a strategic long term environmental overview, and aided by a gradual reliance on technology as a mechanism to control nature, cities may become disconnected from their natural constraints with risks increasingly managed by a protective and technocentric methodology. Within this paradigm a degree of exposure to water risks are accepted on behalf of the public by a combination of public and private organizations, many of which may have competing concerns, such as housing provision or profit generation for shareholders. Therefore, institutional structures, governance processes and the role of science and technology are all key influences on the effective management of water in society.

Progress and nature

> To believe in progress is to believe that, by using the new powers given to us by growing scientific knowledge, humans can free themselves from the limits that frame the lives of other animals.
>
> (Gray 2003: 4)

It is difficult to imagine a more unnatural artifact than a city. The environment is intensely artificial, utilizing hard composite materials that almost inevitably transmit a feeling of separation from the natural world. Ascertaining where this 'control' of nature originated is difficult if not impossible, as differing cultures have interacted with the natural environment to varying degrees, and humanity has routinely used natural resources to improve standards of living. It should also be noted that humanity has always exerted a control over the environment, as evidenced by the axe, the plough, the draining of swamps, or any number of related instruments. Over the last few hundred years, the sheer weight of population combined with the power provided by technology enabled humans to achieve a greater influence upon nature than ever before (Hulme 2009). Consequently, it is now acknowledged that humans could operate as 'geologic or 'geographic agents' (Glacken 1967).

To a certain extent the notion that the natural world can be 'conquered' is a recurring premise, particularly in Western thought (Glacken 1967). It was the evolution in a number of connected fields, which helped to lay the foundation for this dominance. In particular, advances in science, reason and the related challenge to medieval cosmology into this arena, such as the development of laws governing nature, did provide a clear step change in perception (Pepper 1996). Francis Bacon (1561–1626) is widely held within environmental literature as a key figure in heralding a differing interpretation of the relationship between society and nature, perhaps most succinctly represented by his famous aphorism: 'knowledge is power'. Rene Descartes (1596–1650) provides a further example of this change in philosophy arguing that humans were thinking beings distinctly separated from the natural world, and thus can operate apart from their surroundings.

The burgeoning scientific revolution during this period promoted the primacy of science, the need to collect data, the power of evidence, and its interpretation in an objective detached manner. As knowledge increased cumulatively, science was perceived to be a progressive tool to benefit humanity. Therefore, the foundation of modern technocentric attitudes about the use of science and knowledge can be directly linked to both the Baconian creed and Cartesian dualism. In short, the drive to command and control nature can be strongly connected to the advances of the Enlightenment, and specifically with the ascendancy of science as the dominant ideology. A philosophical trend focused on the primacy of humanity that can be easily seen within any city in the world; nature is subservient within the built environment, given discrete and limited space mainly to provide added utility to citizens.

Even the strategies we use to incorporate the natural environment into our cities provide evidence of a detachment, with intensive management regimes exemplifying a desire to control and inhibiting diversity. Hough (2006) cites the humble and ubiquitous lawn as a pervasive image of the urban tendency to dominate nature, creating a highly regulated symbol of control, which inexorably contributes towards a perception of an unaccommodating dichotomy. The prevailing feeling in many quarters has been that ecology relates to the countryside; wild flora and fauna, or conservation. However, the definition of the term is much more inclusive, as it simply pertains to the relationship between organisms and their surroundings. The city can therefore be described as an ecological artifact, encompassing as it does the connections between humans and their preferred surroundings. Indeed, the origin of the modern term ecology is the Greek *oikos*, meaning 'home', suggesting that instead of nature and the city being viewed as opposites, they should, rather, be perceived as interconnected and co-dependent.

It is almost inevitable that we predominately see the world anthropocentrically however and topics connected with *urban* ecology are relatively recent developments, which have had only a limited effect on the built environment. This is despite the value that cities designed to gracefully accommodate and utilize the natural environment could bring to society. Whiston Spirn (1984: 114) highlights a core conundrum of the gradual separation between nature and cities, arguing that:

> More is known about urban nature today than ever before; over the past two decades, natural scientists have amassed an impressive body of

knowledge about nature in the city. Yet little of this information is applied directly to molding the form of the city – the shape of its buildings and parks, the course of its roads, and the pattern of the whole.

Nature has historically been seen as a factor to be tightly managed, a superficial embellishment or an optional luxury within many cities. This convention is slowly being challenged however and the view that by strategically working with nature we can increase sustainability, provide a better environment and limit environmental risks is gaining currency. Within some built environment professions, most notably architecture, working with nature has a long established tradition, Frank Lloyd Wright for example, pioneered the concept of 'organic architecture' a philosophy that merges nature with buildings to create a sensitive, sympathetic and harmonious design. Similarly Geoffrey Bawa has been the principal proponent of 'tropical modernism', an open plan style, specifically designed to reflect the constraints and opportunities of its warm climatic context. A further example is provided by Paulo Soleri who developed the concept of 'arcology', a term designed to encompass a compact and efficient architectural style with an integral ecological dimension. Therefore, two questions become relevant here: first, that spatial planning could learn from related professions and explore opportunities to more strongly link the built environment with its geography and climate; and second, that it may be merely a question of scale – if buildings can be designed and planned to be sensitive to nature, why not a neighbourhood, or even a city?

A vision of a city

Despite the oft used accusation of planning as being overly reactive and short termist, the design of cities on a strategic scale does have a long, although protracted history within the field. Ebenezer Howard (1902: 127) provides perhaps the prime example, stating within his book, *Garden Cities of To-morrow*, that:

> by so laying out a Garden City that, as it grows, the free gifts of Nature – fresh air, sunlight, breathing room and playing room – shall be still retained in all needed abundance.

Howard was a key pioneer of town and country planning and the turn of the twentieth century was a fertile time for considering the city and its relationship to the countryside in a strategic, long term manner. Within the UK, Patrick Geddes, Patrick Abercrombie, Robert Owen, Titus Salt, George Cadbury, Lord Lever and more planning luminaries all naturally envisaged intervention to be on a large, strategic scale and driven by a concern for standards of living and access to environmental goods. The common thread running through these developments was the pursuance of 'blueprint' or master planning; a type of strategic urban design logically extended from architecture and civil engineering. Generally this involved a vision of the desired form of a city, where, for example, sprawl could be contained, workers housed and access to nature provided. It was essentially a reaction to the problems of the age associated with the rise of urban living, unplanned growth and industrialized society. During the post-war period in the UK, apart from a few notable forays into new towns, this view gradually became increasingly rare however. Indeed, in general the top-down master planning approach was criticized as being unsubtle, essentially failing to see planning as a complex, continuous process operating in an environment with powerful private interests. There was also perceived to be a lack of democracy with participation disregarded and the planner presiding as an 'omniscient ruler' (Hall 2002b: 53).

It is interesting to note that after a long hiatus, where planning has moved away from the comprehensive city building outlook of its past, recently this culture has been revived and strategic city planning has again begun to appear. The main drivers for this resurgence has been a new awareness of emerging and interconnected environmental problems, with drivers such as low carbon, waste or environmental footprints providing an alternative theoretical framework for a modernistic urban form. High profile examples of cities being built to these principles include Dong Tan Ecocity in China and Masdar City in the UAE; however, they are not without criticism. Despite the worth of these illustrations as creative, futuristic visions, their perceived narrow interpretation of sustainability perhaps inevitably fails to tackle the sheer complexity of the city. The real need for successful urban living should not necessarily focus on creating entirely new cities from scratch, but, rather, to consider the needs and threats to the multitudinous *existing* urban areas and pursue adaptive strategies for their contemporary problems. However, it should be noted that the resumption of utopian city building, as also pursued in the aftermath of the Industrial Revolution, does show both a valid reaction to the strength of current concerns and the importance of spatial planning as a mechanism to address impacts by considering strategic and integrated solutions.

The factors that have influenced the nature of urban form and function have been predominately economic in origin, and in developed cities environmental risks have been predominately addressed from a technocratic perspective or underwritten by economic tools, such as the availability of state or private insurance. The potential level of impacts experienced by this approach does open the question of whether strategic city building, as conducted by Howard and his contemporaries, does deserve a fresh re-examination, utilizing principles appropriate to existing cities and their exposure to modern environmental risks. Spatial planning does have a long tradition in city design, but the array of influences means that environmental considerations may not be a key structuring factor. In many cities there has been a disconnection from their natural geographical context and it is easy to forget that essentially cities are an artificial construct thinly superimposed over an active, changing and occasionally unforgiving landscape. Moreover, even newly planned 'sustainable' cities, such as occurring in China or the Middle East, can be criticized for the way they interpret the concept and interact with nature. Concomitant with this view is the perception that natural risk can be effectively managed, and that engineering can remove any environmental constraint. An approach that is rightly being questioned in the face of a rising incidence of exposure to 'natural' risks and disasters, such as flooding and drought, that have affected urbanites in every corner of the world. The frequency and severity of which should also raise similar questions to those experienced by our forefathers and eloquently articulated by an English Romantic poet: do we need to recognize hubris and change our perceptions of nature, and in particular climate, in order to help cities adapt, endure and prosper?

Mastering the weather

The relationship between weather, and in particular rainfall and civilization, has a long and distinguished history. Radar and meteorology pioneer Robert Watson-Watt (1935: 1) provided a useful deconstructed perspective in his book *Through the Weather House, or the Wind, the Rain and Six Hundred Miles Above*, when he suggested that:

> civilization, whatever the dictionaries may say, means getting above the weather . . . the oldest mother of invention was the need for devising ways of doing what we want to do, in spite of the weather.

The need to both exploit beneficial climates and protect against the more severe ravages of nature has inevitably occupied humanity and helped shape our urban forms. The weather is widely renowned as a very British obsession, its discussion a national pastime permeating into daily conversation. Although the sheer changeability of the weather system in this part of the world means that this truism does have a basis in fact, stronger evidence is provided by the findings of a distinguished line of British scholars who have conducted research into subjects associated with rain. Examples include Luke Howard first classifying clouds into their now familiar Latin names in 1803, Charles Macintosh inventing the raincoat in 1823, and Lewis Richardson pioneering the use of mathematical formulae as a tool to forecast weather in 1922, all of which helped to cement the reputation of weather as a matter of great import within British society. The perception of a cultural monopoly is misplaced however. The Greeks were the first to question the processes of the precipitation in a scientific fashion, and although their conclusions were imperfect, and occasionally contradictory, it was hugely significant that they considered the natural world to possess its own physical integrity and formed theories to explain natural phenomena. For example, Anaxagoras argued that rivers are created from precipitation, whilst Aristotle doubted that rain alone could count for all the water in rivers.

However, the first real advance in our understanding of the weather, which moved beyond theory towards scientific data, came in 1687 when Edmund

Halley devised an experiment to measure the amount of water that could evaporate into the atmosphere. He came up with an unexpectedly gigantic figure providing evidence that water vapour could account for river flow and helping to form the basis of our understanding of the hydrological cycle. Further scientific advances were made over the next few centuries, mainly driven by the need to protect society and its efficient functioning from the negative effects of the weather.

Another key development came in 1850 when a serious drought occurred in England, the severity of which caused concern amongst Victorian society that a lack of water could impinge on the huge advantages accrued from the Industrial Revolution. A crucial problem, which no doubt resonates with current climate scientists, was to move beyond the uncertainties of folk lore in ascertaining precisely how often this event had happened in the past in order to provide a basis for understanding how often this would occur in the future. This problem was essentially the genus of the ubiquitous meteorological phrase 'since records began'. As a result of the drought George James Symons decided to measure rainfall and started the process of accumulating national records by putting a very successful advert in *The Times* newspaper advertising for rainfall collectors. Using a standardized rain gauge these like-minded individuals sent him their measurements, which he subsequently published in a monthly report, creating a legacy of the oldest rainfall records in the world and crucial historical evidence of precipitation patterns for modern climate scientists.

It is clear that the driver for advances in this area has usually been scientific curiosity allied with expedience. The impacts of rainfall have always provided a spur for research and knowledge creation, from the need to provide roads that can cope with precipitation, and hence the invention of Tarmacadam, to more modern attempts to artificially seed clouds to produce rainfall. The huge progress made in this area over the last few centuries, and the undoubted success of many technological innovations, has led to a predictable feeling in more developed countries, and one rooted in the Enlightenment, that perhaps during the twentieth century we have 'mastered' the weather – in that we can control both its most severe impacts and, through an advanced collection and distribution network, secure its effective circulation. Arguably, this has also contributed to a gradual disconnection from nature and a sense of indignation and a culture of blame, directed at all those connected with climate and the built environment, when the weather again impinges upon people's lives as it has inevitably done throughout history. We are learning anew that we are not above the effects of the weather and cannot master water. As a result, the cities most exposed to risks may have to alter their behaviour, as water is again a real threat to the success of urban areas – one that many nations thought they had all but eliminated. In short, urbanization and the effects of climate change have helped shatter the myth of hegemony and have consequently revived a research agenda more familiar to our Victorian forefathers – just how do we protect society from the powers of nature?

Unpacking 'natural' disasters

'So how did your grandmother die?'
    'Natural causes.'
    'What?'
    'Floods.'

(Michael Ondaatje, *Running in the Family*, 1983)

A cursory look around a developed city can convey a sense of safety and security from natural hazards. The hard permanence of the built environment provides a feeling of shelter from climatic events and the intensely urban milieu assists in the sensation of a disconnection from the forces of nature. In reality the city is firmly embedded in its geo-climatic context and experiences positive and negative feedbacks, as shown by the Urban Heat Island effect or watercourses utilizing their floodplain and inundating housing. We are increasingly aware of the delicate balance of the natural ecosystem; concepts of environmental limits, sustainability and carbon footprints are permeating into the mainstream, but perhaps incongruously the infrastructures of cities are equally fragile and exposure to risks can result in systemic failure with devastating effects. Indeed, the threats inherent in urban based living are amplified, as cities are the nexus of our physical, economic, social, political and cultural capital.

Despite cities being the hub of modern risks, perhaps counter-intuitively cities are also seen as a place of safety and are the frequent recipients of migrants in the aftermath of rural floods or droughts (Blaikie *et al*. 1994). Urban areas are also subject to unintended, manufactured secondary impacts of natural hazards associated with a lack of institutional and community resilience and a high degree of interconnectivity, which blurs the understanding of the true causes of the disasters and the possible contribution of humanity. When unpacking the debate between what may be termed a natural or man made disaster, and observing the apparent correlation between events and populated areas, it is helpful to consider how a natural event *becomes* a natural disaster; and what key circumstances must be present for this to occur. A review of the definition of the term 'disaster' does aid clarity:

> A situation or event which overwhelms local capacity, necessitating a request to a national or international level for external assistance; an unforeseen and often sudden event that causes great damage, destruction and human suffering.

(Scheuren *et al*. 2008: 2)

The main determinant is evidently the effect on people and places; by this definition even a very extreme hydro-climatic event is not a disaster unless it has significant impacts upon humanity. Regardless of whether a threat is of natural or artificial origin, such as an earthquake or a terrorist incident; a disaster, by definition, must correlate to society. Consequently, wider social, economic and political factors influence the vulnerability and exposure to risks, and, considering the climate change science, perhaps even the strength of the hazard. These aspects may therefore offer potential avenues for intervention, as opposed to a reactive and narrow focus on providing hard infrastructure. Logic dictates therefore that addressing spatial planning issues, such as how and where we live or access to decision making, can proactively decrease or increase the exposure to, and impact of, natural hazards. Figure 1.2 displays the steep rise in incidence of worldwide reported natural disasters from 1900 onwards and contains information pertaining to a wide variety of climatological, geophysical, hydrological and meteorological disasters.

How natural are 'natural' disasters?

An analysis of the information suggests some disquieting conclusions for the success of risk management during the latter half of the twentieth century, with an upward trend mirroring advances in preventative science and technology. The sheer volume of disasters reported within this sober looking graph also has a huge social impact. Between 1990 and 2003 the number of people worldwide who were annually affected by natural disasters rose from 90 to 255 million, with a cumulative total over the period of 3.4 billion. In reality however the impacts cannot be neatly contained by a discussion of the number

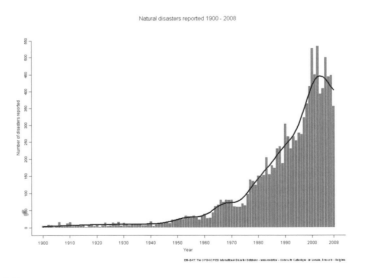

Figure 1.2

Natural disasters reported, 1900–2008
Source: EM-DAT 2008

of people affected; as in addition to more quantifiable data, such as mortality rates or insurance losses, there are less tangible primary and secondary costs encompassing environmental, social and health factors, making the real costs of hazards more pervasive and corporeal.

On a cautionary note the difficulties in obtaining absolutely accurate information on a global scale mean that we should approach data sets such as this with caution (Guha-Sapir *et al.* 2004); nonetheless it is still valid in identifying indicative trends, especially over the recent past when recording and reporting has been more reliable. Although some part of the huge increase in natural disasters over the period may be as a result of better reporting methods, the real growth occurs from the 1980s onwards – a time when effective communication networks were already established. But even if we analyze the dataset with a prudent eye, it is clear that both wider geo-climatic causes and socio-economic drivers could contribute towards greater urban risk. If we identify a natural disaster as operating at the intersection between natural and human environments, we need both an extreme event and a population suffering its effects. Four aspects therefore provide possible answers, either individually or collectively;

1   there is a rise in the severity of natural weather patterns;
2   societies may play a role in amplifying the hazard;
3   people are increasingly exposed to risks from extreme events; and,
4   people are more vulnerable to experiencing the effects.

Taking the former of these propositions, there is clear evidence that our changing climate is contributing towards the incidence of more extreme events; however, we should be cautious when identifying climate change as *the* major factor influencing disaster occurrence (Scheuren *et al.* 2008). In actuality, the main drivers are suggested to be a combination of climate change, rapid urbanization in the developing world and a resultant increased settlement in at-risk areas (Guha-Sapir *et al.* 2004). This also provides evidence that all of the above options are exerting an influence, with some aspects eminently more controllable from a spatial planning perspective than others. Whilst it may be incorrect to say with absolute confidence that we know natural disasters or hazards are increasing from a climatic perspective, we can unequivocally say that humanity is becoming increasingly subject to the constraints of geography and climate via a rise in the volume of people exposed and a way of structuring society that is detached from nature; complex, interconnected and vulnerable.

In response to the rising impacts the concept of 'resilience' has been recently advocated to describe how cities can attempt to 'bounce-back' from disasters, and to the effective embedding of contingency features into planning, governance and response systems. This term has been widely appropriated within urban risk management and the built environment professions, partly due to an acceptance of the inevitability of disasters and a deeper understanding of the ability to wholly prevent them, and partly as a result of its pliable applicability to multiple professions. Although the term does offer promise in moving towards a city less exposed to flooding and water stress, it does need to be considered in direct relation to the evolution and application of risk management in society and particularly how the concept could be useful for spatial planning, these aspects are discussed in more depth in part III.

There is clearly a symbiotic and fluid relationship between cities and natural hazards and, as Pelling (2003: 7) asserts: 'urbanization affects disasters just as profoundly as disasters can affect urbanization'. For a city to be successful it needs to be reactive to socio-economic and environmental threats, and consequently we need to adapt urban areas to respond to changing circumstances. The ability to influence climatic extremes is effectively beyond the control of individual cities, as it inevitably requires the cooperation of a varied number of international agencies and robust political agreements. The exposure to extreme natural events is therefore exacerbated by anthropogenic forcing across a swathe of fields, from spatial planning to the content and application of government policies to the mechanisms to facilitate local and city wide protection. All of which provides a robust argument against any disaster being solely attributable to nature, in reality there may be no such thing as a 'natural' disaster.

Conclusion

On 28 October 1944, Winston Churchill stated during the rebuilding of the House of Commons, that: 'first we shape our structures; thereafter they shape us'. Embedded in this observation is the truism that synergies exist between people and places; not just in the architectural stage, but in the way these buildings influence our behaviour and decision making. This chapter has suggested that many cities evolved in a haphazard fashion; increasingly disconnected from weather and climate, and that urban areas may be experiencing current problems as a result of past decisions. Further, although technology and progress ensure that cities may not be abandoned as in the past, the nature of globalization means that cities experiencing these impacts may struggle to prosper in a competitive world.

Escalating urbanization and an increasing reliance on the economic value of cities associated with modernity has created an intense need for effective protection measures. The gradual disconnection of the city from its environment should also be revisited, as, for example, cities are both the prime generators of greenhouse gas emissions and a main recipient of climate related hazards, whilst urbanization both creates a demand for water and reduces the capacity for infiltration. The need to predict and provide has always been a core of planning and the uncertainty inherent in modern cities lends weight to the argument that these forecasts also need to be more inclusive and anticipatory, resulting in a drive towards more prophylactic spatial planning where preventative policies guard against potentially devastating future impacts.

Although there are differing ways to define a city depending upon its boundaries, population and urban structures, for the sake of clarity and accessibility in this book the term is used as a notional device to encompass all significant settlements. The key message here is not one of semantics, but, rather, the interaction between the built and natural environments, one which is relevant to most urban areas regardless of scale. The book as a whole contends that the current vulnerability to flooding and water scarcity is partly the result of historical development paths and governance processes, and that our exposure and vulnerability to these risks during the twenty-first century will depend upon how we act now and in the near future. A core aim is to stimulate debate in some small way by investigating the potential for spatial planning and land use to assist the development of a more resilient city, with particular regard to ability to manage water more effectively on a strategic scale. It investigates the principles influencing a city more resilient to water hazards and discusses the ability of spatial planning to move towards this goal.

The use of vivid, descriptive terms like a 'resilient city' has a long history within planning and related movements. The power of allegory, such as the 'Garden City' or 'City Beautiful', is frequently used to describe trends; painting a picture of an urban area with both detail and imagination. In many cases its application may be in retrospect, allowing the identification and framing of past movements and a means to understand the developing relationship between people and places. It is clear that we are aware of problems in the past, and also have an insight into the possible scale of the impacts affecting urban areas in the future, but currently these prospective issues may not yet be significantly affecting us enough to alter our present management strategies. We therefore need to have the courage to think long term about the form and function of cities and build in resilience *without* first having to experience an inordinate level of suffering. Whilst long term decision making may not be evident within society in general, fortunately it is a central core of spatial planning and other built environment professions. Girardet's (1999: 7) deconstructed view provides an apposite conclusion to this opening chapter and a link to the following on 'Drivers for change', simply stating with regard to pursuing a sustainable future: 'since we have never been there before, we may as well try our best to arrive there safely'.

2   Drivers for change

· ·

It is profit which draws men into unmanageable aggregations called towns . . . profit which crowds them up when they are there into quarters without gardens or open spaces; profit which will not take the most ordinary precautions against wrapping a whole district in a cloud of sulphurous smoke; which turns beautiful rivers into filthy sewers.

In 1887 William Morris made the above observation in a speech entitled 'How we live and how we might live'. Morris was one of the emerging brand of socialists concerned with the wide ranging effects of a narrow focus on financial objectives. His point is relevant not just by pointing out that a constrictive emphasis on economic issues can bring negative socio-environmental feedbacks, but also that to change practices you first need to be aware of the drivers behind them. The previous chapter contended that past land use decisions, a gradual separation of the built and natural environments and a lack in strategic, long term thinking may result in an increased exposure of urban areas and their populations to natural hazards. Moreover, to be successful in a competitive world, cities need to adapt to changes in risk and reconsider the linkages between their structures and the local geo-climatic context. This chapter brings the debate from the past towards the current and future context by examining the trends and impacts of the main drivers with regard to both urban form and the relationship of its citizens to water: namely population growth, urbanization and the resultant impact on the natural environment and climate.

From *Homo sapiens* to *Homo urbanus*?

For the overwhelmingly vast proportion of human history the population of humanity was estimated to be less than a few millions. Amongst other factors this total was constrained by limited availability of basic resources, poor health and welfare provision, a lack of technological advancement and local environmental constraints – most notably the limited supply of energy sources

(Mumford 1961). The last two hundred years or so has seen an explosion of progress in each of these areas and, as a result, the long standing and steady trend in global population has fundamentally shifted and the world's population has grown at a startling rate. At the start of the twentieth century the amount of people in the world was estimated to be 1.65 billion, this figure has since increased dramatically and in 2005 the Earth's population was a hugely expanded 6.5 billion. This growth is expected to continue and between 2006 and 2050 the total global population is predicted to rise by a further 2.7 billion to around 9.2 billion, an increase equivalent to the entire world's population in 1950 (see figure 2.1).

Within the same period, a review of the growth of cities also provides an insight into the extent of urbanization, the demand on resources and how humanity has chosen to live. In 1900 only 220 million, or 13 per cent, of people lived in cities, whilst in 2007 3.3 billion, more than half of the world's population, inhabit urban areas. This figure is expected to maintain its upward trend during the majority of the twenty-first century and by 2030 it is estimated that the urban population alone will reach 5 billion, or three out of every five people, whilst the level of rural population will decline during this period (United Nations 2007). The average annual growth rate of the world's urban population is estimated to be 1.78 per cent between 2005 and 2030, almost twice the rate of increase of the total population (Tibaijuka 2007).

Significantly, the vast majority of this growth will be centred on more developing nations, amongst other issues placing strain upon local water resources and the potential exposure to hazards. Thus from a global perspective, practically all the predicted growth in population will be contained within what will be rapidly expanding cities. The rise in urban living is equivalent to ten new

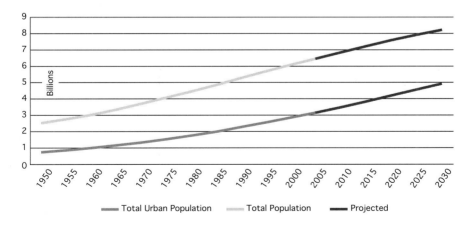

Figure 2.1

Actual and projected world population growth
Source: United Nations 2005

cities the size of London being built every year until the mid-2030s. It should also be noted that the trend isn't necessarily for new cities, but for existing urban areas to be greatly expanded, a development that has led to the birth of the term 'mega city'. An analysis of both the current numbers and estimated projections provides an insight into the increasing intensity of the twenty-first century drivers shaping cities and also their potential escalating effect on related issues such as water supply and flood risk management. The scale of possible impacts has led some observers to highlight the potentially devastating risks of overpopulation on resources and risks, typified by the view of Ehrlich and Ehrlich (1990: 18) that: 'arresting global population growth should be second only in importance to avoiding nuclear war on humanity's agenda'.

The year 2007 has been widely identified as a pivotal point in human history: the time when we predominately became an urban species. Moreover, when considering the high projected rate of growth, one suspects there will be no going back. This development has led some to suggest that we have evolved from *Homo sapiens* into '*Homo urbanus*': a mammal whose natural habitat is the city. However, examination of the population data suggests that although 2007 may appear *numerically* significant it is not a pivotal point, as the real revolution occurred during the eighteenth and nineteenth centuries when humans developed the knowledge to intensively exploit additional energy resources in the form of stored sunlight present in fossils. It was this development more than any other that provided the mechanism for a highly populated future urban world. Further, although the world's urban population may have recently exceeded 50 per cent, within individual countries this figure was surpassed a long time ago. For example, within England, the world's first industrialized nation, according to the 1851 British Census 54 per cent of people lived in urban areas (Best 1979), whilst North America and Europe combined reached the majority urban total of 52 per cent by 1950 (United Nations 2007). In addition, by the year 2000, 75 per cent of Europeans had chosen to live in urban areas, and by 2020 it is anticipated that in seven European countries, over 90 per cent of the population will be urbanites (European Environment Agency 2006). The stimuli for the differing waves of urban to rural shifts from the 1800s onwards are therefore tightly linked to the growth in their respective economies. Many countries in the developed North underwent similar population explosions as now occurring in the global South, but growth in more affluent countries has now become relatively stable, even though cities continue to expand.

Population growth and land use

The nature and location of this increase in urbanity does provide significant cause for concern. Much of the growth will not be concentrated in existing mega cities, but in significantly expanding what are currently small to medium sized urban areas, the vast majority of which will be located in Asia, Africa and South America. Worryingly for issues connected with spatial planning, hazards and water, illegal building is a common feature of rapid expansion (Green 2008) and it is estimated that around 95 per cent of this new development will be 'unplanned' (Gentleman 2007). This raises massive concerns as to the huge, unintentional increase in risks, such as exposure to water based hazards, and sheds some light on the rise in natural disasters highlighted in the previous chapter. The key issue therefore is not that we are suddenly an urban species, as in many countries this has a surprisingly long history, but that we so closely align urban life with progress and prosperity, and that this desirability and the resultant impacts of rapid growth is spreading unerringly to the developing world. However, the occasion of urbanites outweighing rural dwellers does provide a noteworthy footnote in the story of humanity and an opportune moment to reconsider the places where we overwhelmingly desire to live and what these trends may mean to our relationship with the natural environment.

It should be noted that the actual land area occupied by cities is surprisingly small considering that they account for over half of the world's population. The United Nations (2007) utilized satellite imagery to estimate that the total amount of urban area (which also includes greenspace as well as built-up areas) only covers 2.8 per cent of the Earth's land. To put this in perspective, every urbanite on Earth occupies an area less than half the size of Australia. Although there are implications for resource use, with regard to interpreting risk the area of land appropriated for urban use is far less important than considering just how it is used. Consideration of the rise in urban populations and the actual space taken up by cities also reveals a strong trend in suburban urban sprawl. From 2000 to 2030, it is projected that the world urban population will increase by 72 per cent, whilst the actual built-up, developed area will grow by as much as 175 per cent (United Nations 2007). Cities are therefore expanding into their hinterland and developing quickly on what could be valuable non-urban land uses. Land is, after all, a finite resource and within cities how it is used, and its relationship to the surrounding land, is of critical importance both now and for the future. Regardless of the trend for sprawl, we are still living in a relatively dense urban environment and whilst this can be very valuable for sustainability goals, it can also raise issues for the role of nature within the city, the exposure to natural hazards and the effective management of water.

It is clear that we are living in an age of a dominant and rising urban population. The implications of this trend inevitably have consequences for how cities interact with their geographical context, and in particular with water. Drought is a term utilized to describe a long period of low rainfall, and in reality, many cities may not be exposed to this impact. Climate change may influence precipitation patterns and some cities will experience a constriction of supply as a result, but even if the volume of water stays the same rising populations will have to cope with increased demand and water scarcity may affect areas for the first time. Already stressed water resources will be affected by the sheer growth in numbers, whilst the vast increase in urbanization, from housing to retail to transport infrastructure, will reduce the amount of groundwater resources by decreasing infiltration.

The rise in urbanites will also increase the exposure of people to coastal, fluvial or surface water flooding, a process greatly exacerbated by the rise in hard surfaces and the strain on drainage systems associated with urbanization. The nature of city expansion means that these additional people may not just be located in places more vulnerable to water risks, but the potentially unplanned nature of development means that management mechanisms may not be able to intervene. Indeed, it is estimated that the number of people exposed to floods will double from 1 billion in 2004 to 2 billion by 2050 (United Nations University 2004). The impacts will not just be a one way process however, with humanity becoming increasingly vulnerable to water based hazards, the volume of people and the rise in cities will also negatively affect the natural world, which in turn may produce powerful feedbacks on society.

The world is becoming increasingly connected and just as the actions of one nation can impact another, the impact of a global trend, such as population growth and urbanization, can have wide consequences, for example with regard to energy requirements, resource use, food production, deforestation, space for crops and living, etc. Civilization is centred on the consumption of resources and production of wastes, a practice which is exaggerated within more advanced cities. Unfortunately, the rise in urbanization is predicted to be concentrated in less developed countries that understandably want to replicate the consumption-intensive lifestyles enjoyed within affluent cities. This will inevitably create a hugely unsustainable aspirational time bomb, as the largely unplanned growth can only increase the exposure of cities and citizens to natural hazards. Regrettably, within the current development paradigm, the sole mechanism to lift a country out of poverty is to consume energy and resources; or perhaps more directly to produce CO^2. Over the last two centuries the world population has greatly expanded and people all over the world have headed to the city, but what could this mean for the environment as a whole and how we interact with water?

Awareness of the impact of humanity

> Primroses and landscapes, he pointed out, have one grave defect: they are gratuitous. A love of nature keeps no factories busy.
>
> (Aldous Huxley, *Brave New World*, 1932: 29)

Aldous Huxley's celebrated novel of a futuristic society is firmly entrenched in the state of the world at the time, wherein the Great Depression and the post-Fordist culture had exerted a powerful, and some would say, profoundly negative, societal influence. The description of a dystopian society centred on the need to consume to be happy, has, like all accurate social satire, a lasting resonance long after its publication. Currently, the main indicator of our standard of living is based on economic factors, and in particular earning power, with the ability and desire to consume promoted as an aspiration on a universal basis. Consumption is also the main driver underpinning growth, income generation and a whole host of other incremental improvements and has inevitably shaped our cities down appropriately facilitative pathways. Whilst providing goods and services does bring tangible benefits and can raise standards of living it is the way that this view has been adopted and subsequently become hugely dominant that causes concern for cities, their growing populations and the wider environment.

Cities are highly unnatural and inexorably parasitical landscapes. The functioning of life in urban areas is inextricably linked to their ability to command resources and capital from their hinterland, as effectively the input provides the stimulus for growth. The requirement to access significant supplies from a variety of sources inevitably leads to questions as to the wider effects of practices with disquiet regarding the impacts of humanity not just confined to recent changes in our climate. In a forerunner of more modern environmental concerns, two thousand years ago the relatively large reach of the Greek and Roman Empires prompted enlightened citizens to comment on its negative influences. For example, in the fourth century BC Plato discussed some of the problems of deforestation and soil degradation, whilst in the first century AD the Roman historian Pliny the Elder spoke against ore mining due to its impact on the environment. More descriptively, around AD 250 St Cyprian the Bishop of Carthage drew attention to the effects of a large scale exploitation of food and fuel resources by the Roman Empire. This concern for the environment of parts with North Africa provided such a sombre observation that one wonders how he would respond to the state of the world today. His melancholic view was that:

> the world has grown old and does not remain in its former vigour. It bears witness to its own decline. The rainfall and the sun's warmth are both diminishing; the metals are nearly exhausted; the husbandman is failing in his fields. Springs which once gushed forth liberally . . . now barely give a trickle of water.
>
> (Dale and Carter 1955: 114)

As these examples demonstrate, the relationship between population and resource use does have a surprisingly long history, but it was Thomas Malthus (1766–1834), an English economist and demographer, who famously catapulted the issue into much higher prominence by writing: 'An essay on the principle of population'. The article introduced what is now known as the 'Malthusian dilemma' and drew attention to the apparent disparity in human population growth, which increases *geometrically*, e.g. 2–4–8–16, and food resources, which he argued only increase *arithmetically*, e.g. 4–5–6–7. These trends, he suggested, could only be a recipe for disaster, and as population outstrips food supplies, factors such as famine, disease and war will inevitably bring the population back into balance with its resources. Although happily this theory has not been reflected in practice, awareness on the reliance of a continued supply of key resources to enable prosperity was explicitly highlighted and gained pace as the Industrial Revolution emphasized this deep-seated correlation. The desire to change practices at this time therefore was not necessarily to protect the environment, but, rather, to ensure constant supplies. Indeed, the first use of the ostensibly contemporary term 'sustainability' was suggested to be in 1713 by Hans Carl von Carlowitz, who wished to alter German forestry methods in order to guarantee a continual supply of timber for mining (Wilderer 2007).

In addition, in the nineteenth century an unnerving realization that coal, the fuel of the industrial age and basis of much of the new prosperity, might actually be a limited resource led to questions on the need for effective consumption and supply practices within the British parliament. In hindsight, the Industrial Revolution provided a localized case study enabling the tension between social and environmental concerns on one hand, and economic growth on the other, to be identified and considered. Eventually a number of these impacts were at least in part addressed not at source, but via a series of managerial interventions aimed at addressing standards of living connected with poor environmental conditions: one of which was the development of the town and country planning system.

The point at which social concerns made the transition on a significant basis to more recognizably conventional environmental fears is difficult to explicitly identify, and is likely to be the result of a gradual incremental process. However, Rachel Carson's classic 1962 book, *Silent Spring*, has been widely credited as being one of the key factors responsible for launching what could be considered the modern environmental movement. She was a marine biologist whose work led to a US ban on DDT insecticide, successfully arguing that it indiscriminately kills insects and indirectly affects birds and mammals higher on the food chain. The title of the book refers to a powerful passage, where she states that:

> Over increasingly large areas of the United States, spring now comes unheralded by the return of the birds, and the early mornings are strangely silent where once they were filled with the beauty of birdsong.
>
> (Carson 1962: 103)

The latter half of the twentieth century subsequently witnessed some key developments, as concern for the impact of humanity upon the planet, its ecology and our collective future, gradually entered the scientific mainstream. For example, in 1970 the Club of Rome produced a model to examine the future paths of five major trends of global concern: accelerating industrialization, rapid population growth, widespread malnutrition, depletion of non-renewable resources and a deteriorating environment. The analysis contained within the resultant text, *The Limits to Growth*, was criticized as being Malthus revisited as it argued that economic expansion could not continue indefinitely and would start to produce significant negative feedbacks over the medium to long term (Meadows *et al.* 1972). With regard to this view permeating into the political mainstream, a real step forward occurred when the United Nations started to take an interest in how society should plan for the future by establishing the World Commission on Environment and Development (WCED) in 1983. The recommendations of the WCED argued that there was a need for all countries to develop policies to pursue sustainable development in order to help facilitate equity between current and future generations. The report came up with some surprisingly unpolitic and strong conclusions, drawing attention to the global scale of impacts, and amongst other factors advocating the need for a new political consensus and a reorientation of technology, which it described as the key link between humans and nature (WCED 1987).

Arguably a similar case study to the more localized and relatively manageable impacts of the Industrial Revolution is occurring today, the only difference is one of scale; the global size and complex connectivity of which makes its recognition and repair both difficult and reliant upon the cooperation of an enormous array of differing actors and agencies. Political, technological and scientific progress has advanced human power and can provide cumulative enduring benefits, but the belief in 'progress' rooted in the Enlightenment and encompassing a wide variety of social, economic and philosophical aspects has gradually tapered to one overriding aim. We are now in an age of endless expansion, in which ever increasing amounts of material prosperity are seen to be desirable, and growth under the current governance paradigm is evaluated and pursued on a predominately economic basis. But just how substantial and enduring is this progression?

An improved means to an unimproved end

A competitive and global free market economy has been widely identified as a key mechanism to ensure that resources are used efficiently, with an approach aiming to maximize benefits and minimize costs (Harvey and Jowsey 2004). This model however may not adequately incorporate the true cost of development, as many environmental and social impacts are difficult to accurately quantify and therefore may not be included in calculations. It can be argued that these externalities essentially represent a market failure and the planning system is one amongst a number of statutory and regulatory tools to address this distortion. Scientific and technological advances can be cumulative, in that knowledge can be incremental, further developed and the findings can profit society in general, but the ideology of incessant economic growth is increasingly seen to provide both a narrow distribution of benefits and an enormously unequal allocation of costs.

Significantly, these advantages may also not be as sustainable, tangible or enduring as perceived, operating within an arguably unprincipled and flawed interconnected capitalist framework, which was ruthlessly exposed by the global credit crunch. Ironically, the perception of a cumulative snowballing effect may occur, but not in the way promoted in the current growth ideology, as instead the economically dominated development philosophy could eventually result in mounting negative social and environmental feedbacks with cities. The credit crisis brought a realization that economic benefits were not secure as envisaged, which consequently helped crack the veneer of short termism and newly promoted the value of stability and strategic thinking as key aims. A series of quarters of negative growth has shaken the world and challenged approaches, but a significant shift in practice has not taken effect, and the endless economic growth paradigm remains paramount with substantial emergency investment in financial institutions and industry being seen as an overwhelming priority. This ideology has a close link to cities as the main engines of both growth and finance, and has thus helped shape urban form down appropriately facilitative modes.

The view that there is a 'myth' of progress is excellently unpacked by the philosopher John Gray (2009), who argues that there is a secular faith of endless advancement, more akin to a religious sect, that resonates with humankind's most unappealing traits of destruction, transience and conspicuous consumption. Moreover, some observers argue that the goal of continual growth is unsustainable, destructively myopic and can only result in failure, as for example Pearce (2006b: 70) asserts: 'the very suggestion that there can be infinite growth in a finite space with finite resources is an obvious absurdity'. The impacts of the rising level of humanity upon the planet has led to a re-examination of the view first raised by Malthus, and since expanded on by numerous authors, that we need to re-examine the connections between how we live and the impacts on society. The concept of sustainable development has gone some way to merging the anti-growth agenda of the neo-Malthusians with a more pragmatic recognition that growth can be beneficial: in effect attempting to bridge the environmental versus economic impasse. Despite sustainability becoming firmly established in the global mainstream we are however still witnessing a lack of recognition for its core concepts of needs, limits and equity. Almost three hundred years from its first use, and far on from the Brundtland report, societies have never been as unequal, the environment has never been under so much pressure and people have never been exposed to more risks.

The global reach of modern cities has also heightened concerns as to the existence and effect of impacts, and the short term use of resources to aid economic ends. Further, the sheer scale of urban centres as dominant consumers of intensive resources broadens the primary and secondary impacts from the traditional hinterlands to having a worldwide influence. Simply put, urban dwellers tend to produce less and consume more, driving demand for a whole host of resources, but in particular for energy and water. After examining evidence of lifestyles, energy demands, consumption and powerful behavioural trends you could make a strong argument that humankind is set on a negligent course of a gradual unthinking razing of the Earth's resources: an exceptionally short term view jeopardizing long term standards of living. On the face of it, this statement may appear to be an extreme opinion common to hard environmentalists, but it is worth noting that in practice the view has thoroughly permeated into the political and scientific mainstream – it just hasn't necessarily consequently influenced the behaviour of institutions and governments. On reflection, you could argue that this seemingly radical statement actually represents scientific and political consensus; a plethora of documents from powerful agenda set-ting bodies, such as the United Nations or the IPCC, make this case absolutely clear. Challenging the normalization of the global economic and technical hegemony is proving to be difficult however despite a growing awareness that 'humanity's material purpose has become its only purpose' (Satterthwaite 2004: 22), and even more damaging accusations that humanity is in the midst of creating a mass extinction event, similar in scale to historic, more natural catastrophes (Wilson 1993).

The argument that a gradual disconnection from environmental constraints may have caused societies to collapse in the past may become more telling in a future world of 9 billion people. The migration towards vast resource inten-sive urban centres, inevitably concentrates both risk and capital. Furthermore, their hard surfaces and consumption patterns affect the hydrological cycle; increasing exposure to, and vulnerability from, direct and indirect hazards. It is acknowledged however that cities are vital for generating prosperity; therefore Henry David Thoreau's contention in his classic 1854 novel, *Walden*, that all anyone actually needs is a large box in order to protect themselves from the elements does not reflect the pragmatic tone of this book; rather, his related observation that the economic emphasis of modern life may offer an illusion of progress or as he succinctly put it, an 'improved means to an unimproved end'. The contention therefore is not for a hairshirt sacrifice, as cities are vital for improving standards of living; rather, a wider recognition of equity, limits and consequences: both on the environment and on ourselves.

The drivers provide an insight into this view, as the extent of the *current* problems connected with water pale into insignificance when considering the possible intensifying effect of these incredibly powerful future trends. We are becoming increasingly aware of the links between the natural and built environment; yet the nature and operation of cities may result in a growing trend for artificially driven risk with regard to issues such as water resources and flooding. The environmental impact of activities and growth is causing ecological damage to the point where humanity is not only gradually reduc-ing the diversity of the planet but we may also be making it less hospitable as a habitat. Nothing provides a more visible and potent reminder of this issue than consideration of climate change.

A changing climate

Science increases human power – and magnifies the flaws in human nature. It enables us to live longer and have higher living standards than in the past. At the same time it allows us to wreak destruction – on each other and the Earth – on a larger scale than ever before . . . Throughout all history and prehistory, human advance has coincided with ecological devastation.

(Gray 2003: xiii)

In 1972 the crew of Apollo 17 took the first clear image of Earth illuminated by the sun, a picture that was subsequently entitled 'blue marble' due to the glassy appearance of our planet. The photograph has been variously described as being amongst the most important environmental images ever recorded, depicting a beautiful and vulnerable planet visible in its wider context. For the modern day, the same picture taken at night would arguably provide a much more disturbing and consciousness raising picture; moving the debate from an awareness of context to an understanding of implications. Seen from space, intense and highly visible worldwide energy usage transforms the Earth from a dark blue marble to a gleaming, luminous bauble, with huge swathes of continental land masses lit up and individual cities plainly visible from the atmosphere (see figure 2.2). In a similar way to how the blue marble photograph provided a spur to the budding late twentieth-century environmental movement, this contemporary image can provide comparable insights centred on current challenges, how we currently live and what future threats this may bring.

Knowledge enabling the intensive exploitation of fossil fuels has allowed humanity to access a historic cache of solar energy, which has greatly raised the quality of life of the users. It is only recently however that the medium to long term effects on Earth's climatic system, and the resultant feedbacks on our climate, are beginning to be understood. It is tempting to start a discussion on climate change with a dry, empirical overview of the scientific basis for the phenomena. However, as the scale and effect of the impacts become more widely and consistently experienced the need for this technical preface, and the perception that climate change is simply a theory, is receding. From changing plant growing patterns, to species migration, to more extreme weather events, every year personal climatic indicators are visible to the layperson around the globe. Scientists and policy makers now clearly agree that our climate is changing, and crucially that human activities are the cause, but this accord is now also permeating through to the general public as unusual weather patterns and tumbling climate records contribute towards this lay reinforcement and become linked with large scale negative impacts.

Figure 2.2

Europe and North Africa at night
Source: Image courtesy of NASA/Goddard Space Flight Center Scientific Visualization Studio

Climatic impacts

Notwithstanding the argument that data on current and projected climate change is becoming less essential as a mechanism to demonstrate that the Earth is experiencing a period of warming, an overview of the information still provides an important contextual aspect as it gives an insight into drivers, the need to act and some projections with regard to the potential impacts on cities and societies. Whilst natural fluctuations in climatic systems are expected, there is now an unambiguous scientific consensus that human activities, and in particular the burning of fossil fuels and land use change, are influencing the Earth's climate. Perhaps surprisingly the IPCC, the foremost authority in the field, suggest that it is likely that Earth would now be experiencing a natural relative cooling period without the external forcing generated by anthropogenic actions (IPCC 2007a). Despite this trend there is evidence that over the last 100 years the Earth has warmed at a faster rate than at any other time over the last 1,000 years (European Environment Agency 2004) and during this time there has been an average rise in global surface temperatures of around 0.75 °C.

Further, since instrumental records began in 1850, 11 of the 12 warmest years were experienced between 1995 and 2006. It is also predicted that this rate of warming will accelerate over the early part of the twenty-first century and by the 2030s an average temperature rise of 0.2 °C is expected with continental land masses warming more quickly than the sea (IPCC 2007a). Changes beyond this time depend heavily on how we act in the interim. Figure 2.3 shows the variations in the Earth's surface temperature during (a) the past 140 years, and (b) the past 1,000 years. The zero represents the mean temperature between 1961 and 1990.

The IPCC estimate that it is *very likely* (>90 per cent probability) that the cause of this global increase in temperature is anthropogenic produced concentrations of greenhouse gases (GHGs) largely generated since the onset of the industrial age. It has also made worrying projections of an average increase in surface temperature during the twenty-first century of between 1.1 and 6.4 °C relative to the period between 1980 and 1999 (IPCC 2007a). The variation in the figures depends upon factors such as uncertainty between differing

Variations of the Earth's surface temperature for:

(a) the past 140 years

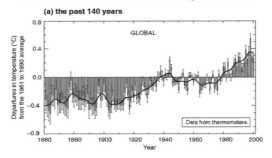

(b) the past 1,000 years

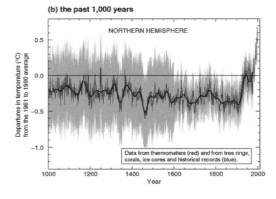

Figure 2.3

Variations in the Earth's surface temperature
Source: IPCC 2001

models, the presence of system feedbacks and the degree of mitigative action taken to reduce GHGs. Given this uncertainty, differing scenarios have been developed to help understand how the global average temperature may change dependent upon how we act in the meantime. But under each future scenario, and in every part of the world, the temperature is set to rise and climates will change, inevitably altering the relationship between water, citizens and the city. Moreover, even in the unlikely event of immediate, synchronized and effective preventative global action being taken, it is predicted that warming will continue until the twenty-third century due to lag and inertia within our climatic system; as essentially the warming we are presently experiencing was generated by historic GHG emissions.

The influence of human activities on climatic systems also extends beyond a simple warming trend. Scientists predict that there is a higher likelihood of extremes in temperature being experienced, such as heat waves, and that we have contributed towards changing wind and precipitation patterns. As a result we have both increased the land areas exposed to drought and the frequency and intensity of heavy rainfall events. Indeed, the United Nations estimate that around 70 per cent of disasters are now climate related – up from around 50 per cent since the 1980s (Tibaijuka 2009). Clearly this rise in uncertainty engendered by a changing climate is significant for our quality of life in the twenty-first century and has key links to designing urban resilience.

It is difficult to ascribe meaning to dry scientific predictions of climatic changes when they are considered in isolation, especially in a world where there may be a marked difference in diurnal temperature without even considering more significant season to season differentials. However, these sober sounding, quantitative figures on rising temperatures hide a series of genuinely terrifying twenty-first-century impacts from widespread desertification and hunger, to the collapse of marine life, to an increase in the incidence of 'natural' disasters (Lynas 2007). Civilization can, of course, live in extreme environments, and has the technological potential to adapt to changes in risk. However the changes in climate will inevitably have significant impacts on the success of urban areas, and in particular the relationship between the natural and built environments. Every city will experience effects from climate change, but we can also identify characteristics of urban areas that will be most vulnerable, and therefore the ones most in need of adaptation measures. Settlements located on coasts and river flood plains are most obviously at risk, but they are joined, for example, by cities whose economies are heavily reliant on the availability of climate-sensitive resources or those in areas of decreasing precipitation. Urban areas prone to experiencing extreme weather events can also expect a higher incidence of occurrence, whilst escalating populations and the resulting urbanization will make many cities newly vulnerable to water stress and flooding, such as caused by intense precipitation events overloading sewerage and drainage systems.

It should also be noted that the impacts of climate change will not be equally distributed, and relatively speaking, there will be both winners and losers, with the latter greatly outweighing the former. A prime example is Bangladesh, with a population of 160 million, making it currently the seventh most populous nation on Earth. It is possible however that an increase in storms, escalating flood events and rising sea levels may mean that this country will not exist in anything remotely like its current form in the lifetime of someone born today. The economist Sir Nicholas Stern (2006) has also argued that the costs of not tackling climate change are far greater than previously thought and water based hazards are at the forefront of these effects.

Although the scope and scale of the impacts may vary according to geographical location and the severity of warming, in general cities can expect to experience some of the following effects that will impact upon their relationship with water (IPCC 2007a):

- hot extremes, heat waves and heavy precipitation events will become more frequent;
- a rise in sea levels during the twenty-first century of approximately 0.2 to 0.6 m;
- natural disasters, such as flooding and storms, to become much more commonplace and severe;
- increased runoff and earlier spring peak discharge in many glacier and snowfed rivers;
- a predominately negative change in ecosystem structure and function; and,
- an increase in water consumption requirements.

In short, not only will the climate affect rainfall patterns, potentially exposing urban areas to a higher risk of flooding and water scarcity, but it will also change how much water we need to both live and create attractive, biodiverse and habitable spaces. Although the impacts of climate change will vary, it is very likely that there will be a net annual cost that will increase over time. For example, the most current report from the IPCC (2007a) states with a high degree of confidence that Northern Europe will be gradually subjected to increased flood risk as precipitation patterns are intensified. These figures provide a compelling argument of the need to understand and move towards a more resilient city; where urban form and function are connected to the natural environment in a manner complementary and appropriate to their geographical context.

Responding to drivers

The agenda for the future city can be understood in terms of both mitigation and adaptation, both of which are challenging remits considering the strength of population and urbanization drivers. A coherent and pragmatic management response to a changing climate would therefore aim to contribute towards reducing emissions of GHGs in order to limit the effects, whilst also planning for a more uncertain future by increasing the resilience of the built environment to any consequent impacts. With regard to water and the city a similar mitigative and adaptive approach can be considered, where society both addresses factors which may drive the strength of hazards, such as urbanization, whilst simultaneously changing to limit the exposure and vulnerability of cities and their inhabitants. This strategy will be unpacked in more depth as the book progresses.

It should be recognized that the capacity to adapt is explicitly inherent within cities due to their dynamic nature as centres for social and economic activity, the existence of networks, and the availability of all types of capital, governance institutions and knowledge. A greater understanding of the current and future threat to these advantages leads to a powerful argument that we need to take proactive steps to adapt our cities, the engines of prosperity, to ensure that the consequences can be either avoided or managed. The onus is on the built environment and related professions to synthesize information, recognize the danger in societal trends and respond to these emerging challenges. The alternative leaves us continuing a relatively short term, reactive outlook, increasingly exposed and subject to preventable hazards. Adapting to the impacts of the rising tide of humanity, related urbanization and climate change will be key to the success of our twenty-first-century cities, as Diamond (2005: 498) argues:

> the world's environmental problems will get resolved, in one way or another, within the lifetimes of the children and young adults alive today. The only question is whether they will be resolved in pleasant ways of our choice, or unpleasant ways not of our choice.

A continuation of these practices that we know, without doubt, damage our biosphere conveys much regarding the evolution of humanity. *Homo sapiens* literally means 'wise human' and was coined to describe the emergence of a more highly developed human, with the ability for abstract reasoning and problem solving. Considering the absence of wisdom in many of our activities, and in particular continuing practices which we know are making our planet increasingly hostile, a more accurate term of the evolution of man would not be '*Homo urbanus*' as previously stated, but perhaps '*Homo oeconomicus*', translated as 'economic man' (Jung and Jung 1993: 86), or even more directly '*Homo myops*', symbolizing the age of myopia. The continual exploitation of fossil fuels without care for our climatic system, which could be excused in the past, is becoming increasingly difficult to justify in its present format. Although this practice has brought significant economic and social advances as the scale of usage increases cities are experiencing serious side effects, whereby both natural and social drivers are combining to drive urban risk. Clearly, we have developed into a civilization where our aspirations of a high standard of living are largely dependent upon an intensive use of energy, and challenging this concept is going to prove a significant task. Cities don't necessarily have to sacrifice growth or standards of living however; a strategic view of the city combined with an increased understanding of risk can help urban areas become more resilient.

Conclusion

The challenges produced by these drivers clearly have implications for the current and future safety of citizens and the success of cities. The need to respond and protect our urban areas from risks suggests that we may require a change to a more long term outlook; considering the impacts of natural hazards to a much higher degree and adapting urban form to be more resilient. Essentially if we want our cities to continue to be the drivers of prosperity we may need to reconfigure the relationship between the built environment and its geo-climatic surroundings. The central epigraph for this chapter is elegantly described in Guiseppi Tomasi's (1896–1957) great Italian novel, *The Leopard*, set in the privileged aristocratic environment of 1860s Sicily. When discussing the imminent decline of the nobility due to the threat from Garibaldi's impending revolution the character Tancredi argues to his high born uncle Don Fabrizio that: 'If we want things to stay as they are, things will have to change.' The implicit message for water and the city is that these drivers will have negative effects, and societies may need to consider radical changes in order to protect the lifestyles that many currently enjoy and others aspire to. So although the book may make a case for a seemingly revolutionary re-examination of the relationship between cities and the water environment, the motives are essentially conservative: the need to protect people and places from risk.

Population growth, urbanization and the way we live will have effects on a global to local scale; from an anthropogenic forcing of the world's climate to an increase in the exposure of areas within cities to natural risks. The intention is not necessarily to argue that cities are not valuable or that people should settle for a lower standard of living; rather, to draw attention to problems on the horizon and respond to emerging threats. It should be recognized that people, cities and nations will always want to improve their quality of life, and that urban areas are widely perceived to be the primary mechanism for achieving this. Therefore, there is a real need to act to influence governance mechanisms and the form and function of cities before they experience rapid expansion and the worst effects of related drivers, as future vulnerability will be a legacy of previous decisions.

The material in this chapter necessarily makes sobering reading. However, examining global trends of the past, present and future provides an important context to decisions concerning the kind of cities we want to build in order to maintain or increase our quality of life. The overriding narrative has been designed to create an argument that we should rethink the management of areas in which we have predominately chosen to live, and adapt to emerging socio-environmental threats. Moreover, whilst the moniker *Homo myops* is deliberately provocative, it should be seen as a warning rather than an inevitability. Humanity possesses an incredible ingenuity and can harness technology and knowledge to adapt cities to twenty-first-century requirements. The first step is realizing the scale of the problem, which in turn provides the inspiration to act. As this chapter has demonstrated, the drive for prosperity has proven to be a double-edged sword, combining an increase in quality of life, but at the expense of the environment and creating the potential for a detrimental impact upon our own security and success in the long term. Self-interest has proven to be a valuable and persuasive motivation in the past, and if the impacts of our current behaviour become strong enough, this natural drive could prove to be highly beneficial in the future by re-examining the relationship between water and the city.

Part II

The problems of
water in the city

3 Too much water in the city

· ·

> For six days and six nights the wind blew, and the deluge and the tempest over-whelmed the land.
>
> (*The Epic of Gilgamesh*)

Any investigation into an excess of water in urban areas first needs to acknowledge that there have always been floods, and writings concerning such events go back thousands of years, from the Noachian events described in the Bible to the great deluge experienced by Deucalion in Greek mythology. Although dramatic flood legends have permeated into a diverse array of cultures worldwide, a more conventional and sober description of events stems from the rise of writings by monastic historians and other diarists who give a surprisingly rich and lucid account. For example, the *Anglo Saxon Chronicle* (Britannia 2007), which provides an important account of British history from the Middle Ages up to 1154, records one of the notable events of 1014 as:

> This year, on the eve of St Michael's day, came the great sea-flood, which spread wide over this land, and ran so far up as it never did before, over-whelming many towns, and an innumerable multitude of people.

It is interesting to read that despite the relative frequent nature of flooding many of these notable events were referred to by their early chroniclers as 'unaccustomed' or 'unnatural' in some manner (Doe 2006), an observation also habitually reflected in more contemporary reviews of disasters. There was equally a common belief that a flood may be caused by the wrath of God, perhaps as a punishment for sinful behaviour, or even as retribution for parishes that were too tolerant of witches (Von Storch and Stehr 2006). These opinions are now broadly recognized as having no scientific credence; surprisingly however similar 'medieval' ideas do still receive support. For example, in the aftermath of the 2007 floods in the UK a number of Church of England bishops suggested that the flood was God's punishment on the country, citing an array of possible crimes ranging from moral decadence, the exploitation of developing nations or even the introduction of pro-gay legislation (Wynne-Jones

2007). Further, a 2005 *ABC NEWS* and *Washington Post* poll after Hurricane Katrina was reported under the seemingly progressive headline of 'Most Say God Not A Factor In Hurricanes'. However, the data revealed that 23 per cent of respondents saw the event as a 'deliberate Act of God'. The range of reasons for the celestial retribution was unclear, but one State Senator suggested that the citizens of this area: 'have always been known for gambling, sin and wickedness. It is the kind of behavior that ultimately brings the judgment of God' (ABC News 2005).

The view that floods are unusual, extreme or even divine inevitably contributes towards the exposure of people and places to inundation by helping to create a feeling of helplessness to the whims of nature or higher powers. Even if proactive, defensive measures are taken to control an excess of water within the built environment, from the simplistic method of raising settlements to the more advanced technique of systematically holding back water, the culture of protection can lead to complacency or the potential for increased damages if the defences are breached.

In developed nations it is easy to forget how vital the effective management of water is to humanity's survival; we both need continual availability and protection from its potentially devastating impacts. In simple terms, the main risk within urban areas from water is centred on regulating a consistent level of supply: either too much or too little can have devastating consequences. The volume of precipitation around a city region may not be static; therefore, the focus is on accessing water then transporting it to households and industry, whilst simultaneously intervening to ensure protection against different climatic events. In practical terms this is much more difficult than it sounds, as the ability to influence the operation of the urban water cycle is subject to a number of key encumbrances; not least the nature of urban form and the way that urban stormwater is managed. The artificial nature of the water management system within cities discussed in this chapter also provides an insight into why the closely related, but superficially antithetical, subjects of flooding and water scarcity, should be considered as inextricably linked. In short, our ability to control climate and the surrounding geography is very limited; the onus is therefore on the role of science and technology and the effectiveness of our governance and management frameworks; chief amongst which are controls over the use of land.

Flooding and land use controls

> Civilization has been a permanent dialogue between human beings and water.
> (Paulo Lugari)

Since the advent of an interventionist approach to prevent flooding, the management of water has historically been placed within the remit of experts, such as the drainage of the English Fens by imported Dutch engineers in the seventeenth century or the scientific modelling and skilled construction of the ultra modern Thames Barrier (Halliday 2004). The approaches conducted by these valued members of society have gradually changed in emphasis however, especially in response to repeated or severe events occurring in areas previously thought to be protected. In particular, during recent years, the reliance on engineered defences has been questioned, as repeated severe flood events, increasing knowledge on the effects of climate change and a deeper understanding of the contributory role of urbanization has helped to expose the limitations of a predominately narrow technocentric approach.

The wider realization of the practical problems in providing an effective defence against floods has recently helped to usher in a new narrative that we should recognize the limits of technocentricity as an absolute method to control water. The emergence of this view has heralded a long term transition from historic self-protection to industrial engineered defence to the need to work with nature in developing more sustainable methods of management (White 2008); a more realistic and rational outlook, cognizant of the uncertainty and constraints inherent in flood risk. This changing stance has been reflected in the pragmatic tenor of recent policy documents titles whereby in the UK for example, the message is that we should 'learn to live with rivers', 'live with the risk' and 'make space for water' (Institution of Civil Engineers 2001; Environment Agency 2005; Defra 2005). A belief also reflected in a number of other countries, such as the related 'room for the river' guidance released in the Netherlands (Ministry of Transport, Public Works and Water Management 2006).

Conversely, just as urban processes can generate an increased exposure to risks, they can equally facilitate a beneficial decrease by an effective analysis of risk leading to a coherent and appropriate land use response. Crucially, the importance of spatial planning in this role is now being widely realized as the limitations of the technical engineering approach designed to control nature has become more apparent. For example, the *Foresight Future Flooding* report in the UK explicitly identified planning as the most sustainable and effective method of intervention over the long term in order to both minimize costs and limit impacts (Evans *et al.* 2004), a view which has now become generally accepted. Not only can planners influence the location of either development or natural spaces, significantly they can also influence the type of development, from retail outlets to critical infrastructure; and other related factors, such as the construction materials used, the stormwater management regime and the relationship with its surrounding environs.

The power of planning therefore goes way beyond a narrow spatial interpretation and encompasses wider influences, such as the function and management of land, and also strongly links to the risk and resilience agendas. This deeper understanding of the potential of planning is beginning to be acknowledged as the rising incidences and impacts of 'natural' disasters bring the complexity of the interactions between the city and the natural world into sharper focus.

The UN-Habitat (2007: 205) division also specifically identifies the need to change the perception of planning as being predominately about facilitating growth and development, highlighting its wider potential to manage risk, stating that:

> Land-use planning is perhaps the most fundamental tool for main-streaming disaster risk reduction into urban development processes.

The effectiveness of land use controls is most easily understood by considering what would be the consequences of either their absence, or more probably, an inability to keep pace with burgeoning growth. Rapid unplanned development has occurred to a greater or lesser degree in a number of the countries most vulnerable to natural hazards worldwide: from the slums of Latin America and the Indian subcontinent to the urban explosion in China. Whilst there are building practices and controls in almost all countries, implementation can be patchy and frequently growth can occur independently with risky construction practices commonplace (Bosher 2008). Therefore, the key to ensuring that planning controls fulfill the potential encompassing remit, as outlined by the United Nations and others, is to design, apply and monitor the mechanisms successfully and combine this with a strategic long term consideration of land use within a city. However, in practice achieving this aim is much more difficult than it may sound.

The evolution of flooding and land use

As the land use planning system is concerned with balancing economic, social and environmental issues, in practice some of the negative effects of runoff should be regulated by controls: either influencing the water and sewerage companies or the built environment professions. For instance, methods such as planning policies, building regulations and advice from wider consultees, such as the relevant environmental protection agency, may all theoretically have the power to mitigate the negative impacts of water on society. However, despite the perceived parallels between land use controls and water quality and quantity controls, the two areas have usually developed independently of each other, presenting significant differences in fields such as management, regulation or administration. Within England, for example, effective and formalized land use mechanisms have existed since the establishment of the planning system in 1947, and over time you would expect that these would have dovetailed with water controls to form a mature, sophisticated and complementary relationship. Yet, inquiries into recent flood events have frequently highlighted poorly structured, or ineffectual, governance systems as a key factor to be improved.

In reality, the seemingly sophisticated land use planning systems as practised within many advanced nations are not necessarily successful in managing current urban flood risks, suggesting that although there is potential, there is scope for significant improvement. Indeed, from the late twentieth century onwards there was an increasing incidence of problems associated with the management of precipitation across most developed parts of the world. Moreover, in the face of both a changing climate and a more urbanized environment, planning systems were rightly accused of being slow to react to and manage potential problems. Perhaps more seriously it was also suggested that neither the power nor the knowledge existed in order to enable planners to provide the expected level of protection. This was partly due to traditional land use controls focusing heavily on spatial factors, such as the restriction of development within a floodplain, and they have only recently attempted to manage land use, runoff and flooding from a catchment wide viewpoint.

The way that the severities of floods are also expressed may also lead to a false sense of security. The notional recurrence interval, where floods are frequently articulated as being a 1 in X-year event, is based on historical data. The utilization of this information would therefore be entirely valid in the case of flooding occurring in a static, unchanging environment. However, the previous chapter provides strong evidence that risk management in cities should be viewed as being very dynamic, and influenced by powerful outside agents such as climatic variations, population growth and urbanization. Whilst information on recurrence intervals can be of use in providing a retrospective indication of the relative strength of an event in comparison to past floods, its veneer of scientific certainty regarding *future* risk should be viewed as illusory. In reality, the urban system is subject to such significant variability that its value in aiding strategic decision making is actually of limited value. Indeed, a recognition of this statistical uncertainty has helped drive the shift from probability based approaches towards risk and resilience, as has happened in many countries in incremental stages since the late 1990s. Yet, there are still policies in operation that may focus on reducing the probability of flooding, which has a different emphasis than the emerging narrative of engaging with risk.

Mirroring the rising knowledge on how to manage flood risk within all those professions connected with water and the city is a deeper understanding of the different sources of flood events. Ascertaining the extent of flood risk necessarily demands an engagement with uncertainty; in practice we essentially use capricious and imperfect knowledge to provide a basis for action in how we use and manage land. For example, in the UK it is estimated that around 15 per cent of all urban land is at risk from coastal, estuarine and fluvial flooding, despite formal land use controls operating since the mid-twentieth century. However, in reality this should be taken as a very low and arguably improbable figure of *genuine* exposure to flood risk.

Box 3.1 The changing nature of flood risk

In practice each new flood event may help provide additional data on the exposure to inundation; information that is periodically reviewed, especially after high profile events. For example, in the aftermath of the autumn 2000 flood events in England up to 2 million properties were officially identified as being at risk of flooding (National Audit Office 2001). However, the wide-scale summer 2007 flood inundated whole areas that were previously deemed to be 'safe' and there was a recognition that to date scientists had concentrated on compiling information on the risk from coastal, estuarine or fluvial sources and there was a gap in knowledge concerning the extent of flooding from elsewhere, in particular from surface water and inadequate drainage (Pitt 2007).

The most current data has again been revised upward to suggest that 5.2 million properties in England, or one in six of the total stock, are now at risk from flooding. With 3.8 million of those newly recognized as being exposed to inundation from the hitherto largely unrecognized source of an excess of surface water in the built environment (Environment Agency 2009a). Therefore, in practice the precise volume of urban land at risk from flooding is both high and uncertain, suggesting that a precautionary approach may be required. Further, this exposure will continue to rise even if all unsafe construction stopped tomorrow, due to a gradual, incremental rise in urbanization elsewhere in the catchment and possible increases in rainfall intensity. Indeed, despite only being newly formally included within calculations of national risk, flooding from surface water is now identified as the main source of flood risk in the UK (Pitt 2007).

This evolution in knowledge is important as within the space of eight years the management of surface water and drainage within cities has emerged from practically nowhere to be recognized as the major, growing threat, making understanding the interaction between climate and the built and natural environments of utmost importance. Part of the reason for this deficiency is that surface water flooding is an extremely difficult source of risk to both diagnose and manage. Indeed, the recent intra-urban flood events exposed gaps in knowledge in many countries; prior to which it may be understandable that no reliable figures were kept on the extent of this risk, partly due to both the complicated governance and management of surface water and emergent nature of the threat. The uncertainty evident in accurately identifying risk and managing impacts strongly argues for a more resilient urban form able to withstand and adapt to natural hydro-climatic variations; identifying the planner as perhaps the key professional in modern water risk management.

As flooding has moved away from being perceived as a natural inundation of the floodplain to an artificially driven and highly unpredictable threat, gaps in management and knowledge have been ruthlessly revealed, providing weight to the argument that cities should adapt to threats and be more risk aware, resilient and sustainable. The difficulties in management have also raised an awareness by the state that it cannot guarantee protection for its citizens, consequently individuals are being given more information to help shift the burden of responsibility. For example, in England some data on flood risk is now freely available online and appears in information given to potential house buyers. Whilst the process of gathering more sophisticated and relevant data is highly recommended to help prioritize and determine decision making, this transformation of understanding within a relatively brief time suggests that it should also be subject to continual review and supported by the implementation of the precautionary principle where our confidence is low or the impacts could be high.

The ability of extreme events to provide a driver to combat institutional and policy inertia should also not be underestimated. History demonstrates that societies may not necessarily be designed to manage threats proactively; in practice it can take an extreme event to create the focused political will to build capacity and implement more effective management strategies. John F. Kennedy famously drew attention to the positive potential inherent within disasters in a 1959 speech in Indianapolis. He cited the example of the Chinese character for 'crisis', which consists of two brush strokes: one meaning danger, the other opportunity, suggesting that each predicament may also offer beneficial possibilities. The advancement of flood risk management provides a good example of this process occurring in practice. Each disaster has also opened a window of opportunity encompassing a spectrum of action from reflection to revolution; improvements which may not be achievable without first experiencing these potentially catastrophic drivers. Yet the extent and consequences of flood risk argue against such a reactive approach; should we only change in direct response to disasters, or should we use scientific knowledge to help predict and adapt? The following section begins the process of substantiating the need for a continued proactive shift in intervention strategies by discussing the scope of flooding before providing an insight into the sources of risk.

The scope of flooding

At this juncture it may be helpful to reflect upon the central theme of this chapter. A useful explanation is provided within Article 2 of the European Union Flood Directive (2007: 3), which simply defines a flood as a 'temporary covering of land by water', but rather more specifically outlines 'flood risk' as being:

> the combination of the probability of a flood event and of the potential adverse consequences for human health, the environment, cultural heritage and economic activity.

The second explanation is important as it links the natural processes referred to in the first definition with the manufactured issues of land use and the city. It also provides an insight into the two factors perceived to be fundamental to the management of risk: probability and consequences, which are discussed in more depth in chapter 5. The understanding also links with the discussion concerning the distinction between a natural or man-made hazard raised in chapter 1, a point central to a deeper understanding of the complex sources and management of urban flood risk.

There is no doubt that cities all over the world are increasingly becoming exposed to flooding from the sea, watercourses or inadequate surface water drainage, making flooding one of the most frequent and widespread natural hazards. Figure 3.1 displays the rising number of worldwide flood events recorded per decade between 1950 and 2000, a trend being experienced on all continents regardless of how advanced they may be. From a global perspective, floods occur surprisingly frequently and hidden within the data in the dry quantitative graph are devastating social and economic consequences. For example, within the month of June 2008 alone there were major floods in the United States, India and China, which affected over 20 million people in total and cost an enormous financial sum to remedy (Rodriguez *et al.* 2009).

Examining the data on the number and impacts of flood events, it would appear that the main difference between more and less developed countries is not necessarily prevention of floods taking place, but, rather, a transformation of losses from predominately being centred on fatalities to instead suffering hugely inflated economic costs. This transition has occurred due to scientific improvements and financial investments in areas such as the efficacy of hard flood defences, emergency response procedures, weather data and early warning systems. The true costs of flood events are very wide reaching, although the scale of the impacts are usually narrowly quantified in either climatic and economic terms, such as it being a 1 in 200-year event or as costing £1 billion of damages. This view can create the equally false impression of impotence in

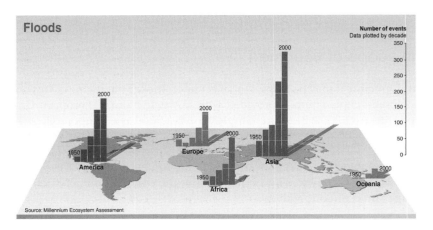

Figure 3.1

Number of flood events by continent and decade since 1950
Source: UNEP/GRID-Arendal 2005

the face of rare, extreme weather events, or can give the resultant impacts a misleading, and sanitizing, financial focus. However, increasing coverage of the victims of flooding and their long term social impacts in coping with the aftermath have latterly provided a much needed humanizing element, better reflecting the realities of the lingering, and occasionally hard to quantify, social and health impacts.

In the same way that floods do not always occur from watercourses or the sea, it should also be noted that flooding may not necessarily be driven solely by rainfall. The term 'precipitation' includes rain, snow, sleet and hail, all of which can contribute to flooding dependent upon locality. Floods can even occur in dry and warm conditions. In Canada for example, a major source of flooding is the spring melt, where warmer conditions can rapidly thaw the heavy winter snow causing intensive runoff and potentially inundating downstream areas. A deeper appreciation of the differing origins, routes and impacts of flood risk is exemplified in the utilization of a source – pathway – receptor model, an approach that has been adopted as a way to better understand certain risks. From a flooding standpoint, the 'source' aspect refers to aspects such as rivers, the sea, or snowmelt, 'receptors' concerns the other end of the spectrum, the people and property receiving the flood water, whilst 'pathway' connects these two facets and may include the flood plain, roads or the overtopping of defences. Although the approach is useful from an engineering perspective, or within other similar areas, such as managing the flow of environmental pollutants, when considered within spatial planning it provides some conceptual clarification but does not greatly assist decision making. The environmental threat is deconstructed, but the approach needs to be supplemented to be effective. The following sections unpack the differing nature of flood events in more depth, outlining the reasons for the varying sources of urban flood risk and providing an insight into their relationship with the city.

Flooding from watercourses

The main source of flood risk is commonly perceived to be that generated by watercourses. Prolonged periods of precipitation, or sharp intensive events, can cause rivers to exceed their bank capacity and utilize their floodplains. It should be noted that the watercourse is acting in accordance with its fundamental principles; it takes occupation of floodplain areas by humanity to transfer a natural flood into a damaging flood. This view was first aptly reflected by the pioneering geographer Gilbert White who stated that: 'floods are an act of God, but flood losses are largely an act of man' (White 1945).

Flooding from this source is known as a 'fluvial' flood event, and from a simplistic perspective may be seen to be wholly avoidable; in the aftermath of flood events it is now commonplace to hear the public and media suggest that planners or residents must be culpable by merely highlighting the definition of the term floodplain. Not all floodplains are created equal however. Although some may be functioning floodplains, others may benefit from excellent protection, while in practice another may not really be in any danger of inundation, being a geographical legacy of historic hydrological processes. A common refrain is to suggest that we should prevent all building on floodplains. However, if we stop developing on floodplains tomorrow, it could have severe consequences for growth and regeneration especially in cities with a limited supply of land and, crucially, may reflect the perceived, not actual, risk. For example, much of London is located on the floodplain, but in addition to the Thames Barrier it is protected by nearly 200 km of walls and embankments. Should we really advocate an immediate stop to all development and regeneration in huge parts of London, even though it is one of the most highly protected areas of the country?

Clearly there needs to be a more sophisticated and targeted response, recognizing the need to balance development with a more scientific understanding of risk. The key therefore is to adopt a selective risk based approach to determine areas where development should be avoided, reduced or managed. As chapter 1 explained, a part of the reason why flood events continue, sometimes regardless of the degree of financial resources designed to prevent them, is the difficulties presented by geo-climatic constraints which can combine with historical development patterns to create a very uncertain legacy of exposure for future generations. This situation is now present in many of the world's most advanced countries. With regard to floodplain occupation for example, in Japan roughly 50 per cent of the population live on floodplains, whilst in the United States approximately 17 per cent of all the urban land is within the 100 year flood zone (Millennium Ecosystem Assessment 2005), but these areas might not necessarily be at risk from inundation.

In addition to issues of natural capacity in response to precipitation, the dominant drainage orthodoxy may also increase the potential for urban flooding of watercourses, especially flash floods, due to the *speed* at which the runoff is conveyed. Though it should be noted that a minority of conventional drainage does incorporate devices to slow down runoff in urban areas, overall the strong emphasis is on moving the water quickly from the urban area to the drainage infrastructure and then into the watercourse. This methodology can cause a number of problems however. A watercourse of limited capacity is required to manage a potentially high volume of water from various parts of the catchment within a relatively short period of time. If the event is of an intense or prolonged nature this may result in the watercourse being overloaded, following its natural processes and utilizing its flood plain. In effect, the watercourse now operates as a drain, a transformation in function that can usually be quickly realized by examining the artificial modifications to many urban watercourses. And like all similar infrastructures, the watercourse has a performance threshold, which can be exceeded. These events are called flash floods and all things being equal are increasingly likely to occur as development and land use patterns distort the natural local hydrological cycle. Figure 3.2 illustrates the impact of urbanization on streamflow levels after a precipitation event, detailing how development can

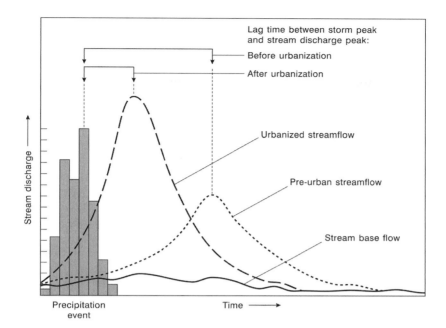

Figure 3.2

Before and after urbanization hydrograph

increase the risk of fluvial flooding by increasing both the volume and speed of runoff directed towards the watercourse.

The emphasis on transporting stormwater at speed not only increases the potential for flash flooding but also reduces the time available to issue effective flood warnings, and the subsequent time available for householders to take preventative measures. Whilst there have been recent advances in this area in many countries, usually due to lessons learned from previous flood events, a continuation of conventional drainage techniques may make significant success in this field more difficult, thus increasing the possibility of economic, environmental and social damage.

Flooding from coasts and estuaries

Inundation from the sea has a long history, particularly in certain vulnerable areas of the world. The Netherlands for instance is famously low lying and records of flood events go back over 1,000 years, with evidence of engineered defences for a similar length of time. Indeed, the Dutch were first recorded as constructing dykes to hold back the sea around AD 1000 and combined these barriers with power generated by windmills to pump water from lower lying areas, thereby freeing land for agriculture and homes. The long tradition of holding back the sea in the face of nature is exemplified by the common Dutch expression of: 'God created the Earth; the Netherlanders created the Netherlands.' A phrase that highlights their historical decision to proactively obtain land despite hydro-geographical constraints, inevitably however this practice has also created a potential exposure that persists to the present day.

Flooding from this source occurs due to the combination of varying contributory drivers, which can all add to increases in water and wave heights, and when these factors merge the consequences can be devastating. The tides are obviously a key aspect, but on their own they can be easily calculated and defended against, it is when they join with more unpredictable wind driven storm surges and drops in barometric pressures that defences can be overtopped. For example, a deep weather depression reduces the pressure on the surface of the sea, which in turn results in a localized rise in sea level. As approximately every 1 mb drop in pressure results in a 1 cm rise in sea level, significant rises can result from more extreme storm events. The shape of a seabed and its relationship with the surrounding coastline can also help cause flooding on coasts and estuaries. In the North Sea for example, surges predominately travel counterclockwise down the east coast of England towards the northern coast of the European mainland, but the sea level gradually gets shallower and narrower, both of which can raise the height of powerful storm surges. One such event occurred in 1953 and although the flood was predicted hours in advance, the lack of flood warning capability and the inability to take preventative measures resulted in the loss of over 2,000 lives on the east coast of England and the northern Netherlands.

Due to advantages such as food supply and trade accrued from settling in this geographical situation many cities are located in coastal areas. It is currently estimated that almost 60 per cent of the world's urban population live in cities that are less than 10 metres above sea level (UN-Habitat 2008), a proximity that can potentially expose the inhabitants to flooding from storm surges. Furthermore, global warming is predicted to generate a rise in sea levels over the forthcoming decades with highly populous and low lying cities such as Mumbai, Dhaka, Alexandria and even New York thought to be particularly vulnerable. Indeed, we have already witnessed a rise in sea level of 17 cm during the twentieth century, with much higher increases expected in the future.

In some parts of the world the lingering effects of the last ice age may also have an impact on exposure to flooding on coasts. As glaciers melt they lighten the weight upon the Earth's surface, which results in a process of isostatic rebound, where the ground gradually rises back towards its equilibrium. However, this may also result in a tectonic tilting action, which lowers the opposite area of land. In the UK for example, the north east of Scotland is still slowly rising since the end of the last ice age some 10,000 years ago, and as a direct consequence the south east of England is sinking slightly. This has resulted in a beneficial offsetting of the relative global sea level rise in this area of Scotland, but has had a detrimental magnifying affect on its opposing area. The area around London for instance is estimated to be sinking at around 1.5 mm per year (Hulme *et al.* 2002), a trend which will amplify the effects of any climate change driven sea level rise. The most typical defence against this source of flooding involved the construction of engineered flood walls, tidal based defences such as the Thames Barrier, or more recently strategies designed to restore wetlands and provide space for safe sea flooding. As with fluvial flood defences, these methods cannot provide protection against all storms, but considering the threat of rising sea levels and the potential for experiencing more extreme climatic events, the consequences for low lying, coastal urban areas could be devastating over the longer term as increasing pressure is placed upon defences.

Box 3.2 The Thames Estuary 2100 Project

The recognition that the drivers discussed in the previous chapter will influence future flood risk along coasts and estuaries is reflected in the Thames Estuary 2100 Project, established in 2002. Uncertainty over the extent of potentially devastating climatic threats such as sea level rise, the height and frequency of storm surges and fluvial flooding have intensified the need for a precautionary approach in this vital region. For example, the projected scale of surge tide increases for an extreme event range from between 0.94 m to 2.7 m by 2100, challenging confidence in both current infrastructure and management strategies. This plan should also be considered in the context of ageing defences and a rapidly expanding urban area with significant numbers of people and assets currently at risk, including around 1.25 million residents and property worth £200 billion (EA 2009c). All of which combine to create an interesting contemporary case study.

As the name of the project suggests, the plan is particularly worthy of note due to its exceptionally long time horizon, spanning until the end of the twenty-first century. One which is aiming to proactively adapt, rather than: 'waiting for the next flood catastrophe to provoke society to action' (EA 2009c: 1). Indeed, advocating proposals over three differing periods: 2010 to 2034, 2035 to 2069 and 2070 to 2100 is an ambitious strategy at odds with the short termist view of many recent approaches to water management. The proposals also encompass a mixture of traditional flood defence techniques, such as improving the existing barriers, with a longer aim to adapt to risks and use land more sustainably by, for example, creating new intertidal habitats and reshaping riverside environments.

The project emphasizes that modern flood risk management approaches, especially when concerned with cities and their hinterlands, have to engage with the wider context of changing climatic *and* socio-economic conditions that are driving the risk. Furthermore, as the level of uncertainty over both the precise scale of the threat and the ability to adequately defend people and places is increasingly understood, the use of land is seen as a vital instrument when managing flood risk over the long term. The scheme is also valuable in highlighting the benefits of both structural and non-structural defence methods; in reality, any argument simply posited of a choice between the two approaches is a false dichotomy – hard walls can be complemented by more natural techniques, such as the restoration of floodplains.

Flooding from surface water and drains

> The city makes its own system of weather.
>
> (Henry James, *London*, 1888)

The influence of the city upon the hydrological cycle transforms the natural process into one heavily affected by the use of land. The way that we have elected to drain our urban landscapes has created an urban water cycle, whose fast management of runoff has helped surface water flooding to become an almost entirely manufactured source of flood risk. Since the spread of urbanization associated with widespread industrialization, advanced urban societies have drained their cities using essentially the same approach. Standing water has been perceived as a hazard and therefore the runoff has been moved quickly, safely and economically into sewers and then into the nearest watercourse. Traditionally, the drainage ideology within industrialized cities has utilized hard engineering solutions, such as underground pipe systems, to transport runoff away from the surface of cities, with the focus on conveying water rapidly away from settlements to prevent localized flooding. Nations have invested significant financial resources on improving this aspect of their infrastructure and it has unarguably brought huge benefits to cities. In particular, it has facilitated the development of crowded urban landscape capable of supporting huge numbers of people and generating enormous economic benefits. In practice, the sector usually enjoys considerable autonomy, yet this drainage orthodoxy, rooted in civil engineering and underpinned by regulations and legislation, creates or exacerbates a number of wider undesirable impacts.

This approach raises the possibility of flooding from two closely related sources. First, *surface water* inundation may occur from an intensive period of precipitation or rapid snowmelt generating overland flow that can pond in depressions. This source is very closely connected to relative elevation, localized precipitation patterns, urbanization and underlying soil. There is a clear relationship with the landscape and permeability of a catchment and flooding can arise prior to the water having the opportunity to enter a drain. Essentially, the hard surfaces of a city perform as a multiplicity of artificial water pathways, operating in a complex and seemingly chaotic manner. The urban streets can therefore be considered as a part of the drainage infrastructure, and like any system can fail under high pressure. Second, *pluvial* flooding can occur if the volume of water entering a sewer exceeds the design capacity. In the same way as flood defences are constructed to manage a specific severity of precipitation event, sewer design recognizes that all sewers cannot manage every precipitation event, due to the massive investment in infrastructure that would necessitate. Therefore, sewer flooding is perceived to be a cost–benefit trade-off; a decision largely made by the profit and liability sensitive utility company and guided by regulations. Consequently, the size, and therefore cost, of sewers is determined by the relative volume of flow they would be expected to manage;

and under extreme demands might not be able to cope.

As the drainage infrastructure is a highly interconnected network, an addition of new housing and its associated urbanization can lead to increased demands on 'downstream' areas, with infrastructure expected to cope with a volume of water perhaps not envisaged during their initial design. 'Urban creep' or the gradual, incremental urbanization of a city has historically not been tackled by either flood management processes or planning systems, yet it is now widely realized that the cumulative impact can increase the risk of surface water flooding both in the immediate area and elsewhere. This new development can consist of the expansion or densification of urban areas, or even by the relatively small accumulation of minor land use decisions. For example, the paving over of gardens with hard surfaces can increase runoff and place strain on drains; research by the Royal Horticultural Society (2006) revealed that in parts of London over 75 per cent of front gardens had been paved over, the majority to provide parking spaces. Essentially these land use changes have operated outside of conventional planning controls, but can both exacerbate flood risk and inhibit groundwater recharge.

As outlined in box 3.1, the shift in the main sources of flood risk away from river and coasts towards surface water has highlighted a number of gaps in knowledge and management. Discussions to address this issue have recently taken place in a number of countries as both the growing risks of surface water and the unsuitability of engineered methods to manage this risk are becoming increasingly realized. For example in a move to better understand and manage this source of flooding in England and Wales, the EA have developed a strategy to map the areas exposed to surface water inundation (Defra 2009a). Obtaining robust data is difficult in this field however as it does not just cover the relative elevation of land, but includes flows around buildings, streets and other urban obstacles. The level of detail is also important, as, in practice, it may even be that the height of roadside kerbs or walls could greatly skew actual water flows. Although currently the information is not yet robust enough to influence planning decisions, it is an important step in improving the empirical basis of using risk to influence land use decisions within the city.

Box 3.3 Localized surface water flooding

The town of Heywood in Greater Manchester, UK, provides an example of the problem of surface water flooding due to urban creep occurring in practice. With no real history of flooding, residents were shocked to experience flood events in 2004 and 2006 after short and intensive summer storms. In addition to some institutional failures, the inadequate capacity of the drainage system was identified as a key causal factor, as a process of densification over many years had contributed to a rising demand on the infrastructure, which is now recognized as newly exposed to being exceeded during intensive storm events (Douglas *et al.* 2010). Figure 3.3 maps the level and location of urban infill occurring between 1968 (black) and 2007 (grey) in the town, and helps explain why urban flood risk may not have any connection with

Figure 3.3

Urban infill between 1968 and 2007 in Heywood, Greater Manchester, UK

either watercourses or the sea. We should recognize however that there is a pressing need for new development and successful cities will not only be protected from flooding, but should be able to grow and regenerate; flood risk management is not just about the restriction of either new buildings or urbanization.

Surprisingly, during an investigation into the cause and effect of these flood events there was also an acknowledgement by the water and sewerage company that their knowledge as to the exact location and capacity of the below ground network was incomplete. This was partly due to the sheer age of the underground infrastructure and the inadequate transfer of records when the company was privatized from public ownership in 1995 (Douglas *et al.* 2010). In reality therefore underneath the city there may lie a complex system of formal and informal drainage of which the relevant operator may have an incomplete understanding. The vast proportion of the twentieth century has been spent on either constructing hydraulically efficient drains or adapting the form of urban waterways to perform as a vehicle for quickly disposing of surface water. In practice, urban streams have functioned in a variety of roles from initial suppliers of water to the transportation of sewage to being covered and performing as stormwater drains. Therefore, in addition to largely accurate records of newer infrastructure, old culverted watercourses, ageing combined sewers and forgotten underground hidden rivers may cloud our understanding of the system; making the path of water from initial drain to final outfall an uncertain process. In short, we may know where the water enters and exits the drains, but the information may not be absolute as to either where it goes in-between or the overall capacity of each section of the network. Although we may be able to ascertain where problems occur due to reports of sewer flooding, finding out exactly why and remedying the issue can be more problematic.

To provide an example of the scope and extent of the concealed hidden water network operating in context of a city, figure 3.4 details research in Greater Manchester which used historical Ordnance Survey and drainage maps to detail the location of previously culverted watercourses. It was discovered that the precise location of most of these 'lost rivers' were unknown to both local planners and the water and sewerage company, despite potentially inadvertently functioning as part of the drainage network. This data provides an insight into why flooding hotspots may occur in certain parts of the city and assists in

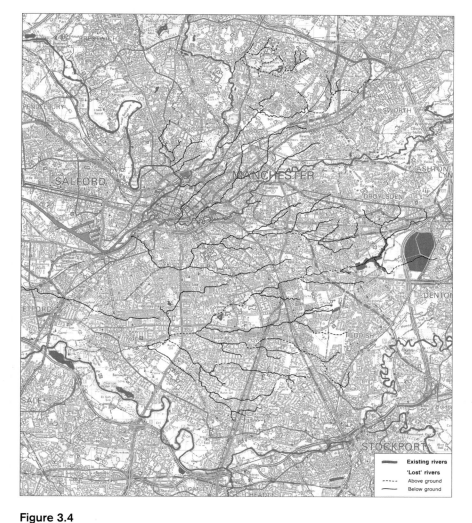

Figure 3.4

Existing and hidden watercourses in Manchester
Source: Adapted by Lawson and Scarle, University of Manchester, from Ashworth 1987

compiling a more accurate record of the below ground hidden rivers that could still exert an influence in draining, and flooding, our cities.

Flooding from groundwater

Perhaps surprisingly in an era of increased water abstraction and frequent water scarcity issues, high groundwater levels can also provide a source of flood risk. In the majority of countries below-ground water levels tend to fluctuate seasonally, with higher levels being experienced in winter and lower levels in summer. The risk of flooding from groundwater sources can be due to a variety of causes, but are mainly associated with prolonged rainfall over an extended period of time, which gradually saturates the ground until the water may rise close to, or above, the surface. Mirroring the spatial nature of other sources of flood risk this is not a problem in all locations, but its natural occurrence is normally related to the presence of specific hydro-geological characteristics, such as chalk aquifers in England, or other areas that naturally have significant seasonal fluctuations. As with surface water, groundwater flooding can also be manufactured by society, for example, in regions with a history of declining heavy industrial water extraction, such as within old mining areas. Groundwater can therefore 'rebound' due to changes in regional employment away from an industrial emphasis towards a more modern service sector, with below-ground water levels effectively rising due to less overall abstraction. A further cause may be associated with land theoretically protected by nearby elevated banked flood defences. In these areas, groundwater flooding can occur due to high water levels in watercourses, even if no defences are overtopped, as water flowing through and under ground can cause inundation, especially in basements.

Protection against this source of flooding is understandably difficult to achieve. Not only are there poor records in comparison to flooding from rivers or the sea, but engineering solutions are also limited due to their being little practical way of adequately containing or channelling the water. The event can also take some time to subside and may last longer than flooding from other sources. It can however be predicted due to the slow pervasive nature of groundwater recharge and the ability to monitor aquifers within catchments. As warnings can be disseminated in advance of a groundwater flood the losses tend to be predominately socio-economic in emphasis. An important aspect of any solution is the initial need to map areas at risk and some countries are at various stages of this process, for example the European Union Flood Directive makes mapping this data a requirement for all Member States (European Union 2007). Although short term defence may be difficult, longer term strategies are available. For instance, a logical proactive solution for the water aware city region may be to sustainably manage the problem by focusing groundwater abstraction where possible on areas at risk from groundwater flooding in order to improve the relationship between the natural and built environments.

Unpacking spatial vulnerability

Although advances in modelling, improved data collection techniques and more innovative spatial planning can go some way to perpetuating the general success of the interventionist, technical engineering approach utilized during the twentieth century, knowledge concerning the future uncertainty of urban risk suggests that a more precautionary approach to land use should be considered. As the United Nations (UN-Habitat 2007: 165) point out:

> The concentration of infrastructure and buildings in cities, including their spatial layout, is a key source of vulnerability in the face of disasters. However, with adequate planning and design, capacity for regulation, and commitment to compliance or enforcement, potential risks in the built environment of cities may be reduced.

In practice however achieving this aim is problematic. An investigation into the differing sources of flood risk has shown that, climatic considerations aside, the threat of inundation is predominately a spatial one and surprisingly manufactured. Nowhere is this better exemplified than when considering embedded vulnerability within exposed areas. The harsh experience of flooding has contributed to a growing understanding of the intricacies of flood risk, which goes beyond a geographical or numerical view of exposure within the built environment. The relative importance and functions of buildings protected behind defences is now starting to be considered. There is now a growing awareness of the level of vulnerability, particularly connected with critical infrastructure and emergency response capacity, which has been absent in previous land use decisions. A striking example of how this can create a problem in practice occurred during the January 2005 floods in Carlisle, UK. The city was protected from fluvial risk by a series of hard engineered defences, which were breached under pressure from an intense precipitation event, whilst surface water drains were similarly unable to cope with the deluge. As a result 3 people were killed and 1,844 properties flooded. As figure 3.5 shows, these properties included a fire station and police station, greatly impeding the capacity for effective operational response, and highlighting how we could consider reconfiguring the urban form to be more resilient in times of crisis.

The summer 2007 floods in the UK also uncovered a potentially far more significant vulnerability of critical infrastructure. During the event, a number of electricity substations and water supplies failed, as did parts of the telecommunications network, causing social upheaval and exposing holes in emergency planning strategies. Moreover, in the aftermath of the event a confidential UK government study leaked to the BBC revealed that hundreds of these critical sites supplying water, sanitation, heat and power services to millions of people are at risk from flooding (Shukman 2008). These historic decisions run the risk of amplifying the impacts of any flood event from a narrow geographical focus into a manufactured disaster affecting much larger swathes of society.

Figure 3.5

Carlisle fire and police station both unfortunately inundated during the 2005 floods
Source: Supplied by FreeFoto.com

Consequently, spatial decisions as to the location and type of development can create long term embedded risks on much greater scales than may be initially realized and can bring a series of unforeseen secondary impacts.

It is clear that the decision to place critical buildings in an area at risk from flooding, but protected behind defences, can create huge problems if breaches or overtopping occurs. Moreover, it may also generate a cyclical legacy between a suffering of ill effects, the construction of remedial defences and the possible exposure of critical infrastructure to even more extreme events in the future. Perhaps it may be more sustainable to reconsider exactly what we value as critical infrastructure and take a precautionary long term approach to its location. Similarly, the relative vulnerability of people is also now becoming acknowledged as an issue, as it is recognized that the young, elderly and infirm may be considerably less able to take action to escape from flood events. Therefore, flood risk management and land use decisions should reflect the modern notion of spatial planning as being about a deeper and more complete understanding of both people and places.

Wider flooding impacts

In some parts of the world flooding is seen as a welcome event that greatly benefits people and local habitats. The annual Nile flood for example has been widely celebrated in Egypt since ancient times and has played a key role in fertilizing the surrounding land. Most ecological systems however are not adapted to profit from, or even weather, the occasional urban flood and as a result can suffer devastating consequences, particularly by the pollutants contained in the water. Utilizing watercourses as mechanisms to drain the city may also bring ecological problems even if no flooding occurs. For example, a combined sewer is designed to transport both sewage and stormwater, and, during periods of heavy loading, it may discharge the polluted contents via an emergency overflow straight into a watercourse. Whilst this does lessen the risk of flooding within homes it can cause serious contamination within rivers. A recent high profile example of this type of incident happened following short intense storms in London during July 2009. Although no one was flooded, almost a million tonnes of untreated sewage was discharged to the River Thames (Kilvington 2009), a process that inevitably kills fish and damages the water environment, highlighting the wider impacts of the limited perception of the role of stormwater management.

A drainage system that separates sewage and surface water can also create problems; in particular that of diffuse pollution within watercourses. This is becoming a more significant and difficult to manage concern as pollution emitting from the end of pipes is becoming better regulated and monitored. The effect occurs within separate sewage systems due to runoff washing and carrying contamination off the urban environment, such as oil from roads, and transporting it untreated straight into a watercourse. In addition to the obvious impact on the aquatic environment, diffuse pollution can also result in higher water treatment costs, and therefore water bills for consumers. Furthermore, using the natural channel to transport runoff inevitably brings a lack of consistency with regard to the flow height and strength, with watercourses performing like a drain and reacting quickly to rainfall. As a result, watercourses may run very high and fast when removing storm runoff, or in periods of relative drought very low and slow; either of which can bring significant detrimental impacts for flora and fauna.

In addition to the environmental impacts, flooding episodes can also have a serious lasting impact on the health of the householders. The amount of research examining the health effects has grown in recent years and the consequences of flooding include premature death, various clinical problems, drug and alcohol increase and treatment for depression. The consequences of floods include both physical and mental problems from both the immediate event and its lingering aftermath due to the necessity of dealing with agencies such as insurance companies, loss assessors, builders and repairers. The true cost of flooding therefore goes beyond the purely economic and can include factors such as loss of confidence in authorities or a higher burden on long term support services, such as counselling for anxiety and stress.

Conclusion

> Water is a very good servant, but it is a cruel master.
> (C.G.D. Roberts, *Adrift in America*, 1891)

Flooding is a worldwide natural event that only becomes a disaster with an interaction between either people or the built environment. The spatial nature of the sources, pathways and receptors of flood risk points toward the possibility of an integrated spatial and managerial solution. The rising amount of both flood events and socio-economic impacts suggests that the prevailing methods of dealing with an excess of water in the city may not be as appropriate within a twenty-first-century context. This outlook has gained in currency in the reflective aftermath of recent flood events, leading to the sought after transition from flood defence to the broader concept of flood risk management. To combat the increasing incidences of flooding there have also been improvements in the way that advanced societies aim to manage these events, such as a greater conceptual clarity regarding the differing sources, pathways and receptors of flood water or attempting to devolve responsibility for exposure to flood risk from the state to the individual. However, this is a transition still gaining in maturity as the sheer complexity of urban flood risk becomes more fully comprehended.

An investigation into the differing variety of flood risk provides a degree of illumination. The main overriding theme is that a surprising amount of the problems connected with too much water in the city are clearly self-inflicted. An initial deficiency relates to a lack of knowledge concerning the extent of both natural and manufactured flood risk, evidenced by recent urban flood events inundating many areas that were previously perceived to be safe. Additional problems are provided by previous spatial decisions, such as building on functional floodplains and locating critical infrastructure, emergency response agencies and vulnerable people in higher risk areas. Governance and management issues have also been highlighted. In particular, that of flash floods being artificially generated by urban runoff and sewers having a limited capacity.

Flooding from these human-made sources has also exposed a limited ability to adapt to changing circumstances. Considered as a whole, you could even raise a strong argument that the conventional surface water management techniques aren't fit for their modern purpose; being narrowly focused on rapid conveyance almost regardless of the wider social, economic and environmental impacts. Additionally, the historically based methodology for calculating flood recurrence intervals is itself inappropriate as a decision making tool for urban environments subject to such dynamic pressures. It is important to note that the actors and agencies may not necessarily be at fault, they are operating a long established methodology within an agreed legislative and regulatory framework; the focus may therefore be in challenging and changing the calculation of risks and the broader management of water in the city to achieve multiple benefits.

As this and the previous two chapters have argued, it is clear that the built form and the gradual nature of risk exposure have constrained effective and sustainable responses. A more appropriate long term strategy may be to consider a fundamental change in the relationship between the city and its surroundings. A common analogy to portray this situation is the well-known story most widely described as Boiling Frog Syndrome. If a frog is placed into rapidly boiling liquid it tries to escape, but if it is placed in a cold pan and the water is slowly heated it does not notice the imperceptible change in temperature and risk and is eventually killed. Slightly disappointingly for those searching for an appropriate metaphor to highlight the slow and arguably unsatisfactory reaction of humanity to pervasive gradual threats such as climate change or urban flood risk, the scientific verdict is that in practice the amphibian does perceive the danger and jump out of the pan, regardless of the speed of temperature variation. The debunking of this popular environmental anecdote should not be seen as signalling its final demise however. The key to the story is not necessarily connected with the poor responses of amphibians to changing thermal conditions; rather, in their ability to recognize risk and enact change concerning their constraining environment.

Similarly, as a more realistic view of the practical constraints in effectively managing flood risk is permeating through into political and managerial thinking, a more critical analysis of the nature of urban form and its relationship with the surrounding environment should be considered. The scope and extent of worldwide urban flood events underlines that they can be both difficult to predict and prevent, regardless of the level of development of a nation, and, as a result, the perception that we can control nature is being increasingly challenged. Indeed, if scientific advances have revealed one key message it is that future flood risks are much more uncertain than previously thought and cities are becoming progressively exposed to natural threats as a result of very powerful external and internal drivers. The unclear nature of true flood risk, as powerfully demonstrated by the largely unpredicted and extensive intra-urban flooding of recent years, provides a compelling argument for an engagement by all those connected with the natural and built environments with the adaptation agenda and in particular promoting resilience within cities. This involves utilizing the precautionary principle to manage scientific uncertainty to ensure that where possible the location, design and function of future development does not increase future hazard, exposure and vulnerability. Consequently, the pursuance of more sustainable and competitive cities would be analogous with a society adapted and resilient to water hazards; this includes addressing problems of too much water, and, as the next section will argue, too little.

4   Too little water in the city

Water, water, everywhere, nor any drop to drink.
(Samuel Taylor Coleridge, 'The Rime of the Ancient Mariner', 1798)

It is worth reminding ourselves that all the water that ever has been, or ever will be, is currently on the planet. It is a closed system, which simply cycles water between solid, liquid and gaseous states. The amount of water resources that are available for drinking is only a fraction of this total however. Some 97.5 per cent is saltwater and of the remaining freshwater, two thirds is frozen in the ice caps with most of the rest difficult to access below ground. Considering that we are perceived to inhabit a watery blue planet, fresh drinking water is actually only a minuscule fraction of the total water supplies. Therefore, the effective distribution and management of this resource by society for a myriad of purposes, including drinking, agriculture, economic development and maintaining healthy ecosystems, should be of critical consideration. Yet, human catastrophes associated with a lack of water have been commonplace, despite having enough freshwater supplies on a global scale to provide for everyone. As many settlements may be located far away from vital water resources the solution therefore is largely spatial and managerial; with the problem connected with collection, storage, effective distribution and appropriate usage.

There are key differences in the scope and impacts of water scarcity that make the problem of too little water in the city quite divergent to that of flood risk. Like flooding, drought can affect almost every city in the world; the problem is however a relative one. Droughts affecting advanced industrial nations tend to mean a temporary restriction in use, whilst elsewhere the consequences may result in a complete cessation of supply. The consequences can therefore vary from a minor socio-economic impact to widespread and prolonged loss of life. However, cities from all over the world have become insulated from the most serious impacts of water scarcity, and in practice it is generally subsistence agricultural communities that suffer the most severe impacts from drought. This point also reinforces the enormous contribution of the urban water supply infrastructure in protecting people from the constancy of critical water supply concerns.

The second distinction is temporal, in that floods are rapidly developing disasters, whilst droughts can be more pervasive and long term. They can therefore be predicted well in advance, but can still be difficult to prevent or manage. These two aspects are however both tightly linked via spatial planning and land use management, due to decisions such as where to locate buildings and people, the permeability of the urban landscape and how water should be used or preserved. Consequently, previous and current land use decisions can affect the scope and extent of urban water supplies far into the future.

The exploitation of water

With such an array of indispensable structures carrying so many waters, compare, if you will, the idle Pyramids or the useless, though famous, works of the Greeks!

(Sextus Julius Frontinus, *On the Aqueducts of the City of Rome*, AD 79)

In almost direct contrast with how the supply of water is seemingly taken for granted in many modern societies, the value of water in ancient times was widely recognized and lauded. Further, as the above quote concerning the Roman aqueducts from the ex general and then water commissioner, Frontinus, displays, their utility was evaluated favourably to other works within similar civilizations. Indeed, Pliny the Elder wrote that in the opinion of many Romans the city's water infrastructure was its most noteworthy achievement. As water availability is a key facet of life and civilization, securing its supply has had a huge influence on the development, expansion and continued success of cities. The access to clean water was undoubtedly a reason for the huge population expansion in ancient Rome; advances that helped it become the most populous city in the world for over three centuries (Modelski 2003).

For the vast proportion of history the exploitation of groundwater resources was but a small proportion of total water usage. However, advances in technology and scientific knowledge during the last hundred years or so have quickly shifted this situation and a consistent supply of water has brought huge social and health benefits, and enabled the expansion of populations and more intensive agricultural production. Improvements in geological knowledge, drilling and pumping have all played a role to the extent that it is now argued that groundwater is the world's most extracted raw material (Foster and Chilton 2003). The modern sources of drinking water depend upon the geo-climatic context, but usually consist of abstraction from aquifers, interception and storage within reservoirs and lakes, and if these supplies are scarce, then modern energy intensive desalination strategies can be pursued.

Although countries such as Norway, Canada and New Zealand have excellent water resources, as a consequence of rising demand in many areas of the world groundwater is being consumed at a much greater rate than it can be replenished. It may be surprising for many people to learn that a number of major rivers, such as the Colorado and Yellow River, now actually run dry before they reach the sea (Pearce 2006a). Even in perceived rainy climates such as the UK, the Environment Agency (2009b) estimate that by 2050 summer river flows could decrease by between 50 and 80 per cent. Intensive abstraction therefore places great strain on ecosystems and on current trends may place a question mark over the future security of supplies. The rights to abstract and use water from the ground can belong to the government, or licences can be sold to companies or individuals who can all draw upon the resource. However, as the case of the Murray–Darling basin will later explain the total volume of legal water abstraction can exceed sustainable levels, creating new areas of water scarcity, which place strain on both socio-economic well-being and the conservation of terrestrial and aquatic ecosystems. As detailed in chapter 2, this situation will, of course, be exacerbated by climate change and population growth detrimentally affecting both water supply and demand.

The scope of water scarcity

> Take one world already being exhausted by 6 billion people. Find the ingredients to feed another 2 billion people. Add demand for more food, more animal feed and more fuel. Use only the same amount of water the planet has had since creation. And don't forget to restore the environment that sustains us. Stir very carefully.
>
> (World Economic Forum 2009: 2)

Since 2002 the right to water was identified as a basic human right by the United Nations, recognizing both its fundamental importance and its wider role as: 'a prerequisite for the realization of other human rights' (United Nations 2002: 1). Although water has now been formally recognized as critical for life and health, its widespread availability suffers from key constraints – from both the manufactured political and economic spheres and the natural geographical and climatic realms. In reality, despite huge technological and social advances throughout the last few centuries, concern as to securing adequate water resources is gaining worldwide currency. Scarcity is however a socially constructed and relative concept. The United Nations (UN-Water 2006: 2) recognize the need for a broad interpretation of the issue, defining water scarcity as:

> The point at which the aggregate impact of all users impinges on the supply or quality of water under prevailing institutional arrangements to the extent that the demand by all sectors, including the environment, cannot be satisfied fully.

Advances in science and engineering have largely solved the problem of water quality in all but the most underdeveloped cities, but although safe supplies of water are now taken for granted, the amount available is coming under increasing pressure. In more technologically advanced countries the idea of a periodic hosepipe ban may cause concerns regarding the future price or easy availability of water, but to an underdeveloped nation suffering from catastrophic drought and poor sanitation, scarcity has a much more critical meaning and the anxieties of the wealthy may appear insignificant and inconceivable. Nevertheless, these differing societies are both experiencing water stress, but as with the case of flood risk, the impacts become more socio-economic orientated rather than focusing on loss of life.

Despite the long history of advances in securing safe and consistent water supplies, on a global scale water scarcity figures are surprisingly high. Based on a measure of freshwater availability per person per day, in 2007 around 1.2 billion people were estimated to be living in conditions of absolute scarcity, with just under half the world's population suffering from the less critical, but still serious, problem of water stress (Comprehensive Assessment of Water Management in Agriculture 2007). Due to issues such as population growth, urbanization, rising demand and climatic pressures, by 2025 around two-thirds of the world's population are expected to experience constraints in supply (UN-Water 2006). Projecting even further into the future, it is estimated that a staggering 7 billion people, more than the current entire world's population, from over 60 different countries, will experience water scarcity by 2050 (World Water Assessment Programme 2003). These social trends place a huge emphasis on adapting our cities, our behaviour and our relationship with the natural environment, for long term societal and climatic changes.

There has also been discussion as to the possibility of 'peak water' being reached during the twenty-first century: an argument analogous to the peak oil concept whereby the limits of natural supplies are reached. As with oil, water will get increasingly difficult to access as easier supplies have already been exploited whilst the resource is expected to be extracted more quickly than it is replenished. Figure 4.1 displays the global reach of concerns as to water scarcity, stress and vulnerability in 2007.

Moreover, the effects of increasing demand and decreasing groundwater supplies are present in some surprising places. The European Union estimate that nine European countries, including Italy, Germany and the UK are water stressed, or approximately 46 per cent of the region's population (European Environment Agency 2009). Indeed, despite the common view of Britain as a rain swept isle, since the 1980s three droughts have occurred, which were expected to happen only once in every 200 years. UK Meteorological Office statistics reveal that annual rainfall between 1971 and 2000 was 1,126 mm (Meteorological Office 2009), yet the average rainfall in London is only 610 mm, a figure surprisingly lower than cities in much warmer climates such as Rome or Istanbul (House of Lords Science and Technology Committee 2006). Therefore, low rainfall totals, combined with impermeable urban areas

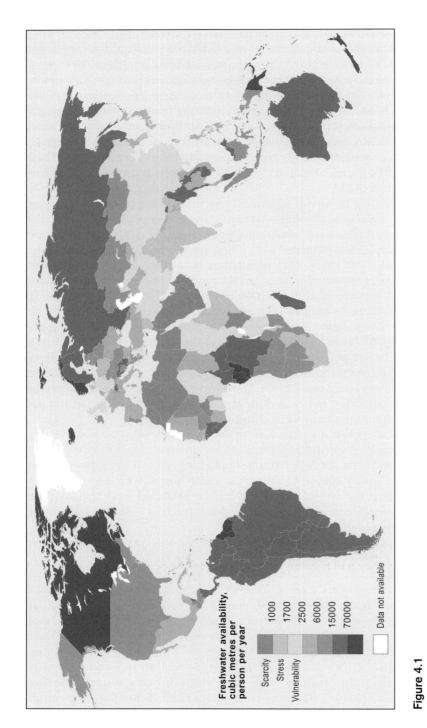

Figure 4.1

World water availability distribution

Source: United Nations Environment Programme 2008

Freshwater availability,
cubic metres per
person per year

Scarcity 1000
Stress 1700
Vulnerability 2500
6000
15000
70000

Data not available

and significant water demand inevitably raises the possibility of water scarcity within populous cities and their hinterlands. For example, in the UK the highly developed south-east has both one of the lowest annual rainfall totals and the highest requirement, raising the possibility of future constraints in supply and potentially influencing the location and function of development.

The water supply infrastructure

> Water is brought into the City through aqueducts in such quantities that veritable rivers flow through the City and its sewers; almost every house has cisterns and siphon pipes and copious fountains.
>
> (Strabo, first century BC)

There is no doubt that advances in technology and engineering have made heroic strides in securing the simple availability of arguably the world's most precious resource. This point is aptly made by the Greek geographer Strabo as he marvelled at the wonder of Rome's early water supply network. The quote also emphasizes that cities have always drawn upon an enormous supply of resources and services from their hinterlands and beyond, not least water and sanitation. In practice, urban areas import and consume huge quantities of fresh water and treat equally large amounts of wastewater, before exporting this usually via watercourses to the sea. Although the two tasks may have been originally developed independently, they are usually managed in a combined fashion, as over time the systems have been amalgamated in both a managerial and spatial sense. The material in this section should therefore also be considered in the context of the operation of the stormwater management network discussed in chapter 3.

Although ancient cultures such as the Assyrians, Greeks and Romans have used dams, aqueducts and other engineered interventions to help provide water supplies for drinking and irrigation, what we would now recognize as a modern water supply network had its origins in combating the growing concerns regarding water quality and health. In London for example, the city's rivers, wells and springs had historically supplied the inhabitants with water, but as the city grew they had become polluted, raising the need both for sewers and safe water. One notable development was the construction of the 'new river', completed in 1613 by Hugh Myddleton. This was a human-made waterway around 20 miles long, designed to bring clean water to the densely populated capital from the outskirts. The innovation had a long influence upon people and places, although its supply was not always guaranteed. For example, in 1855 Charles Dickens wrote of his frustrations to the Collector of Water Rates (Storey *et al.* 1993: 612), stating:

> my supply of water is often absurdly insufficient and although I pay the

extra service rate for a Bath Cistern I am usually left on a Monday morning as dry as if there was no New River Company in existence – which I sometimes devoutly wish were the case.

The artificial provision of water therefore also brought a social dimension, as more affluent areas or individuals could choose a cleaner supply, whilst poorer inhabitants continued to make use of wells, springs, and in London, as the sewage outfalls were directed to watercourses, the progressively more polluted River Thames (Halliday 2004). In general, water supply infrastructure was initially composed in the context of the existing urban form and to respond to predominately economic and health drivers. As the infrastructure became further developed, progressively valued and more widely available, it became increasingly active in shaping the evolution of urban form, from influencing the location of new homes and industry, to commanding land for sewage treatment. Consequently, due to practical economic drivers, the network gradually spread like the branches of a tree to cover the entire city.

The existence of the water infrastructure had an inevitable influence on the use of land, and in practice there was a shift towards expanding urban areas on the basis of the convenient location near to the network. Just as people used to settle near water resources, they now began to live near the highly appreciated piped supplies. The legacy of this original network is still in evidence today with much of it in use well over a hundred years since their initial construction, especially in older metropolitan areas. Moreover, even if the infrastructure needs to be replaced the very same location is commonly used for upgrades, helping to make this facet of the built environment spatially fixed, conservative and relatively static.

In addition to health concerns, the development of this infrastructure was linked to facilitating a society capable of both intense production and consumption of goods and services, and in short the network was perceived to be a driver for increasing the quality of life and economic growth. Indeed, in many advanced nations the heart of the current network is essentially a historical legacy of nineteenth-century capitalist urbanization (Gandy 2004). The development of water supply and sanitation networks should therefore also be seen as a function of modern industrialization and the desire to live in dense urban areas. As a result of their success, water became envisaged as a low cost renewable resource, starting a cultural change to the extent that in many nations water has become largely taken for granted.

The importance of the water supply infrastructure means that although the city may be perceived to grow organically, it is subtly constrained and shaped by what is a largely concealed and static network. Hidden underground, it is naturally subject to an out of sight, out of mind philosophy and over the last few hundred years or so has been firmly posited within the remit of engineers and determined by restrictive cost – benefit calculations. However, it is important to note that the network itself and the underlying management methodology have a lingering effect on urban form, flood risk and water scarcity. Despite these influences, it has surprisingly little formal influence within spatial planning. Indeed, given their pivotal role in enabling national goals to be achieved they enjoyed relative independence, a factor recognized by Marvin *et al.* (1998: 154) who stated that: 'historically, utilities have been given considerably autonomy and powers to conduct their operations unimpeded by wider local public policy considerations'. For example, in countries such as the UK, their importance has provided them with a statutory undertaker status, which gives power to bypass aspects of spatial planning, providing an artificial separation between two very significant and related roles.

The value of water to humanity means that securing access to the resource has greatly influenced the nature of our cities; from their initial location, to the subsequent siting of houses and industry, to attracting new city dwellers. In addition to the actual infrastructure shaping urban form, the methodology has also left a lingering legacy of effects connected with water. However, the management of water within cities shouldn't necessarily be designed around achieving what have become private sector economic goals, as utilities can also play vital roles in reducing water demand, protecting ecosystems and helping limit exposure to surface water flooding. In areas where the supply of water is predominately a commercial concern it will be difficult to reduce demand without restructuring the way income is generated. We need to acknowledge that utility companies can play a major role in shaping future water use in cities; consequently, we should influence and engage with the sector proactively, rather than in a responsive manner. This involves communicating and merging spatial agendas to help achieve more synergetic, strategic objectives. Essentially, we need to challenge the 'supply led logic' (Marvin *et al.* 1998) conventionally embodied by heroic engineering and technofix solutions, and develop a much more sophisticated and comprehensive demand side emphasis to facilitate sustainable, long term growth.

Water and growth

> In their efforts to provide a sufficiency of water where there was not one, men have resorted to every expedient from prayer to dynamite. The story of their efforts is, on the whole, one of pathos and tragedy, of a few successes and many failures.
>
> (Walter Prescott Webb, *The Great Plains*, 1931: 319–20)

In his historical thesis Webb drew attention to the differences between the wet arboreal east coast of the United States and the great plains of the American west, arguing that it was only when settlers adapted their culture, lifestyles and institutions that the area was able to be productively developed. In a separate essay Webb (1957) also prophetically drew attention to the problems inherent in the US government water policy of the time, which utilized high levels of expensive irrigation to create agricultural land in naturally arid, desert-like conditions. A central point of Webb's argument is that landscape moulds life, and the environment forces human change and innovation to overcome geographical realities. Moreover, that decisions made on the location and operation of water supply infrastructure can also affect water scarcity far into the future, partly due to its ability to fuel population expansion.

Box 4.1 Water scarcity in Las Vegas

A fine example of this argument in practice is provided by Las Vegas, one of the most iconic world cities. Established at the turn of the twentieth century within the arid Mojave desert of Nevada the settlement prospered with the construction of the nearby Hoover Dam, which in 1935 was both the world's largest electric power generating station and concrete structure. Additionally, water supply was supplemented by the creation of two new reservoirs in Lake Mead and Lake Powell. The availability of cheap water resources and power was designed to detach citizens and city leaders from the natural geographical constraints of inhabiting a desert and provided an innovative technological solution, the success of which greatly increased growth and quality of life. However, considering some of the current problems it is ironic that the city name actually means 'the meadows' in Spanish.

Almost three-quarters of a century after these pivotal constructions, Las Vegas residents are now being paid to tear up lawns, swimming pools are banned in new developments and only the high profile strip-side hotels are allowed to have fountains. The mayor of Las Vegas painted a blunt picture of how a gradual realization of a future of low and decreasing water supplies has changed perceptions of the value and free availability of the resource stating: 'to put it bluntly, in this town we are going to drink what we flush' (Laurence 2004: 1). The city of excess once hailed for making the desert bloom is now increasingly vulnerable to its geographical context and the consequent constraints inherent in the arid American west. Further, it is now recognized that technology, once the driver of this celebrated city, can only provide a partial shelter from the limitations of nature.

Aside from geographical or climatic concerns the rate of urban growth is also a key factor. Indeed fast growing cities, such as Lagos, Mumbai or Nairobi, may suffer an infrastructure crisis as people spread faster than the ability to finance water and sewerage networks (Gandy 2004). For example, Jakarta, the capital of Indonesia, currently has a population of 12 million, but more than three-quarters of these citizens are without access to clean water. Moreover, the sanitation networks only serve around 10 per cent of the population, with the rest using informal latrines (United Nations Development Programme 2006). As a result, when frequent floods occur they bring health challenges, such as typhoid and dysentery. This problem can only deteriorate as the population is predicted to double by 2025, bringing fears of an impending infrastructure crisis.

In more developed nations the level of sprawl in a city is also an influence, as a compact urban form can greatly reduce water use and energy requirements. In

Melbourne, a part of the world very sensitive to water supply issues, it has been estimated that a more compact urban form has the potential to save 100 GL a year of water. Conversely, a continuation of the business as usual model means a 50 per cent increase in residential water use by 2045 relative to 2001 (Kenway *et al.* 2008). Transporting water over a sprawling urban landscape can also take vast amounts of energy, which, of course, has implications for the related sustainability and climate change agendas. The value of water as both a driver and constraint for growth helps to link water use with city planning and design. It is important to note however that this relationship is brought into even sharper focus when considering the wide ranging direct and indirect uses of water discussed within the following sections.

Domestic water use

> Children of a culture born in a water-rich environment, we have never really learned how important water is to us. We understand it, but we do not respect it; we have learned to manipulate it, but have never really learned how to handle it.
> (Ashworth 1982: 26)

In the space of a few generations an easy supply of water has completely transformed our view of the resource to a degree that would be unrecognizable by our ancestors. Within cities the easy availability of water has resulted in an incremental increase in daily usage to the extent that water is now used for a multiplicity of trivial uses. Indeed, over the twentieth century total water use increased sixfold, double the rate of population growth. The consumption of water is also far from evenly spread; being predictably much higher in industrialized, wealthy nations. For example, in developing countries people may use 20–30 litres a day for washing, drinking and other household uses, whilst in Germany this is approaching 200 litres and in the United States it is as high as 575 litres.

This total may also vary within countries with, for example, the residents of the desert city of Pheonix, Arizona using on average over 1,000 litres per person per day (United Nations Development Programme 2006; see also figure 4.2). The relatively cheap costs of the resource has fuelled the development of water intensive lifestyles within wealthy nations, with an increasing demand for consumer products associated with economic growth such as power showers, dishwashers and swimming pools. The growth in population is also a factor, with each new household and each new person increasing demand for water. And, as chapter 2 demonstrated, the rise in both global and urban populations will provide a further significant stimulus for water use. There is unsurprisingly therefore a correlation between GDP and water use, a trend that can only raise total water usage as countries such as China, Brazil and India grow into more advanced, wealthy societies.

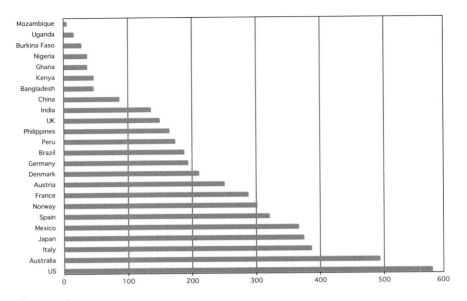

Figure 4.2

Average water use per person per day, 1998–2002 (litres)
Source: United Nations Development Programme 2006

It is now commonplace to advocate the use of water efficiency measures to try and reduce demand. A major method advocated to reduce demand is a focus on technological developments, such as toilets that use less water, universal water metering or greywater recycling. Another key mechanism is an attempt to influence personal behaviour, which, for example, may focus on persuading people to take showers instead of baths. Despite the broad agreement with these measures however strategies to reduce the daily water consumption per person are not estimated to make an enormous difference to the overall usage. In England and Wales for instance, despite advocating a suite of domestic measures such as compulsory metering, rainwater harvesting and greywater recycling, it is hoped that personal daily consumption will decrease from the current average level of 148 litres per day to 130 litres per day by 2030 (Environment Agency 2009b).

Domestic water use is only a minor part of the story however. Trends in water use have been conventionally divided between the domestic, industrial and agricultural sectors, by far the biggest user of which is agriculture, accounting for around 70 per cent of all freshwater withdrawals, with industry and homes being responsible for 22 per cent and 8 per cent respectively (World Water Assessment Programme 2009). Strategies to address water scarcity should therefore also include agricultural and industrial concerns, especially where water resources are starting to impact on either people or ecosystems.

It is clear that in many developed, wealthy countries water has been treated as a freely available, ubiquitous resource – belying its cardinal and elementary value. Perhaps the best illustration of this is provided by examining how we use water outside of drinking and cooking purposes. For example, our entire system of managing sewage has evolved to use water simply as a cheap method to flush away waste, yet in many countries of the world this technology would be seen as an incredibly decadent and profligate use of a precious resource. Furthermore, we produce all domestic water to drinking water standards, a significant proportion of which we then use for a variety of non-potable purposes. Given the intensive energy requirements, and the rising carbon agenda, it may seem a waste of energy to continue this practice. For example, should we use quality drinking water to wash our cars? In the future, considering the prospect of rising consumption demands and the possibilities of dwindling supplies, utilizing water for these purposes may be seen as a relic of a bygone age.

The mechanisms used to transport water from producer to consumer can also be inefficient. In many countries sections of the networks designed to carry public water supply are in a poor condition and a significant portion of the intended water supply is commonly lost through leakage. Across Europe the leakage rates as a percentage of water supply from water networks is estimated to range up to 50 per cent, with even advanced countries such as France and Italy scoring a relatively high 30 per cent loss rate (European Environment Agency 2003). The nature of the infrastructure however means that it is difficult to reduce these figures down towards a very low figure. In practice leakage reduction is an economic calculation between the costs of the loss and those of repair, and a situation may occur where only the major leaks are addressed.

The rapid expansion of world population since the onset of industrialization has highlighted how the management of water needs to be subject to cooperation and partnerships to equitably address pressures on supply. This is especially the case considering the fact that natural catchments and other water resources may not reflect the harsh realities of political boundaries. For example, the drainage basin of the Danube crosses 19 different countries, providing both problems in management and the need to allocate costs and benefits in a reasonable fashion. Perhaps inevitably the increased competition in some parts of the world for precious supplies of water can cause international tensions, such as the disputed water resources between Israel and Palestine, or with the United States and Mexico concerning the Rio Grande (Pearce 2006a). Considering a future of changing climates and inexorable rising demand, water has also been identified as a key potential source of future international disagreements. This is not a new phenomenon however; Gleick (2008) identifies an enormous number of historical conflicts involving water, from ancient Babylon and Persia, to more contemporary disputes. The international dimension of water resources is much more complex than it initially appears. Whilst it may be straightforward to grasp the simple allocation of water resources within nations it is much more difficult to unpack the industrial and agricultural purposes for which that water is consumed, and a key element is to consider the issue of virtual water.

Virtual water use

Water promises to be to the 21st century what oil was to the 20th century: the precious commodity that determines the wealth of nations. How a country handles its water problem could spell the difference between greatness and decline.

(Tully 2000)

Water has always been a key driver for economic growth; it can however be considered to exist in a number of forms beyond the common understanding of solid, liquid or gaseous states. An emerging and increasingly important issue being highlighted when analysing water use is the related subject of 'virtual' water. This term refers to the volume of water needed to produce a good or service (Allan 1998), and develops understanding of water consumption from its traditional focus on withdrawals from limited sectors, towards the reasons for that consumption and consequently sheds light on the relevant socio-economic drivers. Importantly, the concept highlights how the production of some commodities are hugely water intensive and can place a hidden strain on local water supplies and natural ecosystems. The figures comparing the difference between direct and indirect water usage per person are enlightening. In the UK for instance, the average person consumes approximately 150 litres per day, but taking virtual water into account this total rises to a staggering 4,645 litres per day (WWF 2008). The reason for this vast increase is largely centred on consumption of meat, dairy, cereals and clothing products. For example producing a ton of rice or wheat can take 3,000 m^3 and 1,300 m^3 of water respectively, whilst the value for producing meat is even higher as a ton of chicken has been calculated to account for 3,900 m^3 of water with a ton of beef costing a huge 15,500 m^3 (Hoekstra and Chapagain 2007). It is also interesting to note the countries that the UK imports this virtual water from, including drawing upon the resources of countries such as Spain, Germany, Ghana, India and the Ivory Coast – many of which are already exposed to water vulnerability.

The issue does present a worrying trend on a global scale. The rising demand for clothes and food closely associated with increases in GDP are expected to increase global water consumption. Global meat consumption alone is expected to rise by 56 per cent by 2025 (WWF 2008). Moreover, the parts of the globe with the fastest growing populations may also be the ones that desire the consumption rich lifestyles of more advanced nations, inevitably presenting huge problems for local water resources. There are no easy answers however. If, for example, UK supermarkets decide to stop importing horticulture from southern Spain, and instead grow products in greenhouses in southern England, you would essentially be reducing domestic virtual water use but increasing energy and conventional water use. A more seasonal, locally sourced diet can help, but the vast proportion of water use is hidden, making its subsequent management a complex issue. It is also heavily linked to international trade, and therefore any reduction of international exports may bring considerable socio-economic impacts.

Box 4.2 Water scarcity in the Murray–Darling basin

In short, the spatial distribution of the production and consumption of a huge number of commodities may not actually reflect the constraints of local water resources. In practice, a country experiencing water stress may be exporting virtual water in the form of a relatively low value product to a country with much higher water resources. To give an example, Australia's Murray–Darling basin drains around a seventh of the continent and is one of the world's longest river systems. It is also one of the country's most important farming regions. The catchment supplied a growing volume of its water for agricultural purposes and as a result over recent years river flows have declined, threatening both the livelihood of farmers and an ecological collapse. Consequently, concern has been raised regarding unsustainable levels of abstraction and the efficacy of the use of the water within what is a very dry continent, with one commentator provocatively summarizing that: 'the Murray is dying so that Australia can export rice to China' (Fickling 2004).

The impact of the crisis has fundamentally changed the economic output of the area to such a degree that between 2000 and 2008 Australia's annual rice exports dropped from 1.6 million tonnes to 18,000 tonnes (Gleick 2009), affecting both global prices and local employment. Climate change has also been identified as a key contributory factor in this area, and one that is predicted to exacerbate Australian water resources further. In response to the crisis in 2008 the Australian Minister for Climate Change and Water announced a new, ambitious *Water for the Future* strategy designed to help secure long-term water supplies. Amongst other initiatives the policy intends to buy back water entitlements and set new sustainable caps on the amount of water that can be abstracted from the Murray–Darling basin (Wong 2008). Re-examining the production, export and consumption of high virtual water commodities within the agricultural and industrial sectors can therefore be a viable strategy to increase national water supplies and limit potential economic impacts.

This contribution of water to the prosperity of regions, cities and citizens is vital. Yet, to date the major concern has been on supply issues, not unpacking demand-side questions, indeed the global trade network has not really considered the impact of virtual water to any significant degree. Recently though, its message is permeating through to policy makers and the general public, with especially profligate companies becoming the target of public outrage, such as experienced by Coca-Cola or the Spanish strawberry industry (WWF 2008). The level of consumption within huge multinationals may also become a cause for concern. For example, it may be startling to learn that it is estimated that five food and beverage giants, Nestlé, Unilever, Coca-Cola Co., Anheuser-Busch and Danone, use enough water annually to provide for the basic water requirements of every person on Earth (JP Morgan 2008). Private sector companies may therefore need to review how they utilize water in response to both changing supplies and public perceptions of the value of the resource.

The examples in this chapter show however that cities which rely on either a high level of imports or exports of virtual water as a cornerstone of their success and prosperity, may need to put in long term adaptation measures to protect themselves from either rising living costs or a lack of water resources. Equally, parts of the world with an excess of water could find themselves at an economic advantage. An issue identified by the World Economic Forum (2009: 17) who raise questions such as:

> Will companies relocate en masse from resource-poor countries to resource-rich countries, similar to the situation in the last 20 years where lower wages in emerging countries such as China and India became much more attractive locations for manufacturing? Will water security drive economic decisions?

In reality considering its largely unattributed gossamer influence on food, energy, climate, growth and security, water scarcity is a key threat to the well-being of the entire global economic system. It is predicted that over the next two decades the wider importance of water will be increasingly realized, and, as scarcity becomes more widespread, water will begin to be seen as a frequent headline geopolitical issue. The possibility of looming water problems are even compared with the swift and largely unseen impact of the global credit crunch, with one view that: 'we are living in a water "bubble" as unsustainable and fragile as that which precipitated the collapse in world financial markets' (World Economic Forum 2009: 54).

In short, the message is that companies and people may not be able to continue inefficient practices; and that we need to manage water differently, and more collaboratively, to prevent future economic problems. However, as has been apparent both in earlier sections of the book and in this chapter, it may be that the threat is not adequately perceived until the impacts are beginning to be experienced. An examination of the UK government National Archive records concerning the severe 1976 drought provides a fine example of how governments may have to quickly engage with water scarcity, and also how rapidly the issue subsides when the rains occur.

Box 4.3 The 1976 UK drought

To emphasize the example of the Murray–Darling basin, the limitations of the predominately modern management of water as a seemingly ubiquitous resource have only really been challenged in advanced nations in response to actual threats in supply. For example, in August 1976 the UK experienced the driest 16-month period since records began in 1772. The consequent debates within government, and the strategies mooted in response, illuminate how water scarcity can provide a powerful driver for innovative action. Analysis of National Archive records released 30 years after the event indicates the scope of wider concerns connected with water scarcity. In addition to the more obvious areas, these covered many disparate factors, including the availability of animal fodder, the need to offset decreasing farm incomes, the impact upon industrial output, the potential for an increase in wildfires, concerns over the capacity of the armed forces to respond and the fear of a full scale emergency the following summer. In order to avoid serious disruption of economic and social life the prospective solutions ranged from reducing consumption by up to 50 per cent and exploring the possibility of building a barrage across Morecambe Bay in order to capture freshwater from five rivers before they run 'to waste' (National Archives 2006: 14). Over the longer term, proposals advocated the need for a new national water authority with strong central powers, the construction of new reservoirs and novel far reaching water supply schemes, including the possibility of transferring water from areas of abundance, such as Ireland or Norway.

During the crisis, the *Economist* magazine (1976a: 79) colourfully accused certain water authorities of taking a 'Nero's eye view' and suggested that the Prime Minister, Jim Callaghan, should issue the following 'Churchillian' order: 'produce for me within two weeks alternative plans to trap 5 per cent, 10 per cent and 20 per cent of the rain which would otherwise run into the sea' (1976b: 12); a progressive and prescient suggestion that resonates with much contemporary thought. In response to the drought, and growing criticism concerning inactivity, Parliament hurried through the Drought Act 1976, which provided water authorities with the power to exploit new sources of water and the new, potentially draconian ability to prohibit supply to customers. The government also considered a special finance scheme to enable increased capital works to take place and launched a national publicity campaign to limit domestic usage, such as the suggestion that we should: 'save water, bath with a friend'.

The Prime Minister also produced what was arguably the most effective-ever ministerial appointment. On 24 August a cabinet reshuffle brought Denis Howell to the newly created post of the 'Minister of Drought Coordination', a serendipitous appointment considering the almost immediate subsequent downpour on August Bank Holiday four days later. Despite this instantaneous impact, and ensuing prolonged heavy rain throughout autumn changing perceptions, there was an acknowledgement within government that maintaining public interest in saving water would be difficult when the rains start again. The analysis of the archive data provides an example of how it may take an impending disaster before action is taken and provides an insight into how restrictions in water supply can affect a host of seemingly disparate areas across society. It also highlights how water scarcity has the ability to migrate to the very top of the political agenda within a very short space of time.

Chapter 1 drew attention to the rising threat of disasters within urban areas. It argued that although technology and knowledge can both insulate cities from the most catastrophic effects, as the drivers and risks become more powerful differing strategies may have to be pursued. Although cities may not fail completely as in the past the impacts of water scarcity may mean they fail to prosper and in an interconnected world this can have a huge detrimental effect. The potential collapse of high virtual water commodities within water-scarce regions provides a prime example of this process occurring in practice. This possibility clearly links water use, including both the conventional and virtual understanding of the resource, within many differing professions beyond engineering, and in particular with urban planning. In reality, water scarcity within cities may not bring the huge loss of life that can occur in underdeveloped rural locations, but, rather, be centred on potentially transformational socio economic impacts. Whilst it may sound illogical to discuss these impacts of water supply, considering the devastating human tragedies that droughts have brought to some of the poorest parts of the world in recent years, generally speaking in all but the most impoverished cities enough water is available to sustain people. Moreover, we should also remember that water holds much higher value than being a simple economic good, being vital for the maintenance and well-being of ecosystems. The problem is, as initially highlighted, a relative one. But one that holds real long term problems for even the most advanced and strongest societies.

Reflecting upon water scarcity and the city

Nothing on Earth is so weak and yielding as water, but for breaking down the firm and strong it has no equal.

(Lao-Tzu, sixth century BC)

The Chinese philosopher Lao-Tzu provided one of the first insights into the potential of water to humble the powerful in his influential text, *Tao Te Ching*. It is important to recognize that despite a long realized and incrementally advancing ability to control the resource, it has lingering and pervasive effects on the functioning and success of societies that heighten the need for effective management. Indeed, ensuring a safe supply of water has shaped the development of cities from their initial siting, to the extent and productivity of agricultural land, to the location of modern industry. As technology enabled humanity to access high volumes of the resource to promote growth and public health, the resource became, if not mastered, much less capricious and seemingly under control. This occurred to the extent that even the most arid and remote places on Earth could now secure clean water, inevitably changing our everyday perception of its value. There is no doubt that advances connected with the availability and cheap cost of water has utterly transformed how we value and employ the resource within a few generations. The extent of this modern cultural shift is highlighted by the fact that even though water is arguably the world's most precious resource in many advanced nations we simply flush it away down the toilet. It is not stretching the imagination to think that in the future, people may view that approach with incredulity.

However, regardless of advances in technology there are still billions of people experiencing degrees of water stress and there have been a number of worldwide catastrophic episodes of drought. Indeed, the failure to secure safe water supplies for large parts of humanity, despite having the knowledge and resources to do so, is arguably one of the key failings of the twentieth century. The problems may not be supply orientated, but, rather, centred on effective distribution and management, and, as demands increase countries with poor water resources may not be able to consume water in a profligate fashion. Issues such as rising demand, changing supplies and a culture of easy access are now combining to create new areas of water stress and challenge long held conventions concerning how to manage this resource. In the industrialized world solutions to water supply problems have been predominately techno-centric and supply orientated. If water supplies have been low we have usually explored the potential for new major capital works or simply increased the volumes of groundwater abstraction. We have even explored the possibility to artificially seed clouds to produce rain, as the power to control where and when rain falls can clearly bring significant benefits. For instance, in March 1967 during 'Project Popeye' the United States artificially seeded clouds in the Vietnam War to disrupt supply lines, whilst in more modern times the Chinese government was rumoured to have performed the procedure to ensure that it did not rain during the opening ceremony of the 2008 Beijing Olympic Games.

It is only when flaws emerge in this interventionist, technocentric strategy, such as exemplified in Las Vegas or the Murray–Darling basin, that either proposals to facilitate more infiltration or reduce demand are seriously mooted. However, it may take a looming national catastrophe, such as the serious wide reaching threat of the 1976 drought, to change perceptions amongst water managers, users and the public in order to shift towards demand-side approaches. One reason for the dominant methodology is due to trends in the governance of water, which in many countries is overwhelmingly seen as a commodity supplied for profit by the state or private sector. In the UK for example, it may appear counter-intuitive that the main agencies charged with promoting water efficiency are the very same companies who inevitably make more profit the more water is used.

Although the influence of planners, architects and others connected with the built and natural environments may appear to be limited in a field traditionally associated with civil engineering, strategies to alter the location, function and operation of the urban form and the relationship with the natural environment can yield significant benefits. With regard to the strategic scale we can consider maximizing opportunities for infiltration or consider the role of water in the economic resilience of the city. Whilst in a managerial sense we can consider options such as promoting water efficiency at the design stage to encouraging the capture and reuse of rainwater. The example of virtual water also demonstrates that related agendas such as food supplies or the production of goods and services for trade can also affect water supplies. Therefore, we need to move away from viewing water use within a narrow sectoral perspective, as in reality water management decisions may also be related to broader societal drivers, climate change, competitiveness or international trade – all key issues for the city. The adaptation of a city or region to water stress also needs to be considered in the context of the predicted rise in population and its impact on related aspects such as food requirements, consumption patterns and industrial output; all of which will operate in the context of a changing global climate.

Water scarcity however should not be considered from a perspective of simply being exposed to it or not. In reality, an understanding of the virtual water imports of one country, such as the seemingly innocuous demand for rice, can have devastating effects on the exporting region. This understanding provides an added layer of sophistication to the conventional view of advanced nations exploiting the resources of those less advantaged. In the case of water scarcity, the spatial distribution of vulnerability and exploitation may mean that this trend is very different, with many industrialized countries becoming the exploited, depending upon their trade patterns. The effects can also be difficult to address, as a lack of water is difficult to reconcile with the conventional view of resource scarcity focused on simply accessing more resources via trade. However, water cannot be practically shipped from South America or Indonesia like tropical hardwood, or finance easily obtained as with economic problems; the onus may be on internal demand and supply solutions. Indeed, the World Economic Forum (2009) suggests that hydrological water bankruptcy may be a real threat for certain countries in the future. In wealthy nations water may not be switched off, but companies and people may have to be prepared for it to become significantly more expensive in the future. Areas of the globe that are severely out of balance with their natural or artificial water resources, like Australia or the western United States, may be the first examples of a socio-economic trend with the potential to strike growing sections of humanity. In effect they may operate as the 'hydro-canary' of the twenty-first century, where a lack of resources is forcing fundamental changes in consumption patterns.

Conclusion

> We must take great care in searching for springs and, in selecting them, keeping in mind the health of the people.
>
> (Vitruvius, first century BC)

Since centralized water and sanitation networks were established in areas such as Paris in 1806, London in 1808 and Berlin in 1856 they have gradually spread throughout all but the most deprived urban areas (Gandy 2004). Prior to this time, water was held to be an incredibly precious resource, as it still is in many of the least developed nations, and securing its supply determined both where people live and how they may spend a significant proportion of each day. The vital importance of water as a tool for survival fundamentally shaped our existence, and the development of technology to efficiently address this demand within cities helped to fuel the urban population expansion during the following two centuries. The influence of the water and sanitation network as a fossilized structure within the city has consequently affected the development of urban form. As with flood risk, decisions concerning a whole host of urban issues, from land use to agriculture to trade, can also create a legacy of exposure, bringing the topic and its remediation squarely within the remit of those concerned with the city and its operation. Moreover, just as the flood risk narrative in the urban environment has changed towards making *space* for water, perhaps the next shift should be more holistic and proactive. This could be aimed at making *use* of water, where society would facilitate both the storage and utilization of the resource.

Of all the achievements of modern industrialized society, securing an easy supply of the world's most precious resource has to be near the pinnacle. A turn of the tap and it is there; effectively distancing humanity from the constraints and problems of the past and providing the fuel for large scale urbanization and growth. The availability of cheap clean water in every modern home has also helped to shift perceptions, and now water is perceived as a ubiquitous and cheap basic good largely taken for granted. And here is the conundrum: water remains the most powerful force on Earth; it can erode rocks, shape landscapes and change the course of civilizations. Examples from Australia, the United States and the UK emphasize that the true value of water only awakens when a threat to its supply is perceived; and only when we reflect upon society do we realize how wastefully we use the resource.

The examples in this chapter mirror the early environmental determinism views of Webb and others in that cities and regions can be constrained by nature. Twenty-first-century cities will have access to the exact same amount of water as was available in the dim and distant past, yet never before have there been so many people on the Earth, so many water intensive industries and such a profligate attitude to the resource. The message here is not one of a catastrophic impending doom; rather, one of a slow recognition of natural supply and demand issues. In certain cities this process will inevitably lead to behavioural changes connected with a growing realization that water resources are much more valuable than previously perceived. This is a very different type of hazard than flood risk, and eminently more manageable. As will be argued in later chapters, technology and changes in how water is consumed can go some way to insulating society, but the spatial distribution of risk means that some cities will have to take this problem much more seriously than others. Moreover, those cities that either quickly adapt, or have access to an abundance of water, could be well placed to benefit. Simply put, we need to consider how we can minimize the transfer of costs to future generations; and a central facet to this strategy is developing a deeper understanding of framing concepts such as risk and resilience.

Part III

Towards a conceptual framework

···

5 Risk, resilience and spatial planning

The rain is plenteous but, by God's decree,
Only a third is meant for you and me;
Two-thirds are taken by the growing things
Or vanish Heavenward on vapour's wings:
Nor does it mathematically fall
With social equity on one and all.
The population's habit is to grow
In every region where the water's low:
Nature is blamed for failings that are Man's,
And well-run rivers have to change their plans.

(Sir Alan Herbert, 'Water')

The capricious relationship between water and civilization is aptly reflected in Sir Alan Herbert's poem, which elegantly highlights two key themes relevant to this book: first, that water should be managed to support both human and ecological needs; and second, that society should reconnect with nature and design cities appropriate to their geo-climatic context. The line 'Nature is blamed for failings that are Man's' provides a degree of simplistic clarity that resonates with the results of contemporary reviews of recent natural disasters. Actors, agencies and governance frameworks have all been perceived to be culpable by either causing or exacerbating the impact: disasters may have a natural origin, but a manufactured effect, a notion that essentially raises concerns about how we manage risk in society. It should be noted that there will always be extreme environmental events, from prolonged droughts to flash floods to earthquakes, as our planet is subject to ranges of volatile behaviour demanding judgements on acceptable risks and managerial intervention to protect cities and citizens. With regard to water we do have clear opportunities for reducing uncertainty by gathering data on hazards and using this to better predict the future risks. For example, using precipitation and hydrological records we can calculate with a degree of certainty which regions, cities or even which specific localities are more likely to be exposed to risks, thereby providing an evidence base for future intervention. The way risks are interpreted and the subsequent manner in which these events may be managed may not be effective however blurring the distinction between what are ascribed to be natural or man made disasters.

Towards a framing concept

To operationalize a move towards a water-aware city would require the coupling of spatial approaches with framing principles of action. Indeed, part of the problem in managing the resource thus far has been a lack of a coherent strategic understanding. The typical mechanism to merge agendas affecting the natural and built environment would be to utilize the concept of sustainable development. The methodology has been widely identified as a mechanism to help adapt to changing environments, and, like other concepts such as resilience and adaptation, can potentially apply to all sectors. Sustainable development does potentially provide a mechanism to integrate complexity and heterogeneity, but there are only a few examples of cities that have deeply explored this connectivity, such as Curitiba in Brazil. Despite the resources poured into the concept and its widespread adoption, following this pathway has proved very challenging within cities.

Although this chapter will outline that risk might be similarly contested and socially constructed, this problem is greatly magnified when considering the much broader and less easily quantifiable issue of sustainability. For example, problems inherent when implementing the theory of sustainability into practice are commonplace. The same concept can frequently be interpreted in such a competing manner that it may actually increase uncertainty, a key barrier to effective decision making. This lack of surety also decreases the potential for partnership approaches, which are essential to pursuing resilience in a complex arena such as a city. This issue is most easily understood when considering the scope of the remit to fulfil what are often competing economic, social or environmental objectives.

Moreover, urban areas exhibit a dazzling range of forms and are under such an array of differing pressures that designing transferable effective measures has proved difficult. In practice, there are many pathways to sustainability (Jenks and Dempsey 2006), just as there are multiple measures to address water hazards. Useful as the notion is as a tool to raise awareness of either environmental impacts or social concerns within decision making, the idea is highly contested and provides an imperfect framework for intervention. Although the lack of clarity hinders its application as a coherent overreaching strategy for managing water in the city, it is important to note that a city more resilient to hazards would logically also be more sustainable for both current and future populations. Therefore, the most effective route towards a more sustainable city may require a less ambiguous approach, and alternative notions, such as risk are not necessarily competing, but, rather, complementary.

The framing concept of risk, linked with the related ideas of resilience, uncertainty, adaptation and mitigation can provide a clear and logical structure within which to unpack the nature of the city and its relationship to water. Just as the term sustainable development can be useful as a tool to amplify environmental consciousness, and the precautionary principle has potential for addressing uncertainty, utilizing principles centred on the assessment, mitigation and adaptation to risks can provide a helpful conceptual framework to aid decision making. The development of general concepts to manage risk within urban areas would enable the approach to be applied with some agreement in differing cities according to individual need and hydro-climatic and geographical contexts. Adopting a spatial risk analysis also creates the potential for increased understanding from planning professionals and links to the possibility of pursuing effective public engagement strategies. This information can subsequently be used to design appropriate strategic adaptation strategies to be implemented at differing scales in order to limit the undesirable affects of changing societal and climatic trends.

Lost in translation?

Recently, terms like *risk, resilience, hazard, vulnerability, exposure, adaptation* and *mitigation* have permeated into policy and academic discourse, as they are perceived to offer both conceptual coherence and a useful framework to better understand and address future hazards. In an age of both increasing hazards and demands on land new methodologies to facilitate more effective decisions are crucial. With regard to managing water, these modern notions are recently seen to be particularly useful, as urban populations grow and climate changes. In practice, our ability to effectively manage water will be significantly shaped by the way in which the built environment professions interpret the concepts and use them to inform responses.

Considering the widespread use of these terms, you would be forgiven for assuming that there would be a consensus on their understanding and usage. The terms are often sprinkled liberally and occasionally confusingly however and in some quarters have been likened to the wide and varied interpretation of sustainability (Wisner *et al.* 2004), which has been utilized in unforeseen and often contradictory directions. Indeed some observers even indicate that it is this lack of specificity that may have contributed to its growing popularity of terms such as 'resilience' in the social sciences (Klein *et al.* 2004). In some disciplines, such as economics and sociology, notions of risk have been considered since the mid-twentieth century, but accord has still been difficult to achieve. For example, in a 1992 Royal Society report there was a general split between social scientists and physical scientists as to the nature and meaning of risk (Adams 1995). Douglas (1992: 58) also highlighted how separate professions may interpret risk differently within decision making, arguing that:

> When faced with estimating probability and credibility, they come already primed with culturally learned assumptions and weightings . . . they

have set up their institutions as decision processors, which shut out some options and put others in favourable light.

Given this contention in basic conceptualization it is important that the use of these ideas is subject to deep consideration in order to be effective. In spatial planning the application of the terms is relatively new. Although their use is becoming enshrined in policy, it is usually applied and interpreted in a narrow and procedural manner, perhaps reflecting both the inchoate field and the nature of spatial planning. The use of Flood Risk Assessments provides a good example, as they are designed to supply a firm estimate of the probability of inundation, in order to give an indication of how flood risk can be weighted against other concerns. Yet evidence from practicing planners suggests that they are unsure as to the actual authority claimed by the deterministic probabilistic judgement, as in practice perceived risk must be stochastic and uncertain (White and Richards 2007).

To successfully integrate risk and related concepts within decision making processes there is a fundamental need to provide a degree of conceptual clarity, as the way a topic is defined can have significant repercussions for policy and its subsequent interpretation within land use and management decisions. For example, it has implications for the way that problems are weighted in order to assign priorities for action, or it can affect the final allocation of responsibility or accountability. Considering the role of humanity in influencing and accepting levels of risk, it is clear that understanding and defining the concept has to be related to power and culture: both with regard to the ability to act and the perceived apportioning of blame. Moreover, whilst institutions or agencies may have key roles as risk managers, as hazards become more interrelated and complex the contribution of the public in determining their own exposure will become more important.

This chapter begins part III of the book by expanding the debate on from the problem and the need to act, towards developing an understanding of the conceptual framework related to the future management of water in the city. We know that inconsistencies in precipitation patterns will occur due to climate change and citizens will be increasingly at risk from flooding and drought. A key part of the planning system therefore should be aimed at providing sustainable, adaptive responses that increase the resilience of cities and citizens; but what do we mean when discussing concepts of risk, resilience, exposure, uncertainty and vulnerability? What are the links to spatial planning and water? And how can the terms become more useful to decision makers?

The evolution of risk

Risk is an everyday occurrence; from the moment we awake we are consciously making decisions about how best to manage a series of minor risks, from avoiding hitting traffic jams in the daily commute to ascertaining priority to work tasks. An awareness of differing risks is therefore omnipresent. The statistical understanding of the related area of chance also has a long history, perhaps best exemplified by the ubiquity of gambling, one of the oldest diversions. Originally, there was a view that many future events were, at least in part, reliant on chance or the whims of gods, reflecting the belief that exposure to some risks may merely be a product of fate. The transition from a reliance on celestial providence, or the support of Lady Luck, towards a more quantitative basis for understanding risk has occurred in small incremental stages over the last few hundred years.

The move towards a consideration of risk in a more technical sense had its foundation in the maritime ventures of the sixteenth and seventeenth centuries and was related to providing financial compensation for the impacts of acts of nature that could be deemed to be outside of human responsibility (Lupton 1999). In the seventeenth century mathematicians Blaise Pascal and Pierre de Fermat provided a further development by solving the Pacioli Puzzle, a probability problem set two centuries earlier by a Franciscan monk concerning how to split the remaining pot of a gambling game that ends prematurely. In essence they invented the theory of probability and provided a basis for forecasting future events. The development of our understanding of risk increased further in the following centuries with advances such as Jacob Bernoulli's Law of Large Numbers and Abraham De Moivre's Law of Averages. Developments that gradually helped move the view of risk from being related to divine providence, or an accident of chance, to an acknowledgement that some future occurrences can be quantified and therefore could influence present decisions. The improvements also provided the basis of a move from the basic estimation of probability to the fields of sampling and distribution, both of which enabled more uncertain outcomes to be estimated. For example, the collection of historic data within actuarial tables now enabled insurance to be taken out on a person's life. This process of collecting records to reduce uncertainty also has similarities with the collection of precipitation data by George James Symons in 1850, which was designed to help foresee future risks with regard to water.

The legacy of the influence of shipping and advances in probability has significantly affected the management of risk. Our understanding and framing of risk had become very statistically focused, and, in part response, John Maynard Keynes wrote *A Treatise on Probability*, which recognizes the importance of numerical data but emphasizes the value of judgement. The scientization of risk and its associated concepts gathered pace in line with advances in mathematics and probability. In the early twentieth century Frank Knight provided an important breakthrough when he drew a distinction between 'risk' and 'uncertainty' within any event, suggesting that risk is when there is a known chance and uncertainty is when you have no idea of the odds of the occurrence (Knight 1921). This initial systematic understanding of risk is useful to reconsider as it highlights the difficulty in assigning clear values to complex and sometimes relative issues and how true risk resists accurate measurement.

As Adams (1995: 29) puts it: 'risk is constantly in motion'.

This complexity in calculating objective values for indeterminate risks leads to a need to recognize uncertainty as a concept in itself and from there to related concerns, such as how to consider the unknown within decisions. This has been attempted, for example, by the creation of climate change scenarios, increasing the knowledge base or incorporating integral resilience. However, relying on science and technology as tools to address uncertainty and risk may not be straightforward. In practice, scientific advances have the potential to create newer risks as society progresses, such as flood defence or water supply infrastructure failure. At the same time, the knowledge generated also reveals more ignorance as gaps in understanding become more apparent. Perhaps incongruously therefore risk may get more uncertain as knowledge increases.

From act of god to act of humanity to act of planners?

In general, our understanding of risk has been heavily influenced by the insurance and legal industries who used new knowledge of statistics and probability to prescribe compensation for future undesirable events. Indeed, the phrase 'act of God' was appropriated by these professions as a useful and durable tool for referring to natural events that cannot reasonably be foreseen and therefore no one can be held liable for. The origin of this phrase relating to unknown factors affecting the potential losses of maritime ventures reveals much about the subsequent management of risk. It essentially suggests that some risks are normalized in our everyday life; they cannot be managed, we just have to accept it. This contributed towards the view that risk was not necessarily to be avoided, but potentially managed via economic compensation. As a result, effectively many risks have been passed from the state to the individual who can gain support from the private sector. Furthermore, the concept, combined with the separation of water issues from strategic environmental planning, has helped shift perceptions of accountability from people towards nature. Whilst it may be understandable that society used to view extreme events as a punishment from God for various actions of impiety, modern knowledge should make this axiom redundant. Hurricane Katrina emphasized without any doubt that the effect of a severe storm of natural origin was a disaster due to essentially very human drivers: from mistakes in the location, design and construction of parts of the city; to the selection, quality and maintenance of protective levees; to a lack of preparedness and subsequent implementation of a disaster response. The terminology is actually incredibly unhelpful as it is essentially a legacy of outdated thought, deliberately blurs the causal link between human activities and natural hazards and can provide a barrier to pursuing resilience.

The acknowledgment that risk is connected to our perceptions and constrained by information in turn forms the basis of the more contemporary standpoint that risk is socially and culturally constructed. Beck (1992: 99) argues that risk had become shaped by statistics and the expansion of the insurance industry and referred to:

> systematically caused, statistically describable and, in this sense, 'predictable' types of events, which can therefore also be subjected to supra-individual and political rules of recognition, compensation and avoidance.

Therefore, the way we interpret risk shapes our responses. This is also related to the argument that there are no natural disasters, only manufactured ones, best summarized by the view that responsibility for disasters should shift from being described as an act of God to an act of humanity. In reality, risks from flooding and water scarcity are socially constructed and the ability to manage them through the planning system is limited by a narrow interpretation of risk and resilience, despite the growing reliance on planning as a key mechanism for intervention. Moreover, in practice spatial planners have a limited understanding of risk as a theory and may in fact be institutionally inhibited from pursuing such notions. For example, they may consider water based risks in a reactive manner alongside development proposals, whilst as the previous chapters have argued, resilience is a proactive outlook and planning should address hazards on a more strategic and long term basis.

A further upsurge of interest in risk with direct regard to water and the city occurred from the latter half of the twentieth century onwards. There was a realization that although humans may be risk averse, institutions are not, especially if they can design or exploit systems to pass the risk on to other agencies or people. Risk in the business and economic fields was essentially seen as a trade-off between the potential for profit and loss, with the added possibility of hedging risks by paying a financial premium. However, a rising tide of litigation against companies that externalized risk onto individuals led to changing practices, such as increased product safety. Therefore, the threat of legal redress and financial liabilities has subsequently affected corporate and institutional behaviour. The response to the Stern Report into the economic impact of climate change demonstrates this process in practice. To influence risk generating behaviour by institutions it was recognized that there was a need to communicate in their language: profit and loss. Essentially, the report set out to monetorize risk, as related studies centred on the social and environmental effects had not sufficiently changed practices.

The shift in risk management towards consumers raises an interesting question: if a disaster is accepted to be an act of humanity, then which section of society is to blame? For example, if citizens are exposed to risks from flooding or drought who is responsible for considering their safety? The individual, an institution, an architect or a planner? Currently if a house floods, the damage is borne by the home owner and insurance company. However, there is arguably no profit or loss decision involved in their side of the transaction as occurs within the corporate understanding of risk. In this case the profit has already been received by the developer whose risk decision is whether the house will sell or not, not whether the house will be exposed to risks from flooding. Therefore, there is no straight choice between profit and loss with regard to water risks from an individual's perspective, just an overwhelming exposure to potential detriment. In essence the planning system performs a risk management service for individuals who work or live in cities, and the citizen believes that the home they purchase has been deemed to be 'safe' by professionals. Planners have already received widespread blame for allowing building on the floodplain, but in the future could they also be liable for losses?

Deconstructing risk

> Can we know the risks we face, now or in the future? No, we cannot; but yes, we must act as if we do.
>
> (Douglas and Wildavsky 1983: 1)

We have already seen that population growth, urbanization and climate change are a powerful series of drivers that will all amplify the risk of water based hazards to citizens, infrastructure and the biosphere. Significantly, these risks should be managed by a number of actors and agencies, principal amongst which are planners and planning systems. Professionals connected with the built environment therefore need to understand how best to interpret risk, engage with uncertainty, communicate the results and translate this into decisions that limit long term impacts. As the previous section has demonstrated however risk is a contested arena and there are a number of differing definitions each of which may influence interpretation.

Risk is the key concept with regard to managing water hazards; all related terms, such as exposure, vulnerability and resilience, are most easily understood as lesser functions within the risk framework. The recent spate of natural disasters within cities has driven a need to engage with the risk management agenda, but spatial planning has an imperfect ability to consider risk as a whole due to artificial professional and policy boundaries. For example, planning's powers focus upon new development, centre on the built environment and often are used within inappropriate spatial scales. They also have to consider what may be competing 'risks', such as flood risk management versus employment provision, or the infiltration of precipitation against the pollution of groundwater. In addition, the rapid emergence of risk within planning has uncovered difficulties in interpretation, as there is no real foundation of bespoke knowledge to draw upon. At the present time therefore planning systems may find it institutionally complicated to be effective agents of risk management. As a result there is a need to be aware of the constraints of the concept and how it can best assist decision making.

Although risk is a subjective and complex issue in itself, when the concept is broken down into component parts, and specifically considered with regard to hazard and disaster management, a degree of valuable clarity emerges. In straightforward terms risk can be viewed in the form of a simple but powerful generic equation: *Risk = Hazard × Vulnerability* (R = H × V) (Wisner *et al.* 2004). From this perspective, the risk of flooding or drought is a function of both the existence of a hazard (the potentially damaging event) and vulnerability (the susceptibility to its impacts), and may therefore be expressed as being the intersection of both an area at risk and a population variably subject to its impacts. It should be noted that the formula is not strictly arithmetic, but is illustrative and risk may be commonly expressed in quantitative terms, such as a percentile or modular scale (e.g. low, moderate, high), in order to better understand the potential of undesirable consequences. It is important to recognize that vulnerability in this instance does not have a narrow focus on land use or the physical environment. It can have a wide remit incorporating social, economic and cultural factors such as class, wealth, access to resources, social networks and ethnicity.

An alternative view is provided by Crichton (1999) who defined risk in a slightly different manner, as resulting from three interrelated elements: hazard, vulnerability *and* exposure (R = H × V × E), all of which must be present in order for risk to be incurred. The addition of the exposure constituent (being subject to the hazard) provides a further layer of complexity and a stronger spatial element than vulnerability alone can provide. For example, if you are elderly you could be vulnerable to the effects of a drought, but the location of your house within an area of high water availability means you are not exposed. Similarly, you could be exposed to flood risk, but not especially vulnerable if your home is constructed using 'flood proof' materials. A different outlook was recently provided by the Foresight Future Flooding research, which defined risk as being the function of *probability × consequences*. The definition of consequences in this instance included people and the natural and built environments (Evans *et al.* 2004). This view also provides a useful slant for spatial planning by simplifying the risk discourse from hazard, vulnerability and exposure, parts of which are only marginally influenced by planning, into one aspect with considerable linkages: consequences.

A final example of the varying differing interpretation of risk is provided by Wamsler (2007) who suggested that the formula should include a recognition of the capacity to respond. In this case risk equalled *hazard × vulnerability × lack of capacity to respond* (R = H × V × LC). This new final component introduces a human and institutional element and has linkages with concepts of resilience and adaptation, key concepts of a city more resilient to water hazards. Consideration of the constituent aspects of risk is beneficial as in practice risk is often considered as one homogenous topic and rarely systematically analyzed (Wamsler 2007). In essence, deconstructing risk into component parts can bring insights with regard to framing this concept within spatial planning and facilitating the design of tailored, effective management responses.

Deconstructing resilience

The relationship between resilience and conventional understandings of risk is slightly more complex. The word resilience is derived from the Latin word *resilio*, which means 'to jump back' and has only recently come to prominence within the field of disaster reduction (Klein *et al.* 2004). The conceptualization of resilience in academia has been fuzzy and contested, and some lucidity is needed to understand this relatively new theoretical construct in relation to water and spatial planning. When discussing the capacity of society to adapt to a hazardous event such as a changing climate, Timmerman (1981) linked resilience to vulnerability, yet it should be noted that although resilience may be a factor of vulnerability and vice versa, they are not true opposites, as increasing one element does not automatically decrease the other. Indeed, there is a strong argument that they should be viewed as two related, but separate, constructs (Manyena 2006). The roots of the notion lie in the field of ecology and initially related to the ability of a system to return to stability or equilibrium after a disturbance (Pickett *et al.* 2004). However, Holling (1973) provided a significant development by linking resilience with a system able to absorb shocks and still continue. This is important as it provides a differing understanding: of a city being able to adapt to *incrementally changing* environments, not just one-off events. Unpacking this distinction is valuable, as considering the drivers changing the relationship between environment and the city it is the latter, more dynamic, understanding that is particularly useful to spatial planning. The meaning has synergies with the term 'proactive resilience' discussed by Dovers and Handmer (1992) and links to the notion of adaptive capacity that has emerged in the climate change fields. Resilience also goes well beyond the scope of the built environment professions, such as engineering, design or architecture.

In addition to recovering from a disaster and adapting to changing normalities, resilience has a strong human element, which focuses on the nature of institutions and the ability of a society to meet the multifaceted challenges of the future, which may incorporate more intangible social and cultural aspects, including ingenuity, resources and support structures (Homer-Dixon 2000). A key feature of the modern understanding of resilience therefore is its ability to connect with both physical and social systems (Godschalk 2003). The ability of resilience to also link these physical and social elements with natural systems should be recognized; whereby the vulnerability of ecosystems to human or natural threats is acknowledged and strategies are adopted to preserve resources (Klein *et al.* 2004).

Douglas and Wildavsky (1983) suggest that although risk may be a function of social organization, the management of risk and its consequences is an organizational problem, and although we may not know the precise nature of current and future risks, we must act regardless. With specific regard to risk and spatial planning, it is clear that we should take risks and the potential for integral resilience into account even though our scope for intervention is imperfect. Taking a disaster management perspective, the resilience discourse initially had an *outcome orientated* standpoint: a paternalistic, technocratic view referring to the ability to cope and withstand unfortunate events. Latterly, the term has become perceived as more *process orientated*, in which resilience is seen as a wider, more encompassing, deliberative process whereby the resilience capacity of both buildings and communities can be enhanced and augmented (Kaplan 1999; Manyena 2006). This contemporary, expansive understanding of resilience provides a key link to risk and has synergies with our understanding of the reasons for the escalation in natural disasters outlined in chapter 1. The growth in people affected may therefore be described as a function of increasing hazard, vulnerability and exposure; all of which can be influenced by spatial planning.

It is important to note that resilience should not just be considered in a land use sense. For example, vulnerability can be alleviated by poverty reduction, another core aim of planning. There is a strong argument that the outcome and process orientated views of resilience can be accurately considered in a broader sense as a flexible method to decrease risk in its entirety, and theoretically could embrace hazard, vulnerability *and* exposure. Initially, you could be forgiven for thinking that the hazard remains constant, as we have no real power over the natural weather generating processes. However, as the two previous chapters described, anthropogenic forces have artificially amplified the hazard, such as by the management of urban runoff. Therefore, a utilization of the deconstructed risk equation can provide a clearer focus for a more resilient city, which should be focused on reducing hazard, vulnerability and exposure; or in short, the consequences.

In order to reduce ambiguity and provide a degree of conceptual clarity, resilience may be incorporated within the conventional generic risk equation in a similar fashion to consideration of a lack of capacity to respond. For example, by adapting the existing frameworks it could be viewed as risk = (hazard − resilience) × (vulnerability − resilience) × (exposure − resilience). Essentially therefore resilience is not an unconnected aim, but is embedded in the concept of risk and may be fundamentally seen as a mechanism to manage the consequences of risk on people and places via spatial planning more effectively, *especially* in the face of uncertainty. This also reinforces the opinion that resilience is not the opposite of vulnerability; rather, that the concepts should be viewed as independent constructs which have the ability to be considered in an integrated fashion. The following section expands on this knowledge by discussing the links between risk, resilience and spatial planning in more depth, arguing that the deconstruction of the concept can help address uncertainty.

Risk, resilience and water in the city

> As we know, there are known knowns; there are things we know we know. We also know there are known unknowns; that is to say we know there are some

things we do not know. But there are also unknown unknowns – the ones we
don't know we don't know.

(Donald Rumsfeld, former US Secretary of Defense, 12 February 2002)

Deeply hidden in this much-mocked opaque assertion is a surprisingly useful
concept, simply constructed: we live in an intensely complex, interconnected
and turbulent world, and, we should recognize that our knowledge is incomplete. To effectively manage risks we need to acknowledge that not all threats
can be either measured or even foreseen. 'Unknown unknowns' appears para-
doxical, yet its message could provide a useful basis for understanding unusual,
unpredictable events and the consequent need for in-built resilience to manage risks. The theoretical grounding of risk and resilience provides a key link
to planning, which in recent years has moved away from an outcome driven
post-war approach based on the regulation and control of land. The modern
view of spatial planning has a wide ranging more strategic, interlinked remit
incorporating both people and places and has therefore become more inclusive and process orientated; in short, an approach much more conducive to
facilitating the many routes to resilience within cities. When predicting a coin
toss or throw of the dice the probabilities are clear and set; with regard to risks
from water and climate this simply does not apply and we need to make decisions in an uncertain world. But how should we consider this within spatial
planning?

Part of the problem in disaster mitigation is that contemporary hazards
may be less directly related to an explicit cause and effect. Indeed, the phrase
'natural disaster' is misleading as it implies helplessness to the whims of nature.
Since the mid-1970s it has become increasingly recognized that the human
element is key (O'Keefe et al. 1976) and that the way that society is structured
can have a huge effect. Indeed, Wisner et al. (2004: 321) convincingly argue
that: 'disasters are essentially historically and spatially specific outcomes of the
process of contemporary capitalism'. Therefore, what we may commonly refer
to as natural disasters may be the result of a techno-economic development
process, which perpetuates socio-economic inequalities and is largely driven
by the private sector and short term institutional thinking. Indeed, it may be
more accurate to use the term 'cultural disaster' for many of these events as
essentially we have normalized risk and have been complicit in increasing the
risk of a variety of threats.

The fatalistic 'act of God' approach to disaster mitigation perpetuates injus-
tice by preventing remedial action and facilitating repeated exposure. Indeed,
the concept would only be valid if the following conditions all apply: natural
disasters are outside of our control; we have very limited scope for accurate pre-
diction; and we have no way to alleviate the impacts. This view also has impacts
on our ability to respond to risks; if we see disasters as uncontrollable events
that harm the built environment there is a tendency to view their management
in both a physical and post-disaster context, inhibiting strategic intervention

(Wamsler 2008). It is important that we change this view, especially considering the strength and inability to positively influence many of the drivers outlined in previous chapters. Indeed, it may be argued that in all but the rarest of cases, disasters should be viewed as manufactured: either intentionally or unintentionally. Therefore, they can at least in part be addressed by society as they are directly related to hazard, vulnerability and exposure, which have clear synergies with the wide remit of spatial planning.

If we accept the argument first put forward by White (1945) and expanded by O'Keefe *et al.* (1976) that disasters are more a consequence of socio-economic than natural factors, the links between resilience and the possible remit of the built environment professions comes into sharper focus. In this instance resilience would link strongly with the sustainable development agenda, as disasters can greatly affect the ability to meet sustainability goals. Presently, sustainable development is perceived to be the overriding aim of many modern planning systems and sustainable measures to manage water are becoming more strongly advocated. Examples vary from floodplain restoration to promoting zero additional runoff from development to encouraging natural infiltration. However, linking spatial planning with either sustainable water management or risk and resilience is still in its infancy (Werritty 2005). Furthermore, to address vulnerability planning could also utilize its influence in related non-water fields, such as poverty reduction and promotion of measures to address social exclusion. By linking resilience with sustainable development, utilizing the precautionary principle and taking a holistic view of resilience we can approach the concept of a city more resilient to water hazards with increased confidence, and provide spatial planning with a clearer agenda for action.

If natural disasters are driven by societal factors, then resilience must also be about facilitating the ability to cope. In part response, there has been a recent move away from a focus on engineering and structural resilience towards integrating more non-structural resilience methods, such as insurance provision or the ability of support services to respond. The 2005 UK flood in Carlisle provides a good example of the need for this in practice. As the city centre became quickly inundated not only was it clear that the area was not adequately protected by hard engineered defences, but also, as chapter 3 explained, that socio-economic influences had made the city highly vulnerable to the effects of flooding. In addition to homes and businesses being affected, critically, many of the police and fire services were located on the floodplain inhibiting their ability to respond and lowering the resilience of the city. Resilience therefore can include structures, institutions, processes and people and in practice it is much more cost effective to consider the concept from a pre-disaster context (Bosher 2008). Importantly, planning is one of the few agencies that can influence many of these areas, but it needs to be considered in a broad strategic sense to have the most impact. Resilience is therefore more than building codes and controlling development in specific locations; it is a holistic view where the concept is seen as an integral part of an encompassing process, not a structural measure tacked on to development.

Once the contemporary, holistic definition of resilience is understood real linkages with the planning system occur as resilience fundamentally concerns people, places and management strategies, all central facets of spatial planning. Consideration of uncertainty is also key, as in cases where an accurate value of risk is impossible to calculate, risk and uncertainty become a matter of judgement and therefore connect with the core skill of the planner and within the remit of the precautionary principle. This complex, reflexive understanding also shares some parallels with current thinking on the role of spatial planning within water management, which is viewed as interventionist and future orientated (Evans *et al.* 2004; White and Richards 2007). Resilience in this instance should therefore be viewed as an ongoing aspiration, not necessarily a mathematical construct to be measured or a specific level to be attained.

The perception of risk

It is also important to consider issues connected with the perception of risk and the way that it is understood. Risk is not a real phenomenon as such and therefore cannot actually be measured. In actuality there are no 'risks', only perceived perils manufactured by society; moreover, the temporal nature of risk as a *future* hazard means that it can never be 'experienced'. Therefore, the concept should be viewed as a constructed danger that disappears as soon as an event occurs, at which point it transforms from a risk into an impact. In actuality risk is stochastic, but perhaps a result of an emergence from the statistical, engineering and physical sciences, incongruously risk is widely seen to be both actual and incalculable. This divergence inevitably provides inherent communication challenges. Therefore, the way that risk is conveyed in policy may not reflect either its complex conceptual nature or the ambiguity in its evaluation. Moreover, the simplistic language of risk calculation may falsely reduce uncertainty to a comforting illusion of deterministic, probabilistic processes within which the inherent gravitas of scientific calculations can attach a misleading confidence to very tentative outcomes. This was a point recognized by Wynne (2009: 308) who argued that the current methodology for managing risk is erroneous and: 'the dominant risk science approach is more than a method; it is a misbegotten culture which inadvertently but actively conceals that ignorance'.

The way that risk is subsequently perceived can also vary greatly between the lay and professional and may not reflect the real chance of detriment in a realistic manner. The general public may believe that if a house is granted planning permission then it must be safe from flooding. Yet this risk is not the only issue in planning decisions, which considers other needs and may make a judgement on why people should live with a small risk of flooding. The expert is therefore in a position of trust, first in processing scientific risk data, and then in making decisions to ensure that the public is protected. Thus risk may be constructed differently by experts and citizens, and consequently amplified and communicated in a diverse fashion by various actors and agencies. This process is not conveyed very well however and the general public implicitly believes that the planner will ensure that their newly constructed house will be completely safe, not only *partially* protected as there was a competing persuasive need to provide affordable housing. The communication of objective versus subjective risks is therefore vital, both between professions to the planner and then to the public. This issue is becoming more important as the realities of risk management are leading a move towards the 'living with risk' agenda, with individuals becoming increasingly expected to make their own judgements on the level of risk they are willing to accept (White *et al.* 2010).

Conclusion

> When the well's dry, they know the worth of water.
> (Benjamin Franklin, *Poor Richard's Almanack*, 1733)

There has been a long gradual transition from a view that powerful forces may shape our destinies; to a heavy reliance on probability; to an awareness that risk may be socially constructed. The view that humanity can cope with the ravages of nature via risk management is related to the Baconian Creed outlook outlined in chapter 1: essentially it argues that if we cannot physically master nature, we can still provide recompense. The level of knowledge currently possessed by society concerning decisions which may increase the risk of natural hazards should render both the act of God axiom and the phrase 'natural disaster' redundant. Some catastrophes are perceived to be rapid, unpredictable events, the timescale of which seemingly makes it almost impossible to prepare and respond to the aftermath effectively. In reality however most natural hazards are slow building affairs and the roots of vulnerability and exposure may be both centuries in the making or related to recent policies.

The development of risk management within society has centred upon the fields of statistics and insurance, and is therefore tightly linked with finance and compensation. Statisticians may argue that risks can be economically quantified and thus addressed by society. Yet, if alternative management options are available, advocating exposure to threats is not a sustainable position, regardless of the ability to be financially compensated. The development of cities in a manner disconnected from hazard does create a legacy of risk and as a society we essentially utilize a system of designing urban areas that unwittingly welcomes the threat. Individuals, businesses and infrastructure are therefore subject to involuntary dangers, yet paradoxically these very same people may be risk averse, raising concerns that the liability for losses could shift towards the experts making decisions. Manufactured risk therefore needs to become more culturally perceptible, both by planners and the public to better reflect the pressures on society. This position also raises questions as to the extent to which uncertainty regarding the existence or strength of a hazard may be reduced to a calculation of probability (Hansson 2009). Whilst packaging risk in this manner can be useful as a simple communication tool we need to move away from a dominant view that risk can be definitively measured; it can't. In reality, attaching a probabilistic value to a highly uncertain event may actually be a highly tentative judgement masquerading as scientific truth. However, the concept of resilience may prove to be very important to tackling uncertainty within practice.

From the late twentieth century onwards awareness of risks has grown to the extent that some observers now argue that it had become a defining characteristic for organizing contemporary society (Adams 1995; Beck 1999). Despite this profile the theoretical treatment of resilience and risk within spatial planning has been soft and the concept has been widely advocated without firmly identifying how the notion relates to the subject. As a result, these emerging concepts may suffer some of the same criticism received due to the almost ubiquitous use of sustainability, which has arguably blurred what was initially a radical construct. Without a degree of conceptual clarity, the fuzzy nature of terms like risk and resilience could lead to an unthinking acceptance and utilization, within which the notion only gets contested when they move from being very pliable and innocuous theories to the world of praxis. As noted by Adger (2000), the concept of resilience should not be transferred uncritically from the ecological sciences to social systems.

This chapter has attempted to rectify this development to some extent by deconstructing risk and related concepts with regard to spatial planning, and embedding resilience with the risk equation. Moreover, considering the component parts of risk can provide a more targeted agenda for action incorporating both outcome and process aspects of risk management. A multiplicity of measures designed to decrease hazard, vulnerability and exposure, or, in short, the consequences of socio-economic processes, are firmly within the remit of planning. For example, planning could address these issues by looking at a wide range of strategies, many of which may bear little relationship to the traditional methods to manage water-based hazards, from focusing on vulnerability by tackling poverty to ensuring that institutions with duties to respond are not themselves located in areas at risk. Furthermore, understanding resilience within the context of water and the city should not necessarily be viewed as a mechanism to 'bounce back', but considering the pressure on cities also as a means to adapt to what will be changing and uncertain circumstances. Therefore, in simple terms, resilience is important because of three interconnected reasons: the ability to address uncertainty, the potential to adapt to minimize impacts and facilitating the capacity to respond.

The geographer, Gilbert White, is commonly referred to as the father of floodplain management (Wescoat 2006). In his influential post-war dissertation White (1945) powerfully argued that people can be held responsible for losses from floods. This viewpoint gradually became widely accepted, and questions surrounding 'which person', 'which institution' or 'which processes' should subsequently be asked in order to lessen future risk. Society needs to take responsibility for its actions: there is a strong argument that given scientific knowledge on the causes of climate change, predicted population growth and ill-planned development, increasing risk from natural hazards should not be a surprise. Allocating blame is not the intention here. Rather, the phrase 'act of planners' is deliberately contentious, designed to raise awareness concerning the ability of planners to intervene – for good or ill – rather than take a firm view of culpability. This point does however clearly link with the need to communicate the nuances of risk better to planners, and especially to the public. We should scale back the inherent claims to scientific authority in risk communication and instead convey the uncertainties involved in risk management, allowing the individual to take greater responsibility. People may deal with uncertainty by following societal messages and guidelines, and if a detriment does happen at least they know they have acted rationally and correctly. Therefore, the process of calculating risk and using it as a basis for judgement can serve to immunize decision making from failure (Reith 2009).

Uncertainty does not have to equal inaction however. We therefore need to develop processes to enable us to act effectively, even if we don't know for sure. The following chapter explores this point in more depth; outlining the principles of a theoretical water resilient city and starts the process of moving towards a more sophisticated and integrated approach to contemporary water management. Indeed, if we don't consider risk management as a central tenet we are essentially relying on faith or luck as a way to consider hazards and ignoring the pivotal contribution of the socio-economic context. As Bernstein (1998: 197) states: 'If everything is a matter of luck, risk management is a meaningless exercise. Invoking luck obscures truth because it separates an event from its cause.'

6 Principles of intervention

Those cities which lie to the rising of the sun are all likely to be more healthy than such as are turned to the North, or those exposed to the hot winds, even if there should not be a furlong between them. In the first place, both the heat and cold are more moderate. Then such waters as flow to the rising sun, must necessarily be clear, fragrant, soft, and delightful to drink. For the sun in rising and shining upon them purifies them, by dispelling the vapors which generally prevail in the morning. The persons of the inhabitants are, for the most part, well colored and blooming [and] in temper and intellect are superior to those which are exposed to the north. A city so situated resembles the spring as to moderation between heat and cold, and the diseases are few in number, and of a feeble kind. The women there are very prolific, and have easy deliveries.

(Hippocrates, fourth century BC)

The above passage appears in the section of the Hippocratic corpus entitled, *On Airs, Waters, and Places*. Although the text is mainly concerned with medicinal matters, it also was one of the first to explicitly link health and well-being with the nature of cities, specifically highlighting how wider environmental factors, such as its relationship with the natural world and the local climate, can affect the quality of life of urban dwellers. Whilst we now know that many of these early observations were incorrect, the principle driving the text is enduring: the fundamental desire to intervene and improve how we live. Considering the wide importance of the city from economic, cultural and social perspectives, it is logical that we should aim to follow in the footsteps of Hippocrates by generating knowledge and adapting urban form in order to maximize environmental benefits and minimize risks. But how should we do this? It is clear that cities will experience differing constraints and opportunities; consequently no single strategy could be applicable for all areas. An understanding of risk, as outlined in the previous chapter, may prove beneficial, but there is a need to develop guiding principles for intervention that can be applicable regardless of context.

A basis for intervention

The desire to intervene and address impacts, such as security needs, poor standards of living and environmental impacts, has a long standing historical foundation. However, the move from ad hoc approaches to more formalized and structured intervention has only occurred in the relatively recent past and in particular since the establishment of the first modern planning systems. 'Spatial planning' is an inclusive term that encompasses a seemingly ever-expanding array of topics, from the longer established housing or transport provision, to more modern objectives, such as designing out crime or improving health. Given this scope it is perhaps understandable that there are many different definitions of planning, but overall there is some degree of consensus on its key characteristics or aims. The remit of planning may be simply described as inherently reactive, future orientated and seeking to rationally achieve end states (Rydin 2003). The outlook is satisfyingly encompassing and has both synergies with initial utopian city building exercises and more postmodern collaborative approaches. It also clearly links to the need to protect society from environmental risks.

Significantly, whilst organizations with the mandate and power to act are now generally in place, in modern societies there is a need to gather data, collate arguments and produce convincing evidence for many changes to be initiated. This process ensures planning is a very logical activity and explicitly links some certainty concerning potential impacts with the process of intervention. Some of the first examples of this important relationship was provided by the work of pioneering social scientists, such as Engels (1845: 92) in his vivid *The Condition of the Working Class in England in 1844* where he described the prevailing social conditions in an industrial city in a enormously unflattering light, stating:

> Such is the Old Town of Manchester, and on re-reading my description, I am forced to admit that instead of being exaggerated, it is far from black enough to convey a true impression of the filth, ruin, and uninhabitableness, the defiance of all considerations of cleanliness, ventilation, and health which characterise the construction of this single district, containing at least twenty to thirty thousand inhabitants. And such a district exists in the heart of the second city of England, the first manufacturing city of the world. If any one wishes to see in how little space a human being can move, how little air – and such air! – he can breathe, how little of civilization he may share and yet live, it is only necessary to travel hither.

In addition to Engel's study of Manchester, similar examinations of London and Chicago by Henry Mayhew and Upton Sinclair respectively both extolled an anti-urban agenda, with the city variously described as being a dark, teeming and threatening place. These investigations carried on the tradition of Hippocrates and were vitally important in understanding the effects of the emerging industrial paradigm on city inhabitants and raised awareness of the need to consider wide scale intervention. Although humanity has continuously attempted to improve the places in which we live, it was the Industrial Revolution, and the resultant squalor and impacts movingly described by Engels, which ultimately led to the birth of formal intervention in the form of the modern planning system. Indeed, as the risks and impacts become more powerful, it is logical that the tools for intervention should respond accordingly.

Although the desire to increase standards of living was the first basis for intervention, as the environmental movement gained momentum and science revealed the global nature of cause and effect, the complex issue of anthropogenic forcing became highlighted. If problems may be caused or received on opposite sides of the world, how can you intervene effectively? In addition to risk, some modern intervention strategies have subsequently been framed around the useful notions of *adaptation* and *mitigation*, concepts that are able to address both the cause and effect of challenging international problems, most notably the issue of climate change. The following sections develop the risk and resilience equation outlined previously and explain how these two complementary ideas can be incorporated within an overarching risk based conceptual framework.

Linking risk, resilience and uncertainty with adaptation and mitigation

As the role of humanity in driving problems on a global scale has been more widely recognized there has been a move to limit our contribution. This is what may be termed the mitigation agenda, which from a climatic perspective can be defined as: 'an anthropogenic intervention to reduce anthropogenic forcing of the climate system' (IPCC 2007b: 878). Or to consider the issue with regard to risk; as society has a role in increasing the hazard we can try to lessen this negative contribution by reducing the driving forces. In reality however these potentially damaging trends may not necessarily be quickly reversed, or even slowed. Therefore, cities will also need to live with the consequences of changes in risk. This is where the sister concept of adaptation becomes valuable. Using the same climatic viewpoint, adaptation may be defined as: 'adjustment in natural or human systems in response to expected or actual climatic stimuli or their effects, which moderates harm or exploits beneficial opportunities' (IPCC 2007b: 869). Or to put the issue in a more simple fashion: as not all the changes can be prevented we need to live with the impacts. Both can be seen as being closely linked with the sustainable development agenda, as they have the capacity to limit social, economic and environmental impacts, and, via the use of mitigation in particular, can help limit long term effects and pursue intragenerational equity.

Within climate change, the focus was initially on developing a mitigative agenda, and, as it was increasingly realized that impacts would occur regardless of the efficacy of any measures, adaptation started to become seen as an equivalent part of the solution. The information contained in part II however suggests that with regard to water, the opposite appears to have been the case; adaptation has been the key area, with mitigation the poorer cousin. Both concepts however do have value in contemporary environmental management and can be applicable to differing fields. In particular, they have value where there is a disconnection between the power to influence all aspects of cause and effect within a short timescale, such as occurs when considering the drivers concerned with water and the city.

The wider relationship between the two aspects is most easily considered in the context of the climate change agenda, which has engaged with both of these notions. Figure 6.1 describes how climate change leads to impacts and vulnerabilities, which in turn informs policy responses. These can either address the mitigation agenda and thus the scale of the climate problem, such as by reducing GHGs, or aim to adapt to the consequences, for example by developing strategies to cool urban areas. Adaptation and mitigation should also not be considered as operating independently. In practice, an attempt to adapt may inhibit the ability to mitigate. Alternatively, maladaptation may

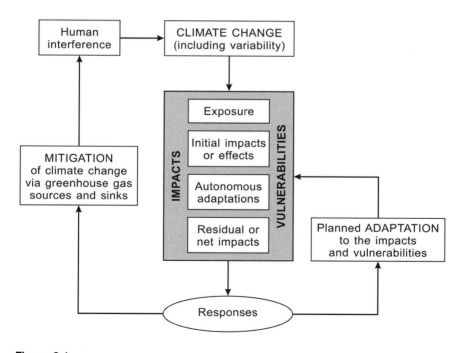

Figure 6.1

Adaptation and mitigation in the context of climate change
Source: Smit *et al.* 1999

occur where the intervention may bring harm as well as benefits. For example, urban densification may help reduce energy use, but could increase the volume of surface runoff or the total exposure to urban risk (McEvoy *et al.* 2006).

Analysing the model in more depth, the difference between *autonomous* and *planned* adaptation is also important. The former is an informal response, such as might occur in less developed nations or natural systems, characterized as reactive with a minimal strategic overview. Whereas the latter is what you might term formal intervention, such as involving mechanisms of the state. Consideration of this distinction, and the effectiveness of governance institutions in taking action, can also help explain the problematic context outlined earlier in the book. For example, the scale of risk does provide a powerful argument that there has been a lack of a planned targeted response in many cities thus far. Moreover, a reliance on the state as the means to manage flood risk may inhibit the drive for autonomous adaptation, such as may have occurred in the past.

There is also a temporal distinction between the two areas, with the impact of adaptation usually occurring swiftly, whilst there may be a long lag time before mitigation actions have any affect. Adaptation can therefore be useful to address rapidly emerging problems, such as flash flooding, whilst mitigation may be well suited to the slower, more pervasive, water resources agenda. Similarly, there is a disparity in the scope of influence, whereby adaptation is stronger at addressing local impacts, whilst mitigation has the potential to affect much larger scales. The two concepts are clearly useful to considering the management of water in the city, but, just as with the case of resilience, we need to reflect upon how they may aid clarity within decision making and relate these useful ideas to the overarching concept of risk.

A conceptual framework of risk

Resilience is viewed as a key idea to tackle risk, particularly in an uncertain arena. As outlined previously, the concept can be understood as being either concerned with restoring equilibrium, or adapting to differing circumstances affecting both the city and its citizens. This dual distinction is important. The former has conventionally been achieved via insurance, or any other form of disaster response; it is reactive, occurs after the event and at its most basic level may require no specific skill or knowledge, apart from relating probability to financial recompense. This approach is commonplace within cities, but it does perpetuate risk by adopting a narrow focus on protection via restoration and is therefore not a particularly sustainable approach. This view of resilience facilitates ad hoc intervention and can be appropriate when the scope of the potential effects are small and a lighter managerial touch appropriate.

The alternative view of resilience, best understood as concerning adaptation to a changing normality, is however more problematic to implement, which perhaps explains why it has not been as widely utilized. As a precursor to this approach there is a need to address difficult questions such as, 'what is the current risk?' Or 'how should society change?' It is therefore reliant on the production of science and knowledge, the ability to predict and project risk, and effective governance. This accumulation of data does however enable an engagement with complexity, which is the basis to developing a long term strategic approach to risk management. As attaining knowledge requires resources, any impacts may need to reach a certain damaging level to demand a less neoliberal approach to resilience. This effect may be seen in the master planning ethos as adopted at the end of the nineteenth century, such as the Garden City movement, and at the start of the twenty-first, as displayed by the birth of various EcoCity projects: as impacts increase so does the desire for planned remedial action. Therefore, to achieve anything more than a basic engagement with resilience may require a more interventionist approach to governance.

These dual connotations of resilience have clouded understanding of the concept within spatial planning. For example, when the resilient city is used as an academic metaphor is it connected with reactively restoring normality, such as by improving responses to a natural or artificial disaster? Or about proactively adapting to future hazards, such as by designing green space in cities to store excess water? Although distinctive, the differing perspectives can be complementary when considered in the context of the risk and resilience equation outlined in the previous chapter. Indeed, developing the understanding can provide a tighter focus and increased conceptual coherence to managing water in the city.

When considered more closely, the differing connotations of resilience can each be considered as having synergies with differing sections of the risk equation. A restoration of equilibrium is essentially concerned with both bouncing back, as catered for via insurance, or with influencing the drivers forcing change to the system, which currently does not yet occur with regard to water. The understanding consequently has humanistic and systemic interpretations. From a planning perspective, the mitigation agenda can therefore be linked with tackling the drivers forcing normality. This may be best expressed as a reduction of the *hazard*, which has links with anthropogenic forcing in a similar fashion to climate change. This may incorporate strategies designed to proactively decrease driving forces, such as urban runoff, and thereby increase the resilience of a city to both hazard and the overall risk. Equally, adaptation appears to be most closely connected with the *exposure* and *vulnerability* part of risk. For example, this may involve the alteration of a form or purpose of a building to increase its resilience to a flood event or addressing pockets of poverty, which may be amplifying vulnerability. In essence this might be best understood as adapting to changing normalities. In sum, reducing the hazard can be connected with the 'equilibrium' metaphor of resilience, such as by reducing the forcing drivers influencing normality, whilst addressing exposure and vulnerability has synergies with the alternative understanding: 'adaptation' to the consequent circumstances.

Figure 6.2 draws upon Smit *et al.* (1999) and illustrates how the differing concepts can relate to each other. It also provides a further insight into how

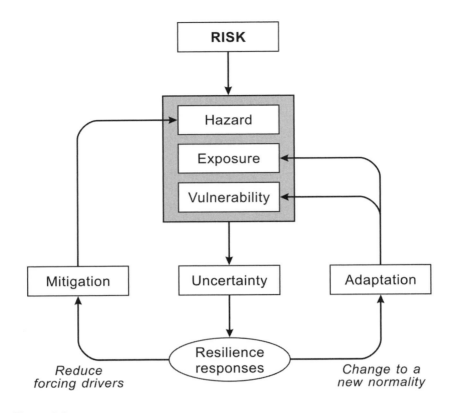

Figure 6.2

Incorporating risk and resilience within a decision-making framework

spatial planning can utilize potentially useful, but ambiguous, concepts such as risk, uncertainty, resilience, adaptation and mitigation in order to help manage water in the city. In this model, risk is determined by the interaction between hazard, vulnerability and exposure. The level of uncertainty in these areas then informs the policy response, which is centred on the need to pursue adaptive or mitigative options. These two pathways incorporate the differing metaphors of resilience. These interventions then feed back into the model to separately influence the three elements of risk and the cycle continues.

This flexible methodology of managing water in the city can ensure a consistent approach and potentially provides a framework for cities to design their own strategies dependent upon their own drivers and constraints. The next stage is to consider how best to utilize figure 6.2 within spatial planning to enable cities to become more resilient to flooding and drought. Prior to any discussion of individual measures however we first need to address the issue of uncertainty, which although could be seen as operating in all aspects of the model, is most prevalent as a barrier to implementing effective resilience responses.

Engaging with uncertainty

> The very term 'planning' implies that society should find a means of handling the uncertainties facing us.
>
> (Rydin 2004: 8)

Natural disasters occurring within urban areas may be described as a product of either inadequate governance frameworks or overly short term and narrow land use planning perspectives. Yet the information detailed within this book provides a strong argument that, historically, our understanding of the vast majority of water risks has been highly uncertain. The significant veiled role of uncertainty, most easily expressed as the degree to which a value is unknown, as a contributory driver of risk should not be underestimated. In theory, high levels of uncertainty within risk management could be addressed via the contested view of post-normal science or the largely accepted precautionary principle methodology; both of which suggest that societies should act where there are high consequences and high uncertainty. However, the previous chapters argue that these approaches have not been successful in intervening within the complex arena of water risks.

As the examples of the early social and environmental pioneers demonstrate, within society there is a need to collate an evidence base in order to inform intervention. A lack of surety concerning both the problem and solution effectively prevents planned adaptation or mitigation, and therefore inhibits resilience responses. As governance mechanisms with the potential to intervene are in place, there is clearly a disconnect between the *theoretical* and *actual* ability to act, part of which may be due to a lack of evidence. Without this secure foundation the management of risk may slip down the order of priorities and pose challenges for collaborative approaches. This situation particularly applies to spatial planning, which has been tightly linked with knowledge of cause and effect, such as the early need to predict and provide, or the more modern notion of evidence based planning.

The most straightforward way to reduce uncertainty in this context is to expand knowledge and science within areas specifically related to water. An increased evidence base could facilitate the implementation of complementary mitigative and adaptive resilience responses. But before we can consider how best to use the information, we first need to consider more fundamental questions connected with the spatial nature of the risk. It is commonplace for the victims of flooding or drought to accord blame, but as absolute protection from these hazards is now recognized as being impossible, societies should initiate a debate concerning protection and responsibility. As a component of this process cities and their inhabitants need to reflect upon risk and uncertainty and enable freer access to information. This step would also be a precursor to devolving a degree of responsibility for disasters away from either nature or the nation state.

Specific questions include: how much risk are societies willing to accept? How certain should experts be before they intervene on behalf of citizens? How, and to what extent, should citizens be protected by the state or other agencies? And how should this occur? Each city will be exposed to differing levels of risk according to factors such as historical development patterns, geographical location or economic structure. Therefore, engaging with uncertainty requires an initial unpacking of the nature of the threat and the current gaps in knowledge within a specific locality. The requirement for intervention will also differ spatially, as in practice some citizens and countries will be more risk averse, or risk tolerant, than others.

To apply the knowledge we also need to consider the uncertainty inherent within the information. This is related to two aspects in particular: the probability of the hazard and the severity of the consequences. Although a complete absence of uncertainty can never be achieved, this shouldn't prohibit our ability to engage with the concept and accumulate data to help inform action. To aid decision making, where possible risk and uncertainty should be quantified in order to help weight the problem against competing concerns. Where a precise value of risk is impossible to calculate, professional judgement and a precautionary approach should apply. Both risk *and* uncertainty should be expressed where possible, thereby facilitating the devolution of decision making away from the expert and providing a qualitative dimension to balance quantitative mapping and modelling data.

In practice, risk and intervention will become increasingly socially and culturally constructed with relative values attached, as risk may be determined one way by mathematicians and another by the non-expert. As a result the value becomes assessed, interpreted and communicated by differing groups in varying ways. For example, certain interest groups may amplify the risks to influence decision making, whether intentionally or not. Intervention therefore needs to balance the variety of opinion: not just what the experts think, but what the citizen's value. An understanding of potential deficiencies also provides a feedback loop into future data requirements designed to further reduce uncertainty and help move towards a city more resilient to water hazards.

The ability of the planning system to influence land use and future development patterns over the medium to longer term is vital in any move towards a more water sensitive city. However, a more effective management strategy requires an engagement with uncertainty to better understand the threat within each urban area. This process can in turn expose gaps in learning which can be used to inform future scientific research. The following section discusses the type of knowledge necessary to move towards sustainable, collaborative and strategic solutions based on the specifics of place.

The production of knowledge

> Knowledge is one. Its division into subjects is a concession to human weakness.
>
> (Sir Halford John Mackinder)

The foundation of any water resilient city is knowledge: both in terms of its generation and effective dissemination. Indeed, this should be viewed as a logical mechanism to reduce the emerging issue of uncertainty. Although there is a need to view risks holistically, the scale and complexity of the problem within cities argues that we could reflect the views of the English geographer Mackinder and deconstruct risks to the city before considering the subject as a complete entity. Even though attaining data across multiple fields may be largely outside the remit of spatial planning there is a clear need for this information to feed into strategic land use decisions. Information produced by, or contained within, agencies that deal with weather forecasting, environmental protection, geological organizations or water and sewerage providers, for example, are all important to accurately assessing risks of flooding and scarcity. Engaging with uncertainty may inform knowledge requirements and limitations, but the information itself provides the potential for a robust evidence base to enable spatial planning to intervene within cities.

Before we consider specific intervention strategies we first need to outline the necessary knowledge requirements. Within many countries that have recently experienced disasters, there has been an upsurge in interest with regard to ascertaining more scientific evidence on the causes and sources of risk. For example, in England there is an ever improving understanding of the areas that may flood, due to advances such as flood risk mapping, modelling of urban water flows and the requirement for the production of flood risk assessments at various scales. As an initial source of information, a map of areas at risk from fluvial, coastal, estuarine and groundwater flooding provides a logical, and achievable, foundation.

A further layer of knowledge is connected with the provision to manage surface water. As chapter 3 outlined, this artificially driven source of risk is very uncertain and policy makers are only recently beginning to understand and address the issue. Further, whilst the location and connectivity of the majority of the below ground surface water management infrastructure is well mapped, in some areas there is evidence that the existence of hidden watercourses and inaccurate mapping records make the true drainage capacity much more uncertain. Therefore, modelling information would be needed on the flow routes of *all* water, from the sources of flooding from watercourses high in the catchment, to the flow paths taken by surface water runoff, to the below ground sewer infrastructure. Planners could use this information to consider aspects such as increased urban water storage, redirecting the flow of surface or subsurface water away from areas at risk, or the identification of areas that should receive restricted levels of new development.

An additional source of information would be the mapping of green infrastructure; defined as the interconnected network of green spaces that conserve natural ecosystem values and functions and also benefit human populations (Benedict and McMahon 2006). Within urban areas there has been a gradual erosion of greenspace, partly because their overall contribution to the well-being of the city is often difficult to quantify and therefore undervalued (Pauleit and Duhme 2000). Yet they can provide vital functions for the management of flooding and scarcity via infiltration, evaporation, runoff and storage (Shaw et al. 2007). Although the floodplain as a geographical feature can currently influence development decisions, the related area of greenspace has no comparable impact on either flooding or scarcity decisions, despite the potentially significant influence on aspects fundamental to water in the city.

Closely linked to this data is information concerning the underlying ground composition. The difference in infiltration potential between sandy and clay soils can be significant, with the runoff generation of clay soils comparable to a highly built up area (Gill et al. 2007). Again, this information does not permeate into decisions concerning urban form and function. This means that areas which may currently be designated and protected as greenspace, and therefore perceived to operate as mechanisms to naturally manage flood risk, may actually provide very little benefit in this area. Further, areas of low density development sited upon sandy soils may bring significant unanticipated benefits in water storage and infiltration, but could be earmarked for densification.

A further data requirement would be concerned with the nature of the existing urban fabric. This is largely available and would need to be examined with regard to the presence of critical infrastructure, vital industries and vulnerable communities. The water resilient city would be able to manage flood and scarcity events with a minimum of impact. Therefore, the need to protect critical infrastructure, such as power stations, water treatment works, or even crucial water intensive industries would be paramount. In less developed nations it is commonplace for the most vulnerable to live in areas at risk from flooding or scarcity, but within advanced, industrialized cities the nature or function of developments has had no real impact on its location relative to water. Therefore, vulnerable buildings such as hospitals, schools or retirement homes, which may have the least ability to cope with a flood event, could be currently sited in relatively high risk locations. Equally, there may be a heavy reliance on virtual water to underwrite agricultural exports, tying socio-economic vulnerability to a consistent supply of water resources. Effectively utilizing this knowledge within land use decisions could positively affect the vulnerability of a city.

A more detailed understanding of the current and future scope of water resources also should influence decision making. Cities and regions adopting unsustainable abstraction regimes may experience potentially damaging contractions in industrial or agricultural output, not to mention possible environmental impacts. A medium to long term strategy aiming to balance water entitlements with resources is crucial in this respect. An understanding of the virtual water resources consumed within local production is important in order to become more resilient to future socio-economic orientated water shocks. These aspects should especially be considered in the regional context of potentially diminishing input from precipitation and rising water consumption. The factors also provide a basis for considering the requirement to promote water efficiency and incorporate technological efficiency measures within the built environment. Furthermore, the data is a prerequisite for addressing scarcity via increased storage, both formally with reservoirs and more innovatively within the city.

As a final point it needs to be recognized that as they currently stand these data sources are all snapshots. One of the main messages of this book is the need to proactively adapt, which requires consideration of present and future risks. The layers of knowledge therefore need to be enhanced with projections on the drivers and the pressures that an urban area may be placed under. For example, estimated population growth and detailed regional scale climate change predictions will assist in the development of the long term strategic view of constraints and opportunities. The development of water specific scenarios could be particularly useful in projecting these risks forward into the medium and long term. Figure 6.3 summarizes the theoretical layers of information needed to reduce uncertainty and help lessen the risk of either too much, or too little, water in the city.

It should be noted that figure 6.3 is illustrative in that to be effective the factors should not necessarily be viewed with regard to the precise spatial boundaries of a city. The nature of urban areas as an intensive consumer of resources means that the catchment or even the region, when considering water use by industry and agriculture, may be the most appropriate scale. We should also recognize that the production of this information does not guarantee a safe, sustainable and resilient city. The data is neutral and can be interpreted in differing ways, and even adapted to different scientific and policy agendas. For example, the mapping or modelling of information may not reflect political or administrative boundaries or future priorities. In addition, the differing sources of knowledge should try where appropriate to incorporate lay information, as there is a long history of tacit, indigenous strategies for environmental adaptation and locally specific knowledge of risks.

The potentially thorny issue of who should produce this knowledge has also not been addressed, as this would clearly differ from country to country. The scale of the assessment would however point towards a city, regional or national body to take the lead. This would be in contrast to the current trend where the onus may be predominantly on the developer, landowner or private sector industry, an approach that inhibits strategic, collaborative responses. It should be noted that not all the information covered in this section exists, but the drive to provide planners with increased data, such as the EU drive to strategically assess all sources of flood risk (European Union 2007), demonstrates that it may not be too far over the horizon. The real challenge will be

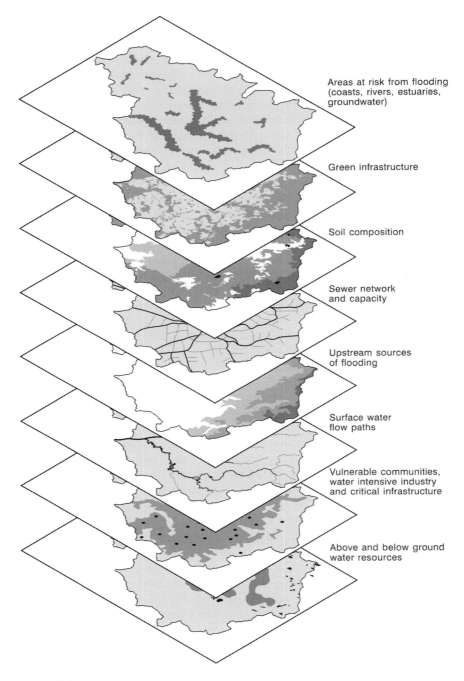

Areas at risk from flooding
(coasts, rivers, estuaries,
groundwater)

Green infrastructure

Soil composition

Sewer network
and capacity

Upstream sources
of flooding

Surface water
flow paths

Vulnerable communities,
water intensive industry
and critical infrastructure

Above and below ground
water resources

Figure 6.3

The differing layers of knowledge needed to move towards a water resilient city to link the knowledge with spatial planning so that it can influence adaptive and mitigative responses in an integrated manner.

The application of knowledge

> In wishing to bring a modicum of natural science to the planning process, I am, like most other planners, seriously hampered by ignorance of the subject.
>
> (McHarg 1969: 47)

The increased risk of New Orleans to catastrophic flooding by a gradual erosion of natural defences and inappropriate development had been highlighted prior to Hurricane Katrina in 2005 (Wisner *et al.* 2004). The data was there, the risk was identified, but it did not influence subsequent decision making to provide either adequate protection or an effective emergency response. Although the production of knowledge can situate risk and resilience within an urban land use context, and place the issue within the remit of spatial planning, it also needs to be applied. Knowledge on its own may be impotent; it is the way that the information is utilized that is vital. This is also particularly challenging, if, as McHarg (1969) identified over forty years ago, the sources of information are outside the core training of planners.

Risk management from a land use perspective does not operate in a vacuum; it needs to be weighted against other local priorities and linked with related issues, such as trade and regeneration. The planner is therefore a key agent of intervention, and data can give decisions a greater evidence base and link science and policy with increased accountability. Whilst the scope of this knowledge can help bridge the gap between policy silos, the actual application of these risk assessments may be difficult to utilize in practice, not least due to the way that the data is presented. This is not to say that the process should be overly scientific and mechanistic however; resilience responses should draw upon the experience and skills of planners in making judgements.

Although skill shortages may be in evidence in the short term, the need to engage with these layers of data is not necessarily outside the comfort zone of architects and planners who are used to considering a wide array of information before making decisions. New skills may be needed however and a wider appreciation of both the rapid and protracted effect water can have on society. The complexity of the issue may require that those professionals connected with the city should develop a greater specialism in hazard management, and foster a new normality within which to embed natural science based concepts such as risk and resilience.

The ability to successfully intervene will be reliant on a number of factors, and in particular financial and scientific resources. This may mean that those cities with the highest wealth may have both the highest risk and the strongest adaptive capacity. Further, levels of historic risk will be spatially different, dependent upon previous decisions; consequently, some cities will require more significant intervention than others. There is clearly a need to do more with less money, which could be achieved by a focus on what may be termed preemptive loss reduction, such as by protecting important assets from potentially catastrophic breakdown. This process sounds like a complex strategy, but it is essentially like wearing a car seat belt. The consequences can be severe so we should adapt behaviour as a result. Promoting urban resilience can also be one of the most efficient ways to allocate resources, as the United Nations estimate that for every one dollar spent to avoid disasters seven are saved in relief and rehabilitation costs (UN-Habitat 2006). Or as Benjamin Franklin more plainly stated when discussing the need for organized fire prevention in eighteenth-century Philadelphia: 'an ounce of prevention is worth a pound of cure'.

Beyond spatial planning

Although forward planning and financial aspects are important, intervention includes more than the availability of economic resources and good pre-disaster preparation: it is also tightly connected with effective partnerships. The application of resilience is therefore not just spatial, but connected with institutions and governance. A partnership approach provides the potential for a coherent strategy, wherein city-wide adaptation and mitigation can function as an integrated, reinforcing network. The notion of 'coping' or within risk management parlance, increasing resilience, should therefore be considered as applicable to multiple audiences and scales: from the state to the individual, from the country park to the building.

In practice, resilience is connected with altering the behaviour of actors and agencies that either increase personal risks or those of others. The array of data can help identify key risks and provide the evidence base to communicate, regulate, or even legislate, any required changes. In reality, you are not necessarily trying to make a city resilient *per se*, but more specifically targeting how and why urban hazard, exposure or vulnerability are driven and taking remedial action. The scope therefore goes way beyond spatial planning and relates to society as a whole.

The volume of data required to help manage water more effectively also throws the inadequacies of spatial planning into focus. The sheer scope of the causes and solutions of risk expand beyond planning and may not even be picked up by any other agency. Within England for example, the planning system has a statutory remit that specifically ties its responsibility to land use and development and there is a clear view that it should not seek to replicate other statutory regimes (Rydin 2004). Therefore, environmental risks need to be placed in a spatial context to be influenced via planning. The areas where responsibility falls beyond the scope of planning, such as when relating to sewerage infrastructure or retrofitting solutions, emphasize the importance of partnership approaches. Moreover, with regard to water management, some of the varying types of data with the ability to positively influence risk are not even widely recognized as being related to the field. For example, the underlying geology of an area can have a huge influence on runoff, whilst brownfield areas are frequently automatically targeted for regeneration regardless of their potential to manage water.

The effective and free transfer of data within and between agencies is also important for strategic, integrated intervention. In practice, information may be held by a variety of institutions with no single agency responsible for collation or dissemination. Therefore, its application within urban decision making can be subject to problems. For example, in the UK there are instances of utility companies holding information on areas that may be exposed to sewer flooding. However, the data remains confidential, meaning planning authorities and the Environment Agency cannot consider the issue within their decision making (Douglas *et al.* 2010). Furthermore, many utility companies may have research concerning how the changing climate in their area may affect water supply and usage over an extended timeframe. Yet, agencies concerned with regional and city development or spatial planning may not have access due to private sector sensitivities. The main principle behind this overall approach would be to collate all information in order to tightly link the hydro-geographical context with the natural and built environment so that the layout and function of urban areas can adapt to current and future risks. Theoretically, multiple agencies could operate to lessen overall hazard, exposure and vulnerability for all concerned.

To date, intervention in the city has been predominately pursued on an ad hoc basis, with individual buildings or developments incorporating a variety of methods dependent upon their particular context. The concept can embrace a much wider understanding than stronger building codes, water efficiency measures or minimizing floodplain construction however. Adaptation and mitigation applied on a holistic, strategic basis has a much higher potential to be effective. You could, for example, have one part of the city performing a high degree of water storage and infiltration to enable a continuation of intense densification elsewhere. Alternatively, you could aim for a gradual shift away from water intensive industry in order to help secure supplies for households and ecosystems. This change in scale is a prerequisite for making a city resilient, as opposed to a building, and has the potential to achieve the best overall reduction in risk for its citizens.

Conclusion

> Ultimately, the resilient city is a constructed phenomenon, not just in the literal sense that cities get constructed brick by brick, but in a broader cultural sense.
> (Vale and Campanella 2005: 353)

Discourses concerning more intervention to improve city living have traditionally been dominated by a social agenda. From alleviating deprivation to improving sanitation, factors such as social reform, wealth creation and advances in health care have transformed standards and helped make cities popular places to live. Advocating intervention in order to increase the quality of life for citizens did not start with the formation of planning systems however. The desire to manage a whole host of risks and become 'resilient' has been in operation long before the term entered the mainstream planning lexicon. The focus should also not be entirely on the built environment. As the quote above illustrates, resilience is strongly linked with cultural factors, such as the nature of institutions, behavioural trends and social values.

In essence, the dominant policy formation model typically follows the traditional scientific approach whereby science identifies and quantifies risks, and then politicians and policy makers respond. Risks connected with such a complex arena as water however, touching upon a host of issues across the natural and built environments, may challenge the certainty central to this approach. Consequently, risks have been tackled in a disconnected and deficient fashion. The scope of the problem also suggests that precautionary or post-normal theories, designed to act where uncertainty is high, have not been effective in influencing decisions. Increasing knowledge does however have the ability to transform intervention from being reliant upon 'post-normal' to 'normal' science. Therefore, cities with more information have a greater chance of implementing reinforcing resilience measures, as not only are politicians and policy makers more comfortable with this situation, but the data can provide a driver for collaborative partnerships across the city region.

In practice, the implementation of resilience to water risks may have been hampered by the lack of an appropriate framework for intervention, disjointed scientific understanding and a light touch approach to management. Whilst a policy of low market interference may be appropriate where impacts are low, as the scale of the effects increase so should the desired level of intervention. As population growth and changes in climate inhibit our ability to separate cities from their environmental constraints we need to develop principles of intervention that can enable cities to be more resilient to risks from water, particularly in an uncertain world. The far reaching social issues of the late nineteenth century and the modern climate change and population agendas both argue for changes to the form, function and operation of a city. Although not all cities will be subject to such wicked, emerging problems, those that are should consider engaging with risk to help lessen the impact of future water impacts.

Indeed, the responsibility to facilitate urban areas that can avoid climatic impacts far into the increasingly uncertain future argues that we could profitably re-engage with aspects of the visionary ideals and perspectives of the master planning proponents of the bygone era. A postmodern interpretation of the same strategic, long term planning principles as extolled over a century ago may provide an insight into how to effectively facilitate cities that are safe and competitive over the medium to long term, especially as the continued success of cities are perceived to be vitally important on both a national and global context. But to do this effectively may require challenging the hegemony of neoliberalism, developing accepted principles of intervention and enabling a broad partnership approach.

The earlier chapters have argued that many of the current and emerging problems associated with the management of water have their roots in unthinking action, inadequate governance or a lack of information as to the scope of potential effects. Therefore, an approach that utilizes a clear conceptual process of risk management can help to increase the resilience of cities and citizens to this hazard. The initial basis of a deeper understanding of the components of risk and its relationship to resilience provides a foundation upon which to consider how best intervention should occur in the city. This chapter has built on this information by outlining how adaptation and mitigation, ideas widely held as important mechanisms to tackle powerful and uncertain environmental risks, combined with an engagement with uncertainty can be used to address embedded hazard, exposure and vulnerability drivers. Essentially, the approach assists in unveiling a multiplicity of risky behaviours and enables cities to pursue resilience in a more strategic fashion. Together these natural science ideas can be amalgamated to produce a conceptual framework designed to better manage water in the city. Significantly, this approach is also flexible, scalable and communicable enabling its application within different contexts. The following three chapters utilize and expand on this approach to highlight in more detail the differing changes we can incorporate into the built and natural environments in order to increase resilience via mitigation and adaptation in the urban area.

Part IV

Planning for a sustainable future

· ·

7 Hazard and resilience in the city

· ·

> The last century has been remarkable for an exceedingly rapid growth of towns. In England this growth has produced serious results . . . Miles and miles of ground, which people not yet elderly can remember as open green fields, are now covered with dense masses of buildings packed together in rows along streets which have been laid out in a perfectly haphazard manner, without any consideration for the common interests of the people.

Take a moment to consider the above quotation and then try and guess in which year it was written. The observation is essentially concerning swift urban growth and urbanization, with particular reference to both the associated erosion of natural capital and the absence of a wider, strategic consideration of the impacts of the strategy on the resident population. Reflecting upon the information contained in earlier sections of the book, the timing is clearly post-Industrial Revolution, but retains a degree of contemporary resonance that challenges a strict temporal demarcation. The quote is actually contained within Raymond Unwin's agenda setting 1909 book, *Town Planning in Practice*, one of the very first 'planning' books published. The longevity of the passage aptly illustrates that concerns regarding city growth, urbanization and the resultant social and biological impacts are clearly an enduring problem, and that seemingly modern issues may have had a surprisingly long history. Indeed, one of the interesting aspects to the excerpt is its lingering applicability – just why is the quote still relevant some one hundred years after it was written?

Within the previous chapter there was an argument that social problems have been the main driver for intervention. The possible anthropocentricity of this view is not necessarily in conflict with the rise of modern environmental issues however; in reality much of the debate has been driven by a need to influence the built and natural environments, and so, as intimated by Unwin, limit the undesirable environmental impacts upon humanity. Yet, the mechanisms designed to influence these aspects of urbanity are imperfect. Notwithstanding the development of modern planning systems and their remit and power to control land use, there is actually very limited scope to alter the *existing* urban fabric. In practice, the majority of the power to intervene is focused on influencing future development. The scope of impacts and the rising value of land do however increase the need to influence embedded risks, as a focus on new urban development can only have a limited effect. Moreover, within spatial planning, disasters have been predominately addressed by influencing the use of land and strengthening building regulations. These policies are much easier to implement when considered on an individual basis; implementing resilience at a city level is much more complex.

The spatial nature of water risks affecting urban areas necessitates the need for a focus on flexible and transferable principles that can provide a basis for effective decision making. Utilizing the concept of risk as a basis for intervention does offer a possible solution, as it is a mechanism able to marry complex social, economic and environmental goals in an intergenerational manner, although its effective application by social scientists and planners may take time to mature. Strategies to manage urban risk by proactively reducing hazard, vulnerability and exposure have the potential to increase resilience in the medium and long term. But to date, part of the problem has been that cities simply haven't reflected upon risk and integrated the required knowledge to enable effective, strategic intervention. The following sections begin to unpack some of the differing resilience responses within the hazard aspect of the conceptual framework, before the following chapters explore the related notions of exposure and vulnerability. These chapters are not designed to provide a definitive list of all the various measures to better manage water in the city; but, rather, to provide an insight into applying the framework in practice and to highlight how cities can move towards a more sustainable urban future.

Managing hazard

In almost all spheres disasters can change normality: from tragedies at sea driving the design and operation of ships, to new policies and procedures to help strengthen buildings against hurricanes. The strategy can adopt a twofold approach, where we can both try to mitigate the strength of the hazard whilst adapting to reduce exposure and vulnerability. From a water and the city perspective, consideration of the hazard essentially connects to the urbanization discourse; how we use land, not just in a simple developmental sense, but also its associated infrastructure, from the roads and pavements, to the above- and below-ground drainage network. It may therefore also encompass the *absence* of development, such as the provision of natural spaces in and around cities.

Water based hazards can be both naturally *and* anthropogenically driven. Theoretically, one mitigative approach therefore can be to influence the natural world, and in particular its climate. The climate change predictions outlined in chapter 2 suggest that the precipitation patterns will be altered and more intense events increasingly common. We could therefore promote a reduction in the drivers for change, such as by a reduction of CFCs, but these issues largely fall outside the scope of the book and have been well covered within the climate change mitigation discourse. Moreover, cities, and even nations, have less influence over the scope and scale of any implementation on this scale. The area where cities can have the most effect is to concentrate on *their* contribution to localized hazard generation, a key anthropogenic aspect of risk. With regard to water and the city this is mainly focused on the interaction between precipitation and the surface of the urban area, including both built-up and natural areas, and the methodologies for managing this resource.

Even if strategies to decrease hazard generated within the city are initiated, external forcing is predicted to have an escalating effect. The predicted effect of climate change on weather patterns has been calculated within the UK conurbation of Greater Manchester. The research discovered that in the 'high' 2080 climate change scenario it is estimated there would be 56 per cent more precipitation, which equates to an 82 per cent increase in runoff, whilst in the 'low' 2080 scenario surface runoff would still increase (Gill *et al.* 2007). It should also be noted that this increase in runoff does not factor in any future growth projections, such as the desire to build an extra 172,400 houses in the study area, along with their associated hard infrastructure, between 2003 and 2021 (Government Office for the North West 2008). Figure 7.1 provides an insight into both the spatial nature of hazard generation within the conurbation and the potential increase in runoff up to 2080.

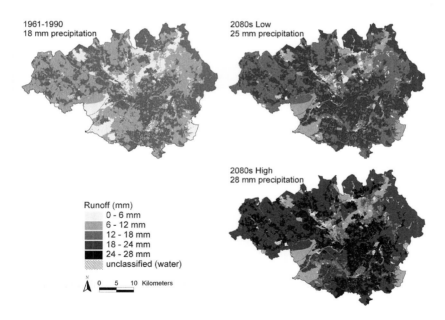

Figure 7.1

Modelled surface runoff from a precipitation event occurring on average one day per winter with normal antecedent moisture conditions in Greater Manchester
Source: Gill *et al.* 2007

The same research also provided an insight into relative drought by modelling the average number of months per year when grass may experience water stress in Greater Manchester. This occurs when the soil water deficit is greater than, or equal to, the limiting deficit and indicates urban areas where grass may suffer from drought due to the soil–climate system. As figure 7.2 shows, it was estimated that the number of months where grass may experience water stress would greatly increase in both the low and high scenarios. The comparison of the 1970s to the climate change projections for 2020, 2050 and 2080 gives an illustration of how even an urban area with a reputation for precipitation may need to adapt in the future. Again, this study did not factor in either future growth plans or potential increases in water use. As a final point it should be noted that the UK is by no means at the forefront of climate change impacts, a similar analysis conducted within the United States, Australia or the Indian subcontinent may reveal much more disturbing results.

The interaction between the surface of the city and precipitation is the key to exploring how to lessen hazard. The problems associated with the management of surface water have gained in prominence despite advances in intervention mechanisms and preventative knowledge and technology. There is a growing awareness that to effectively reduce the negative impacts from the prevailing

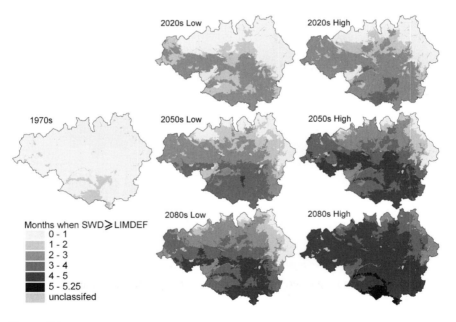

Figure 7.2

Modelled average number of months per year when grass may experience water stress in Greater Manchester
Source: Gill 2006

methodology, which range from surface water flooding to water scarcity to negative effects on ecosystems and habitats, society may have to reconsider how it controls surface water and incorporate a more holistic, strategic view that considers alternative management strategies. There are more sustainable and creative methods of surface water management available however, such as strategies that capture and store precipitation as a resource, or other methods that attenuate runoff, yet their usage is very much in the minority and the use of conventional hard infrastructure approach is dominant. The following section explores issues surrounding the use of alternative, yet complementary, *soft* infrastructure and outlines their ability to increase urban resilience.

Soft infrastructure

> Let the reader imagine Paris lifted off like a cover, the subterranean net-work of sewers, from a bird's eye view, will outline on the banks a species of large branch grafted on the river. On the right bank, the belt sewer will join the trunk of this branch, the secondary ducts will form the branches, and those without exit the twigs.
>
> (Victor Hugo, *Les Miserables*, 1862)

Victor Hugo colourfully highlighted the concealed value of the Parisian sewers by describing them as the 'intestines' of the city, drawing parallels with vital organs that perform similarly critical tasks. The metaphor also serves to emphasize that determining which facets of the city function as infrastructure can be problematic when they may operate in a hidden or unattributed manner. Hard defences or water supply infrastructure can be plainly regarded as an asset, but more natural land uses can also be designed to achieve comparable outcomes but with a less obviously engineered design.

Regardless of which approach is taken, in this respect the mitigation of hazard in the urban environment is centrally connected to the management of precipitation. This can include strategies to control runoff and the capture and storage of water for consumption. Historically, spatial planning has not engaged with precipitation issues in a significant manner, as this has been seen to fall within the remit of environmental protection agencies, civil engineering or water and sewerage providers. This view has been challenged as serious problems, such as flooding, diffuse pollution, environmental damage and low groundwater levels, gained in prominence and proved difficult to manage within existing practices. This predicament has assisted in fostering a growing awareness that to effectively reduce the impacts of runoff, spatial planning may have to engage with surface water and promote a more holistic, sustainable and strategic view.

A key mechanism able to provide an alternative methodology for surface water management is the use of sustainable urban drainage systems (SUDS), also known as best management practices or Low Impact Development. SUDS is a term encompassing a variety of techniques, which can be used singly or as part of an integrated system. They are a drainage approach inspired by natural processes, which have the potential to prevent many of the negative impacts of surface water by altering the focus of drainage design, construction, operation and maintenance to enable a higher degree of consideration to be given to the receiving environment. The SUDS methodology aims to mimic pre-development runoff levels so that even though construction may occur the runoff is managed to a different set of principles lessening the impact on the catchment hydrology. Whilst each SUDS site might only bring a small amount of benefit, the cumulative effects over an entire catchment could be very significant for both runoff and groundwater recharge. With regard to runoff, SUDS have three main abilities: *source control; permeable conveyance;* and *storage and pollution management.*

The first function of SUDS is that they can reduce the quantity of runoff discharging from a site. This is termed *source control* due to its intention to manage the water as close as possible to its source and is commonly the initial stage of any SUDS approach. These techniques can positively influence both flooding and scarcity due to diverting water away from the hard engineered drainage system. An example would be a green roof, which has the potential to capture and store precipitation, or the use of permeable paving, which can allow water to percolate through, rather than flow over, the surface. These methods also create the possibility for rainwater harvesting to reduce water consumption, such as by utilizing the retained resource for landscaping or greywater purposes.

The second ability of SUDS is to slow the velocity of runoff discharging from an area. This may be termed *permeable conveyance*. The methodology commonly utilized within conventional drainage systems is to transport water at speed; this can however create capacity problems either within sewerage and drainage infrastructure or later in watercourses. By reducing the velocity of runoff we not only limit the potential for flash flooding, but also create the possibility for infiltration, evaporation and settlement of pollutants. An illustration of a SUDS technique in this area would be a Swale. This is a shallow vegetated channel that is designed to receive, store and convey water slowly. In areas of low runoff this may not require a further destination, but if required to manage more significant amounts of runoff they can be designed to gradually discharge the excess into either the conventional drainage system or a larger area of storage.

The final capability of SUDS is the possibility of retaining runoff either over the long term or temporarily, which can provide a passive level of treatment. This may be expressed as *storage and pollution management*. An example within this heading would be a detention basin, a retention pond or an artificial wetland. These features can all accept and store precipitation from a site, potentially enabling new development to have zero runoff entering either the drains or the watercourse. The water may be utilized as a resource or allowed to infiltrate and evaporate. Wetlands also have the added capacity to use natural processes, such as those provided by reed beds, to break down and reduce

Figure 7.3

An example of an artificial wetland SUDS system, which accepts runoff from multiple retail and office units at a business park on the outskirts of Leeds, UK

pollutants from runoff. If designed well these storage areas can provide additional functions, such as with regard to local amenity, regeneration, cooling and biodiversity.

Although there are different types of SUDS available dependent upon requirements, all three aspects could be designed to operate as part of one integrated system. This approach may be understood as a 'surface water management train', whereby water would be passed through a series of SUDS measures to reduce the impact of development decisions on both flooding and water scarcity. The methodology can therefore operate over differing scales; from the source, to the neighbourhood, and even on a strategic city level.

From a scarcity perspective, many countries will continue to receive more than enough rain, even taking into account the possibility of reducing supplies via changing precipitation patterns. The onus is therefore on improving recharge, capture and distribution. In effect, urbanization and impervious surfaces link precipitation directly with watercourses via stormwater drains. Conversely, utilizing SUDS helps to reconnect precipitation with the more conventional hydrological cycle, where it may infiltrate down to contribute towards groundwater resources or evapotranspire back into the atmosphere. In addition, less runoff also results in higher water quality due to a decrease in diffuse pollution. Therefore, all things being equal, water bills should fall alongside water treatment costs, providing indirect benefits to citizens and the private sector. The benefits from a flooding standpoint are equally tangible. SUDS essentially reduce the volume of runoff from development providing a mechanism to address the problem of flooding from surface water, drains and watercourses. Significantly, via attenuation and storage, they may also have a role in mitigating the increased hazard of flood risk anticipated from a combination of more intense precipitation events and continued urban growth during the twenty-first century.

The application of SUDS

Notwithstanding these potential benefits, in practice SUDS have found it difficult to break into the ingrained hard drainage hegemony. A problem partly connected with their rapid emergence. Translating their potential into action has proven problematical, and their wide scale implementation has been plagued by a number of persistent barriers encompassing a wide variety of factors, such as policy, legislation, regulation, design, costs, liability and maintenance (White 2005; White and Howe 2005). Within England for example, there has been both increased knowledge regarding the difficulties in effectively managing precipitation in the built environment and, since 2001, a strong planning policy push for SUDS. Despite this, the strength of the barriers has been such that, in practice, the spatial planning system has been unable to achieve anything other than occasional implementation, regardless of the content of national, regional or local planning policies. Although few studies have been conducted on the extent of SUDS use, a recent research project revealed that in 2009 there were only 36 SUDS sites in operation across the whole of Greater Manchester, a conurbation of 2.5 million people covering 1100 km² (White and Alarcon 2009). In simple terms, everybody knows where they stand with conventional drainage, but SUDS are contested, and uncertainty is an anathema to the development and drainage sectors.

The contribution of SUDS to increased urban resilience via addressing anthropogenically generated hazard could potentially be significant if increased surety is provided to facilitate their selection. Considering the layers of knowledge in the previous chapter we need to reflect upon how best SUDS could be used. First, it is clear that source control could be used throughout the city, regardless of location. The space taken up by this approach can be minimal, and it generally assists in reducing the contributory effect of urbanization on runoff. However, infiltration devices may not be equally applicable in all parts of the city. In areas of clay soil for example, their performance may be poor, whilst conversely in sandy conditions they could be very effective. Groundwater levels may also be a consideration. Permeable conveyance systems are similar in that they are related to infiltration devices, but they may require a small amount of development land to be effective. Therefore, in the densest built environment these may not be a practical solution. The problem of land use is further highlighted when considering the use of storage devices, as these tend to be above ground and so can occupy valuable development space. This constraint may mean that their use may be most appropriate outside the urban core, and in particular where they can manage runoff on a neighbourhood scale.

SUDS do offer potential but to become an accepted drainage infrastructure option they essentially need to replicate the agreed and established operational framework as occurs within conventional drainage. There are good practice examples however, and cities within the United States, Canada and Sweden have made advances in implementing SUDS as part of an integrated network, and are receiving benefits as a result. For example Augustenborg is a suburb of Malmö, Sweden. It is a high-density, inner-city location similar to post-war developments in the UK and the United States, which suffered flooding problems from surface water and drains after heavy storms. To solve this problem the area utilized a substantial array of SUDS designed to lessen the load on the drainage infrastructure and has experienced a good deal of success in managing both total runoff and peak storm flows (Villarreal *et al.* 2004).

The SUDS methodology places a high value on the contributory role of nature as a tool to make cities more resilient to environmental risks, this does first necessitate a change in perception of the role of the natural environment however. This issue is further unpacked by the closely related, and equally emerging, concept of green infrastructure. A subject that although similar in principle goes beyond SUDS and recognizes the wide benefits that nature can bring to urban areas, and the valuable and often unseen contribution they can make in the management of urban hazard.

Green infrastructure

> Urban land as a whole will be required to assume environmental, productive and social roles in the design of cities, far outweighing traditional park values and civic values. Many of the problems generated by the city, and imposed on its larger regional environment, will have to be resolved within it.
>
> (Hough 2006: 25)

When studied closely, urban land may not actually be that urban. Interspersed between the hard buildings and city landscape is a blend of greener areas that can directly or indirectly enrich the lives of citizens. The emphasis for provision of green spaces within the city has predominately been to offer a single amenity function, such as by providing recreation or leisure opportunities. Although formal and informal green spaces within and surrounding urban areas may have been planned for a distinct purpose, some will serendipitously perform additional roles heightening their actual worth to the city. This unheralded array of largely unattributed benefits has particular resonance with regard to increasing resilience to both water scarcity and flooding. As Hough identifies in the opening quotation, in areas where the supply of land may be in high demand, promoting strategic and multifunctional spaces becomes analogous with the sustainable use of a finite and valuable resource: the approach essentially delivers a wider series of benefits within a smaller scale.

As this natural functionality has become more widely recognized the patchwork of green spaces connected with cities has been considered to operate as infrastructure – in much the same way as the more established and consciously constructed drains, sewers and highways. In simple terms green infrastructure (GI) may be understood as the natural, outdoor environment. It consists of a wide variety of planned and more natural spaces that are located within and surrounding cities, from private gardens to woodlands, from roadside verges to river corridors. The utilization of the term 'infrastructure' is a deliberate recognition of the prospective valuable contribution that these spaces can perform in assisting the functional operation of the city. Table 7.1 provides some examples of the range of water related GI assets at local and city scales.

An understanding of the differing types of GI also provides a link to the previous section on SUDS, which although similar tend to be smaller in scale and explicitly designed to manage surface runoff. GI on the other hand can provide multiple functions over a huge area and yet may not even be recognized as doing so. However, this lack of regard is changing and GI is beginning to be identified as an innovative method to increase the well-being of citizens outside of a pure amenity perspective. The effects can also be considerable from an ecological viewpoint, as if designed as an integrated network GI can increase habitat connectivity and help maintain wildlife corridors. A particular ability of green spaces within cities can be to help adapt urban areas to a number

Table 7.1 Examples of green infrastructure assets with the potential to influence water and the city

Local and neighbourhood scale	City and regional scale
Private gardens	Rivers
Small parks	Floodplains
Green roofs	Shorelines
Swales	Reservoirs
Street trees and verges	Lakes
Ponds and streams	Canals
Local parks	Recreational spaces
Allotments	Community parks
School grounds/sports fields	Woodlands and forests
Cemeteries/churches	Agricultural land
Brownfield/derelict land	Open countryside

of differing climate related risks, such as by lowering surface temperatures to increase human comfort levels. The advantages can also touch wider agendas such as health, biodiversity and air quality. For example, New York's Central Park is widely described as the 'green lungs' of the city, with the appreciation of the high quality resource only heightened by its dense urban surroundings.

To supplement these adaptive roles, GI can assist in helping reduce the contribution of the built environment in generating additional hazard. The key to managing the impacts and benefits urban water can deliver centres on the interaction between precipitation, the surface of the city and how water is subsequently stored or transported. Green spaces have natural functions in retaining and attenuating surface water, enabling the recharging of water tables and creating the possibility of capturing water as a resource. They also have the ability to store and cleanse runoff reducing both the potential size of the drainage system and the demands on treatment plants. As with SUDS, GI can reduce and slow surface runoff helping to lessen the risk of surface, pluvial or fluvial flood risk. Indeed, Gill *et al.* (2007) estimate that a 10 per cent increase in green cover could reduce the volume of surface water runoff by 14 per cent from extreme events. GI in a shoreline context can not only lessen the risk of flooding in coastal areas but also provide wider advantages. For example, a restored wetland or area of managed realignment aids biodiversity, recreation and flood management and reduces the financial demand to defend land over the long term. GI can therefore assist in embedding resilience within the land use of a city. To achieve these multiple benefits GI should be planned and designed appropriately; with land sited where it can supply the widest array of social, environmental and economic functions.

In order to best maximize the ability of green infrastructure to manage water scarcity and flood risk we should recognize the wider functionality of all green spaces and plan the network to operate in a strategic fashion. For example, in addition to recognized, although nebulous, benefits via infiltration, transpiration, evaporation or storage functions, greenspace could be designed to operate as both temporary flood storage and as a safe flood pathway to transport water into areas with little or no consequences. Greenspace of various functions can be designed to store flood water if sited and designed correctly, and information on upstream sources and runoff models can assist with this aim. An example is provided in Greater Manchester, UK, where Sale Water Park, Withington golf course and an adjoining nature reserve alongside the River Mersey are all utilized for water storage in times of high precipitation. This provides a good example of the multifunctional use of land and an insight into possible sustainable land uses designed to reduce hazard. If capacity problems occur it can inundate low value recreation land, which can quickly, and naturally, recover with no significant financial or social penalties.

The application of green infrastructure

With regard to greenspace provision an initial spatial planning aim could be to ascertain which areas are both currently designated as greenspace and sited upon sandy soils. These locations are actually operating as a natural drain and a groundwater recharge area. Consequently, where their value is high in this respect they could receive added protection within spatial planning. Furthermore, areas that have sandy soils could be considered as appropriate locales to create new greenspace when determining the shape of the urban form over the medium to long term. Densification or replacement development in these areas could be tightly controlled once the lifespan of the current buildings have come to an end. Presently there is an almost automatic assumption that brownfield sites should be regenerated, but if they are performing valuable roles in managing water due to their underlying soil structure, or due to their important storage capacity within the context of the surrounding urban environment, consideration should be given towards preserving them within the greenspace network of a city.

Developing strategies to recharge groundwater resources and provide increased formal storage also lessens the possibility of economic risks from a reduction in water supply affecting both people and high water industries. Water resources as a subject may not be a problem for many cities in that the volume of precipitation exceeds the volume of usage. In practice however inefficiencies in the collection, storage and distribution of the resource, combined with increasing demands, may expose deficiencies in current practices. The problem of relative drought may therefore be addressed by increasing the capture of rainfall within the region. Within the water aware city any strategy to store water would also consider multiple benefits, especially over the long term; for example, where possible new reservoirs could also function as upstream flood storage areas to help manage extreme rainfall events.

Although storage is one of the most effective methods to both manage flood risk and enable infiltration, it is difficult to find an appropriate area to accept large amounts of water at short notice within the urban core. This is where the boundaries between the water resilient city and its surrounding hinterland become blurred. Any consideration of water should recognize that the catchment level is the key scale; therefore, cities may also need to make use of land outside of their administrative borders. Information on flood source areas and flow pathways can be of great use in this respect, as can data on appropriate areas for abstraction and reservoir storage. Upstream storage options should be exploited where possible and low value greenspace or agricultural land could be transformed into temporary or permanent water storage basins, intercepting flow from the upper catchment or coastal areas and releasing pressure on the city core. This may be difficult due to the land being perhaps controlled by a neighbouring Authority or agency, but a city more resilient to water hazards would aim to influence land use situated and managed in diverse locations.

One of the key problems in realizing the potential benefits of GI is quantification: we know via geographical principles that water can be stored, infiltrated and evapotranspire – but just how much? And how do aspects such as local conditions or the design of spaces affect this ability? If you compare this opaque situation with the rigorously engineered and computed functioning of conventional infrastructure, a tension between the potential and practical application of GI becomes apparent. Within the typical understanding of infrastructure, performance is known in all different conditions and an acceptable failure rate, such as drainage exceedance level, is part of the design. We also know how, and how frequently, it should be maintained. As with the case of SUDS, more research designed to lessen uncertainty may need to be required to help transform the use of GI in practice.

It is clear that the combination of both the initial veiled advantages and subsequent ambiguities concerning the performance of GI has detrimentally affected the perceived value of natural spaces within urban areas. Furthermore, this limited understanding of the interaction between driving forces and the built and natural environment has inadvertently helped to generate increased hazard from water risks. If risk is framed within the context of market failure, as can be clearly argued with aspects of urban water, there is an emphasis on market readjustment or other corrective action. Nowhere is this more apparent than when discussing the apparent value of the natural environment, within both urban areas and from a general perspective. This may require a market correction to enable the lack of certainty within GI to be effectively considered within the constraints of the prevailing cost–benefit decision making approach.

This deficiency has also been compounded by the gradual erosion of the natural environment within cities, despite its ability to provide an important, yet largely unacknowledged, regulating function. It may be that the rising costs of this view can help drive a change in the services green spaces are seen to provide within the city. Perhaps the best example of a change in perception concerning the previously largely hidden contribution of nature to society is provided by the Western honeybee. After a decline in bee colonies in the UK and elsewhere awareness was raised concerning their unattributed value to UK farming. It was estimated that their role in plant pollination was worth up to £200 million per annum, in addition to their more quantifiable annual honey output of up to £30 million (Defra 2009b). In practice, calculations of this nature may be a prerequisite to change perceptions and influence institutional behaviour and land use decisions.

As the difficulties in managing water become more apparent within societies, it is logical that the value and function of natural systems within and surrounding cities should be re-examined. The growing awareness of the perceived role of green spaces beyond amenity towards infrastructure is critical in both embedding resilience within cities and preventing additional anthropogenic forcing of water related hazards. The need for land to be multifunctional is also analogous with the sustainable use of a finite resource and the development of places that are less exposed and vulnerable to climatic risks. This argument becomes increasingly important when considering the current difficulties in addressing the drivers for future risks: in particular, population growth, urbanization, and changing climates. The extent and power of this issue means that both GI and SUDS should not be seen as a replacement to traditional surface water methodology; rather, as a means to reduce pressure on existing services by helping to reduce the artificial generation of hazard. The following section expands the discussion to consider the possible role of the conventional, and vitally important, water infrastructure.

Reflecting upon infrastructure and resilience

> The sustainable city needs to be treated as an open or empty concept which is filled by sets of competing claims about what the sustainable city might become.
>
> (Guy and Marvin 1999: 273)

Pursuing one rigidly defined interpretation of the function of spaces becomes increasingly problematic as the supply of land diminishes. Infrastructure has essentially been seen as a constructed mechanism to provide services that sustain and improve society, from sanitation, to transport, to water supply. These functions have unarguably helped to drive growth, quality of life and prosperity, but as the pressures upon these services increase so does the need to develop strategies to expand systems and/or reduce inputs. A failure to adequately respond to the demands on these systems has fuelled fears of an infrastructure crisis in many developed nations, with an ageing hard engineered network struggling to manage expanding twenty-first-century cities. Although effective in its singular purpose, infrastructure of this nature has proven to be expensive to construct and maintain and is prone to obsolescence and failure. In reality, as the initial quote from Guy and Marvin (1999) illustrates, the pathways to a more sustainable city should be more complex and plural.

This chapter should be viewed in the context of the ongoing evolution of surface water management. Just as the historic urban expansions of the eighteenth and nineteenth centuries demanded a change in practices to provide water and sewerage services on an industrial scale, the current problems of surface water runoff and scarcity similarly challenge prevailing methodologies. The strong trend has been for hard engineered intervention, but when considering the future relationship between water and the city infrastructure should be understood to include a much wider array of spaces. The problems facing cities, combined with a continual squeeze on land use, point towards a need to continue to refine the perceived value of land and question what we consider to be essential 'infrastructure' within cities. A point recognized by the European Commission (2009: 5) who state:

Green infrastructure can play a crucial role in adaptation in providing essential resources for social and economic purposes under extreme climatic conditions. Examples include improving the soil's carbon and water storage capacity, and conserving water in natural systems to alleviate the effects of droughts and to prevent floods.

Although hard engineered systems have provided a degree of management of surface water, they have created a legacy of concrete and piped networks that help generate increased hazard for both flooding and water scarcity. The understanding of infrastructure has evolved from pertaining to human-made, physical objects, such as buildings, roads and power supplies, to a more encompassing definition potentially incorporating natural and artificial functions. The rise of the 'green' infrastructure agenda has driven a change in terminology, with traditional structures now thought of as 'grey' infrastructure; only one part of an integrated tapestry. The fundamental premise of infrastructure concerns the provision of necessary structures desired for a society to prosper, and therefore the definition should include important, but often hidden, roles played by the natural environment. This concept is gaining more credence as the wider contribution of parks, wetlands and other more natural spaces are acknowledged; in effect these are nature's utilities, and may perform a variety of unseen, free services, such as draining runoff, recharging water supplies or preserving habitats.

However, when examined closely there may be a perceived tension between the two areas. Indeed, in some respects grey infrastructure may be seen to be part of the process that facilitates displacement of the natural environment – either directly or via its enabling role for other development. Although the competition for space within a city may appear to have placed the natural and built environment at odds, when considering how to mitigate hazard in urban areas they should be viewed as complementary facets of the same managerial strategy. For example, SUDS and GI can offset the need to replace or expand existing water supply and drainage systems. One approach therefore may be to identify our most important green spaces for preservation and expansion in order to reduce the level of required economic investment in hard engineered functions. This point also relates to the ability to allocate financial resources wisely. For instance, with regard to water leakage within the distribution network there does become a point at which the economic cost of repair is reached. Therefore, money might be more effectively allocated to increasing the supply of water via capturing or storing precipitation by softer infrastructure.

The need to pursue resilience with regard to water hazards is also amplified by the fact that hard infrastructure has been selected as the main mechanism for its management. However, infrastructure can and does fail, meaning that a precautionary approach with the risk spread between the built and natural environments may reduce the possibility for anthropogenically driven hazard. Indeed, an awareness of the limitations of engineering combined with knowledge of the extremes of nature argues that there are only two types of flood defence: those that have failed and those that will. For example, even London's Thames Barrier, which protects one of the most valuable areas of land on the planet, is only designed to protect up to a certain scale of event. Furthermore, in all but the most naturally abundant areas of secure water resources, the same, albeit slightly fatalistic, argument may also be applicable for relative drought but over a slightly longer temporal scale. Although hard engineered infrastructure is effective, it should be noted that embedding resilience to water risks in the urban area is constrained by this singular managerial approach to address hazards – in addition to the much more high profile climatic drivers.

Future housing growth and hazard

Although this book has used a notional scale of a 'city', in practice this should be seen as a rather fluid and nebulous concept. The discussion of water resources and virtual water provides a good example as in practice a regional perspective would be more accurate. In reality, many of the problems of the city as a whole, and the individual districts, are externally driven and, where possible, solutions should also have a similarly encompassing scope. Consideration of both the hydrological links between city districts and their respective targets for new housing throws this issue into sharp focus. New development provides an added burden on existing storage and transportation mechanisms. This occurs within the natural environment, such as in a floodplain or watercourse, or within the artificial arena, where it may affect a reservoir, sewer or surface runoff. An area can therefore be subject to increased risk through no fault of its own, meaning that adaptation needs to occur both within and outside its locale.

Box 7.1 Future housing and the risk of surface water flooding

Figure 7.4 provides a schematic of this process. The Greater Manchester region has been exploded outwards into its ten local authorities and neighbouring hydrologically connected districts. Each area details both the future housing targets and the direction of water flow. The figure also provides an understanding of the shape of the catchment, with water from the higher surrounding areas flowing towards the western side of the conurbation. The diagram outlines how the outer authorities essentially export their runoff into Salford, Trafford and the outlying area of Warrington, emphasizing the cumulative nature of risk and the need for adaptation to be closely aligned to future growth. Indeed, if all the housing targets are met, a total of 145,100 new homes, and their associated infrastructure, will be constructed upstream of Salford, an area already at relatively high risk of flooding within the Greater Manchester region. Even if Salford has an exemplary policy to address flood risk, unless its neighbours upstream are similarly proactive, the hazard may rise sharply due to external drivers.

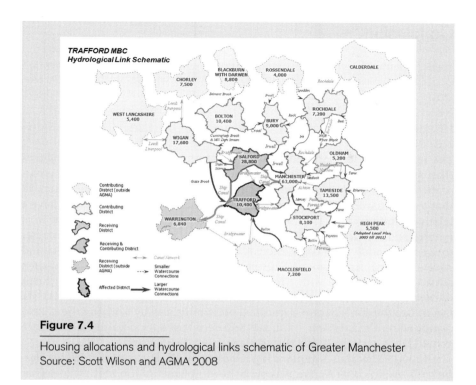

Figure 7.4

Housing allocations and hydrological links schematic of Greater Manchester
Source: Scott Wilson and AGMA 2008

In practice however the power to operationalize adaptation may not be completely within political or administrative boundaries. This is true of the city scale, such as presented by a changing climate, and a micro scale as evidenced by upstream housing allocations. Consequently, the process of critical reflection also needs to include a new commitment to partnership working, where, for example, area X changes behaviour to beneficially influence area Y. A city therefore needs to approach water management in a joined up manner, rather than develop individual solutions for separate areas.

This does raise a series of important questions however. For example, should housing, regeneration or growth proceed on a silo basis regardless of the wider costs? Should an outlying upstream area have to curtail development to allow a neighbouring central urban locality to continue to prosper? If not, how should we try and achieve smarter, more sustainable growth? Is the presence of water intensive industries becoming a drain on water resources for homes? Whilst we clearly need to think more creatively about the transfer of costs and benefits, adaptive measures are available to help limit upstream runoff and downstream impacts; these do however require a broad 'city' perspective to be developed, as is starting to occur in the Manchester region, to be successful.

Conclusion

certain types of land are of such intrinsic value, or perform work for man best in a natural condition or, finally, contain such hazards to development that they should not be urbanized. Similarly, there are other areas that, for perfectly specific reasons, are intrinsically suitable for urban uses.

The notion that land should be sited according to a wider set of principles than market forces is not necessarily a new concept. The quote from the environmental planning pioneer Ian McHarg (1969: 154) underscores the argument that a more naturally appropriate approach to land use planning does have a relatively long history. He also highlighted the need to integrate design with nature and use land in an efficient manner. A view that is essentially a precursor to the more modern concepts associated with sustainability, risk, resilience and natural hazard management. This book therefore draws upon an established school of thought, but with a more contemporary emphasis and a clear focus on water in the city, rather than the environment as a whole. In this respect, we can utilize the concept of risk outlined previously, and by isolating the hazard component of the risk equation, it is apparent that a focal point for resilience should be on strategies to better manage urban precipitation.

Although McHarg's argument is persuasive, in the forty years since his classic book, *Design With Nature*, was published implementation of these ideas has proved difficult, evidenced by the rising potential for naturally driven urban impacts outlined in earlier chapters. Adopting an 'environmental' perspective can prove to be a challenging position when attempting to change the overwhelmingly anthropogenic land use paradigm. The relative success of the Stern Review in repackaging an existing environmental contention, but for an economic and growth orientated audience may provide an example of how to make progress. To be more effective it may not be the message that changes; rather, a transformation of the reasoning. This would entail a readjustment in focus from places to people, and in particular emphasizing the growing economic costs of mismanaging urban water. Indeed, the scope of impacts would suggest that the very same argument would be much more powerful from a humanistic standpoint; we should alter practices, not just due to the effects on the natural world, but because of the potentially severe and growing consequences for cities and their citizens.

The view that areas, which suffer repeated flood or scarcity events, are human made rather than natural disasters has been growing in currency since the 1960s. The present pragmatic focus on working with nature reflects this view and provides an insight into the foundation of the resilient city with regard to water management. In practice, urban areas are not necessarily designed with to cope with twenty-first-century problems. Their form is a result of historical evolution informed by political, social and economic factors, with the perception of infrastructure developing on a similar basis. Essentially these aspects inhibit a coherent and reflexive risk management strategy due to the ability to generate additional hazard. SUDS and GI can provide a mechanism to address these forcing drivers influencing normality, but they should be seen as strands of a wider resilience response centred on pursuing a more efficient use of land – including an array of green and grey infrastructure.

This contemporary understanding of water and the city links heavily with the concept of resilience and multifunctional management. It is clear that cities are becoming increasingly at risk and our ability to control the negative impacts of water is challenged due to the way that the built environment is constraining our responses. In short, floods and droughts can be driven by factors outside of our control therefore a key strand of our intervention strategy should be aimed at providing responses that can embed urban resilience. The paradigm shift towards the more natural management of water also logically leads to a discussion of the future make up of a water-aware city, and the ability of spatial planning to influence a viable alternative.

Whilst GI and SUDS do offer potential, and planning does have the power to facilitate the use of these measures, institutional and governance factors mean that large scale implementation is not straightforward. For example, the inherent constraints within planning to influence the existing built and natural environments means that changing the understanding of infrastructure would enable a partnership approach encompassing wider stakeholders, most notably water and sewerage companies. Moreover, addressing the hazard element of risk can prove to be more difficult than exposure or vulnerability aspects as it necessitates the adoption of a longer, more strategic and proactive view. In reality, the gradual application of resilience to hazard within a city may be a project for the long term; addressing exposure and vulnerability by a focus on adaptive measures can however be implemented within much shorter timescales.

8   Exposure and resilience in the city

···

> for the buildings speak and act, no less than the people who inhabit them; and
> through the physical structures of the city past events, decisions made long ago,
> values formulated and achieved, remain alive and exert and influence.
>
> (Mumford 1961: 113)

The German philosopher Johann Wolfgang Goethe stated that: 'he who cannot draw on three thousand years is living from hand to mouth' and when considering the concept of a resilient city this advice may be a conservative estimate. Although urban planning as a formal organization only has its roots in the late nineteenth and early twentieth centuries, history demonstrates that many settlements have displayed evidence of autonomous or planned adaptation in response to perceived natural and human threats. The notion of 'resilient' or 'adaptive' cities may be relatively recent, but, as the quote from Mumford helps illustrate, the broad themes of protection, durability and recovery have been associated with cities from time immemorial.

The rising trend towards urban living and the escalating costs of hazardous events has resulted in a growing awareness for modern cities to adapt to their local conditions and manage environmental risks more effectively in the face of a changing climate (IPCC 2007a). Consequently, cities need strategies to effectively absorb risk within growing populations. Significantly, this is not just about avoiding new risk; but of ascertaining the degree and severity of current exposure with a view to proactively and strategically retrofitting resilience into the city, from the built environment to our institutions and processes. A more resilient city would have less emphasis on a cycle of protection, warning, emergency response and disaster recovery, with citizens potentially exposed to flooding and water scarcity on an ongoing basis.

The city is imperfect and will always remain so, yet fortunately concurrent with this view is the desire to intervene, to address threats, to redesign cities and to prosper. It is clear that cities can and do adapt to changing circumstances, sometimes regardless of strategic intervention, the key is therefore not can cities adapt, but can its citizens and policy makers? This is not necessarily advocating that we undertake a futuristic visionary process, such as recreating Sir Thomas

More's *Utopia*, but, rather, as Patrick Geddes (1904: 3) argued more practically in the early twentieth century:

> civics as an art, a policy, has thus to do, not with U-topia, but with Eu-topia; not with imagining an impossible no-place where all is well, but with making the most and best of each and every place, and especially of the city in which we live.

The uncertain nature of water risks has been powerfully demonstrated by the largely unpredicted experiences of intra-urban flooding and water scarcity in recent times. This risk provides a compelling argument for 'built in resilience' to these hazards and a new responsibility for spatial planning. A society resilient to water risks would also be analogous with a more sustainable city, one which engages with the concept of exposure to ensure that the location, design and function of future development do not increase threats. As exposure to water based risks is predominately spatial in origin, management strategies need bespoke information embedded in the geography of the area. As knowledge can assist in reducing uncertainty and providing an evidence base for inter-vention, it essentially allows cities and their inhabitants to mitigate the major threats and live with the minor. The following sections examine the subject of exposure in more detail and suggest some examples of strategies to increase resilience within this aspect of the risk equation.

Unpacking exposure

Exposure is most easily understood as the degree to which an entity is subject to a risk. In practice, exposure levels will vary across the city and so the notion can apply to the severity, extent and duration of the perturbation (Adger 2006). The areas affected could include a city's population or the built and natural environment. With regard to flooding and scarcity, the term may be most simply understood in terms of the number of properties located in areas that could be exposed to the risk. It therefore has an evident spatial dimension, which has synergies with controlling exposure by altering urban form and citizen behav-iour. Both the city itself and specific locations within the urban area may be subject to naturally and artificially driven risks, and so spatial planning could usefully consider a wider array of data to provide a stronger 'natural' input into land use decisions. Or as McHarg (1969: 197) put it when discussing the need to coordinate design with nature: 'let us ask the land where are the best sites'.

Although there is a clear spatial aspect, the scope of activities connected with exposure cannot be neatly packaged into a pure land use discourse; exposure is also concerned with differing aspects of capital. For example, this may include a threat to financial, social or natural capital and so exposure can spread beyond the use of land and relate to the operation of wider society. It is also worth highlighting that an area may also be exposed to the same threat to a greater or lesser degree, for example from a minor temporary water shortage to a sustained and debilitating drought. The difference with regard to flooding is less marked however, as even a minor flood can have considerable effects on both people and property. The disparity in perception also means that exposure is inevitably socially constructed with some nations, communities or citizens feeling at higher risk than others. These effects can be subsequently magnified by consideration of the notion of vulnerability, which can deepen the impact and lengthen the duration of the perturbation.

The previous chapter explained that hazard is not static and may be driven by artificial and natural means; as a result it can have a forcing effect on the degree or extent of exposure. Equally, the relationship between exposure and vulnerability is also beneficial to outline. Although the two elements may each be present, it is when the aspects overlap that the possibility of detriment occurs. For example, if an area is exposed but not vulnerable, or vice versa, then the threat of drought or flooding is not realized. In reality, vulnerability may be present throughout a city, but is not distributed equally and so some areas and citizens will be more susceptible than others. This is discussed in more depth in the next chapter.

Although there is a degree of external forcing from hazard, exposure is mainly influenced by historical decisions concerning the nature of the city combined with behavioural patterns and the geo-climatic context. Significantly, the distribution of exposure is uncertain and may be subject to change, such as in the aftermath of an event or the release of updated climate scenarios. For example, chapter 3 detailed the rise in the number of people exposed to flood risk in England from 2 million properties in 2000 to 5.2 million 9 years later – information largely driven by harsh experience. Equally, fears of increasing periods of water stress and scarcity in many parts of the world are creating a deeper understanding of the potential present and future exposure to this risk. Although notional exposure therefore increases with a greater understanding of the intricacies of the risk, human land use activities on a city scale have undoubtedly played a part, from developing on the floodplain to a failure to implement water efficiency measures. The exposure of a city to water risks may also be driven by macro factors; most notably population growth, population density or changes in industry or agriculture. However, the tight relationship of the concept to decision making means that there is significant potential for resilience responses.

Exposure and spatial planning

As exposure may relate to a combination of the location of properties, agriculture and industry, and broad societal trends and policies, spatial planning is well placed to pursue resilience to water risks. There are clear and long established mechanisms in place to directly control land use, whilst there is also a degree of power to indirectly influence the more intangible wider issues, such as desired population growth. Although understanding flooding and scarcity threats as a whole is not yet a highly developed field, there has been some success in addressing exposure as it is arguably the most obvious element of the risk equation. For example, we know that some floodplains and low lying coastal areas may be exposed to periodic inundation, and particularly in more recent years efforts have been made to help shield these places from new development. The role of information here is vital; if the exposure of a city to water risks can be determined measures can be taken to enable the city to adapt. This isn't just relating to extreme events, but also to incrementally changing normality influencing the scope and extent of exposure.

In order to decrease exposure via spatial planning there is a need to unpack alternative sustainable urban futures, many of which are competing (Guy and Marvin 1999). For example, a compact city brings a number of sustainability benefits such as combating urban sprawl, limiting energy use and facilitating public transportation. This vision may appear however at odds with the emerging green infrastructure agenda, which stresses the importance of natural spaces within the city, as they can perform vital roles in water storage and groundwater recharge. How can you measure the desirability of the compact city agenda, a strategy promoting higher urban densification, which is firmly entrenched in many different countries (Jenks *et al.* 1996), with green infrastructure policies, described as a vital 'life support system' and critical to adapting to the effects of climate change (Benedict and McMahon 2006)? That is not to say that these concepts are in opposition; promoting green spaces within cities is not analogous to advocating urban sprawl; in reality, the issues are much more complex. The prioritization of competing strategies will inevitably differ spatially and be influenced by past exposure to risks or future development objectives, which help identify the appropriate resilience responses. The following sections move the debate from the theoretical to the practical by identifying and discussing a number of available responses to help manage water threats within the city. Flooding and scarcity are considered separately with regard to exposure, as the strategies to intervene are not as closely related as when considering the subject of hazard.

Exposure to flooding

The need to consider an idealized vision of a city, one designed to minimize the risk from flooding and drought seems to gain in importance each year as urbanization and climate change increase exposure. Interestingly, the ability of the planning system to think long term and incrementally influence factors, such as urban morphology, greenspace provision and building design, does provide a real opportunity to travel towards a strategic, long term vision of the city region. From this perspective water management would be an elevated consideration with development being in an appropriate location according to hydro-geographic principles, rather than being driven in a typical socio-economic fashion.

The mechanisms developed to manage water in many modern societies have until recently however paid little attention to this view. Exposure was mainly addressed by the construction of hard flood defences, larger drains, or the construction of additional water supply infrastructure. The idea of achieving a similar, but frequently more sustainable effect by influencing the urban fabric or individual behaviour was only recently introduced as a component part of the shift in narrative from defence to management. As the success of the protectionist policy could not be guaranteed, there has been a stronger onus on spatial planning to exert a controlling influence on risk. It should be noted that there will always be a place for hard flood defences, some parts of the city are too valuable to suggest otherwise, but that the reliance and load on defences could be reduced by exploring the possibility of moving towards a more resilient city. Equally, technology will play a key role both in increasing the supply of water to homes and businesses and reducing the demand on water resources.

The familiar refrain by the media and populace in the aftermath of a damaging flood event is 'don't build on floodplains'. Although simplistic, there is truth in this statement. Of the source – pathway – receptor causal chain outlined in chapter 3, within spatial planning we have the greatest ability to influence the 'receptor' aspect – the characteristic that experiences the exposure. Achieving resilience via reducing exposure can be most easily ensured by a focus on property, as the layers of information essentially translate risks into a spatial dimension. In reality, the built environment can prove very resistant to change within cities, not least by deeply embedded economic interests, which specifically inhibited resilience responses. Vale and Campanella (2005) highlight the power of property rights as a stabilizing force on cities and a stymie to their future evolution. They cite the example of Japan, which has introduced land readjustment practices designed to reduce the impact of disasters. In practice however these policies have been able to change property boundaries and the width of streets, but have not fundamentally altered the urban structure.

Addressing exposure is also proactive and strategic, as you need to first comprehend the nature of the risk in order to take remedial measures. The lack of data described in chapter 6 has therefore been one of the key factors in rising urban risks; cities simply didn't have a rich supply of information as to areas which suffered from exposure, beyond a simplistic recognition of functional floodplains. But with a broader understanding of water risks and the city there is a hierarchy of desired approaches which are possible as a risk management strategy: *avoidance*; *resistance*; *resilience*; and *repairability* (CLG 2007). The first of which is related to exposure and the latter three are discussed in more depth in the following chapter on vulnerability.

Addressing exposure to flooding

The most sustainable method is to locate development in areas safe from flooding or to increase the height of the ground level to ensure that water cannot enter – in effect to *avoid* the exposure. As a matter of course this approach should also consider the potential for the construction to generate increased hazard elsewhere. Where the building is already in place or there are no safe sites available, resistance techniques can be utilized to try and prevent water from entering a building. If flooding does occur, resilience and repairable measures can subsequently reduce vulnerability, lessen the possibility of damage and facilitate restoration. These issues are discussed in depth in chapter 9.

As a policy aim, avoidance has been engaged with to some degree. Currently, only one of the geographical layers of information outlined in chapter 6 influences the management of urban form via the planning system; yet this is the most high profile and effective. The ability to map the extent of floodplain inundation presents us with our first predictable opportunity to further the water resilient city: a need to tightly manage new development to avoid risk. A water sensitive view of the city would go further however and consider the possibility of abandoning areas currently at risk and restoring the natural floodplain in order to create extra storage for the flood waters. Godschalk (2003) cites the example of Tulsa, Oklahoma, as a city adapting its form in order to become more resilient. In the wake of repeated flood events there was a concerted effort to remove homes exposed to the hazard by embarking on a process of floodplain restoration that also helped achieve habitat and open space objectives. These newly created areas could be multifunctional green and blue spaces, combining flood storage capabilities with recreational and ecological uses. In short they would function as environmental corridors, or blue belts, to complement the existing green belts, which are predominately socio-economic constructs effective at controlling urban sprawl, but may not contain a high ecological or amenity value.

Utilizing other data sources we can expand our influence way beyond the floodplain however. Mapping the potential for surface water or pluvial flood risk is more problematic, but still achievable, enabling a response to all types of exposure by intervening with regard to either urban form or the infrastructure to manage water. The approach could involve shifting development away from areas susceptible to surface water flooding, or alternatively where the land is valuable, an investment in drainage to reduce exposure. A strategic view of this data would enable a city to gradually become more resilient by altering the location of buildings, defending the land or increasing the capacity to store and transport water. A city scale policy of avoidance would also help to manage the pervasive issue of minor incremental change, which has helped amplify hazard and exposure.

A consideration of the type of future development appropriate for each location would also be beneficial. A water resilient city would not necessarily just bar all development in certain locations. A wider appreciation of the value of land combined with the need for safe and sustainable growth means that the use of land should be informed by the level of risk. High value and critical infrastructure should be located via a more precautionary principle, but certain development could be directed towards areas of minor exposure if they have low vulnerability or can quickly recover without loss of services. In addition to the more obvious aspects of green infrastructure, such as sports fields, or golf courses, uninhabited buildings designed to be resilient may also be deemed to be able to accept this level of exposure. Using this approach, development and growth is still possible, just informed by risk, and if an event occurs the damage and disruption is minimal and temporary.

Whilst there is simply no need to specifically develop on a floodplain as there may have been over the preceding centuries, there is still a requirement to provide safe and sustainable land for new development. Utilizing the principle of siting the most appropriate land use in the best location, undeveloped land, which is presently not fulfilling a role in either flood risk management nor has high ecological value, could be considered for development. For example, areas of greenspace on clay soils may be released for development, dependent upon their having no significant ecological functions that could not be replicated and compensated by newly created greenspace within the blue belts. This land may include areas within the existing greenbelt, which are attractive areas for development and in many parts the greenbelt offers very little recreational, amenity or ecological value, and operates simply as an artificial barrier to urban sprawl. This low value however conflicts with one of the main premises of the space conscious water resilient city: the requirement for land to be multifunctional where possible. Although this view is controversial within the current development paradigm, a city pursuing an avoidance policy would allocate land according to its most sustainable use and aim to make new safe land available to compensate for losses elsewhere.

Densification is usually a problematical subject for sustainable flood risk management. Whilst policies to increase urban density may deter the release of new building land elsewhere, development also increases the volume of runoff in general. The reflexive, knowledgeable city would recognize this apparent contradiction and attempt to open up existing urban areas to better manage precipitation. For example, where sandy soils underlie the city, we could usefully promote the unsealing of hard surfaces in order to promote infiltration and limit runoff. This strategy should not be viewed within a narrow green space remit, there are many possible areas for unsealing, such as car parks, urban squares or locations with low public usage. A further measure could involve improving the multifunctionality of our existing infrastructure. Transport networks, such as motorways, railways and ring roads, could be designed to be at a lower level and operate as sacrificial storage areas in times of excessive precipitation, as the damage would be at a much lower level as long as adequate warning systems are in place (Evans *et al.* 2004).

Densification could also be encouraged in areas that aren't appropriate for surface unsealing. Therefore, essential development and its associated infrastructure could be directed towards areas that fulfil little or no water management role, freeing up valuable land elsewhere. Where new development does take place, planners and architects could adopt a number of measures to ensure that the impact of development on water risks elsewhere are minimized, or even reduced. Design features could include the installation of green roofs and other storage devices, or a policy of promoting pre-development or better runoff levels, especially if data on surface water flow routes presents a risk downstream. Above ground space would be at a premium in highly urbanized areas, but it is possible for water storage to be provided below ground in order to better protect areas of high importance.

The exposure to flooding within a city can be positively influenced to a much higher degree than has historically been the case. A risk based approach would advocate avoidance, but this should be complemented by releasing safe development land elsewhere to enable growth. A consideration of wider issues, such as green infrastructure or ground conditions, also raises the possibility of utilizing land where it can provide the most benefit for the management of water. Although theoretically, using this approach a city may not need any flood defences, the nature of cities means that in practice it is not economically viable to completely circumvent exposure. As with hazard, the contribution of hard engineering as a means of pursuing resilience also needs to be acknowledged. Defences will always be a necessity, as would more innovative measures to promote resistance, resilience and repairability measures, especially within the existing urban fabric. In addition to extra capital expenditure on new structures, this requires a targeted replacement strategy of poor drainage capacity hotspots, changing ageing infrastructure to develop a more reliable network with a higher capacity before overload occurs. Unfortunately, this means citizens can expect to pay for significant new above and below ground drainage infrastructure that can manage more intensive storm events, placing an upward pressure on water bills.

As a final point, it should be noted that on average the exposure to flooding within a city should display a gradual upward trend. The ubiquity of policies to promote growth and increase population combined with the possibilities of more extreme events means that the threat should be slowly amplified. Therefore, a simplistic and basic strategy to increase resilience may really only be able to slow the rate of exposure, rather than remove it altogether. To effectively manage cities and protect citizens requires a reflexive, resilient approach, which acknowledges uncertainty and is able to adapt to emerging threats: as Dawson (2007: 3095) states when referring to the threat of climate change in cities: 'it is no longer tenable to consider urban systems to be static artefacts constructed in a stable environment'.

Exposure to water scarcity

Exposure to a lack of water resources is less about differing locations within the urban area and more about the city, its hinterland and its geographical context. The balance of supply and demand can be altered, although, as opposed to the issue of flooding, the response typically has a longer timescale. In the majority of cities there are usually significant amounts of rain theoretically available to be captured and stored for domestic, agricultural and industrial use. This view does however help breed a complacent view; 'we need more water? Then build more reservoirs'. In practice, new reservoirs or changes in behaviour will take time to be implemented, which also hampers the ability to swiftly adapt to changing normalities or recover if the situation does occur. In summary, although exposure can be reduced by the construction of new supply infrastructure, or measures to reduce personal consumption, the lengthy time lag to completion means cities are vulnerable, especially over the short term. Moreover, urban areas are not static in their consumption of water. As the previous chapters explained, population growth and household consumption patterns provide a driving force on water use. As with flood defence, if you are not investing in new capital projects on an ongoing basis the possibility of exposure may naturally increase.

A reliance on hard engineering to address exposure further creates the possibility of serious problems in the future, especially in the case of operational failure. The supply of these services also serves to provide an 'escalator effect' (Parker 1995) on exposure, wherein after the infrastructure has been provided the perception of risk reduces. This helps drive exposure, which in turn increases the potential damage and the demand for more defences. All of which means that the potential detriment is greater if the structure fails and either inundation or scarcity occurs. In short, when new reservoirs and supply networks are constructed to manage water scarcity, there is consequently less pressure to reduce consumption and more capacity in the system to facilitate future population growth. Furthermore, in a privatized water market corporate income rises alongside consumption; there is usually little incentive for the water company in promoting frugality. The market therefore encourages a circular paradigm of new assets to supply rising needs; without a shock or stress, as occurred in the UK in 1976 or parts of Australia and the US more recently, there is little pressure to act to conserve the resource.

Addressing exposure to water scarcity

In the light of the last few chapters it is perhaps counter-intuitive that densification and brownfield regeneration are seen as an obvious and unchallenged pathway to sustainability. Yet the potential negative effects on surface water flooding and groundwater recharge by redevelopment mean that we shouldn't merely pursue this strategy in a simplistic unthinking fashion. For example, the previous chapter outlined how the use of green infrastructure and more sustainable drainage can reduce hazard. The approach can also help reduce exposure by recharging groundwater and so further resilience by increasing potential supplies. Although infiltration does inevitably percolate downwards, it should be recognized that this is a strategy which will only bear fruit over the very long term, and should be seen as a sustainable principle, rather than short term fix. In practice, reducing exposure to water scarcity should be followed via a twofold approach: increasing supply and decreasing demand. As the supply aspect may not necessarily include groundwater supplies due to the difficulties in renegotiating abstraction rates or facilitating rapid recharge, the focus is on a high degree of city wide capture. Alternatively, the demand angle is mainly centred on influencing usage within the three main sectors: agriculture, industry and households.

The change in water use by agriculture and industry within the Murray–Darling basin after being exposed to a lack of water resources demonstrates how adaptation to drought is not necessarily concerned with the location of property within the city as occurs with flooding. The risk is actually related its broad scale hydro-climatic context and the reliance on the resource for economic success and prosperity. As with Las Vegas, water availability can help fuel growth, but the opposite can also occur. Furthermore, high water use within the non-domestic sectors essentially exposes the city and citizens to potential economic impacts. Although an emphasis on virtual water imports to replace domestic production can increase local water resources, it does transfer abstraction elsewhere, and unless the exporting area has abundant resources the supply may not be very secure. A city pursuing resilience policies would therefore aim to reduce the reliance on sectors which are under threat to a period of water stress or shock. Equally this strategy would involve the identification of critical water imports originating from areas on uncertain, or unstable, water resources. This response would help to increase resilience beyond the spatial dimension into aspects of capital.

The most advanced and accepted demand side measure is aimed at influencing individual behaviour and the usage within a property, such as the government target in England to reduce per capita water consumption from a national average of around 150 litres to 130 litres per person per day (Defra 2008). New and innovative techniques to manage domestic water more effectively have emerged in response to perceived future restrictions in supply, government targets or the possibility of debilitating price rises. For example, there has recently been research concerning the possibility of implementing zero water buildings and water neutral development, but currently there is a gap with regard to skills, standards and political will. From this perspective, rainwater is captured as a resource and utilized for a variety of domestic purposes from landscaping to non-potable greywater functions, such as the flushing of toilets. This approach also reduces the volume of water running from the property into the local drainage network.

In addition to increasing the supply of water to homes, steps can be taken to reduce demand. An example of a measure in this area would be the utilization of water management devices, such as household metering and the adoption of technological devices that can better conserve the resource. In particular metering has been seen to bring a demonstrable effect, with a number of studies in the UK and continental Europe consistently reporting reductions in water consumption of between 10 to 15 per cent (Herrington 2007). To aid consumer education and reduce sectoral energy requirements, households could also have a third tap fitted to add to their current hot or cold options. This resource could provide a supply of water cleansed below drinking standards that could be utilized for a variety of non-potable purposes. Other measures could include advice concerning garden watering or the purchasing of water intensive technology, such as power showers. These strategies could all reduce the exposure of a household, and, by extension, a city if they became common-place. Significantly, this approach could also be applicable to the current built form with retrofitting these devices a real possibility, especially as they directly reduce water bills.

Balancing the need to provide economic orientated benefits, such as housing, jobs and infrastructure, with complementary environmental goods and services is a central theme of contemporary planning, particularly as the broader benefits of green and blue infrastructure are realized. The effective protection of green spaces within the city is also vital, as once developed they are usually never regained, emphasizing both the longevity of land use decisions within a largely inert built environment and the need for cities to pursue sustainable long term policies. But planners are also charged with promoting economic development, providing new housing and linking with regional agendas to facilitate the success of an area – all of which may increase the exposure to restrictions in supply. Merging growth objectives with an understanding of risk is a necessity to enable planning to meet multiple objectives and prevent significant added hazard and exposure within a city and its wider region.

The consequences of either not reducing exposure, or a narrow focus on hard engineered constructions, is both a population at risk and a recurring financial penalty to defend areas from flooding and to capture, store and transport more water resources. For example, the flood defence budget in England has gone up from £272 million to £800 million per annum within the space of 15 years, and there are still calls for this to be increased further. Each new defence also increases the overall year on year maintenance burden, which, all things remaining the same, decreases the amount of budget available for new defences the following year. An increase in water consumption will also mean additional capital expenditure on infrastructure to capture and transport the resource, with costs to the consumer possibly rising due to increasing asset management expenditure.

Obtaining new scientific data on exposure to risks also necessitates additional costs, as in reality increased knowledge lessens uncertainty over whether, and how, to respond. The costs are spread across government, the private sector and the consumer, and are a rising and unwelcome burden on society. Outside of hard engineering, the main mechanism for decreasing, or at least containing, these costs are through changes in the built and natural environment, and therefore via spatial planning. The key is consequently to strengthen the linkages between traditional technical and engineering responses and emerging social and managerial processes. Essentially, this requires planning for the sustainable success of the urban areas from a longer term, strategic viewpoint; in general terms giving urbanity more of a safety culture. Not just with regard to an individual development, but applying similar principles to the city. Therefore, the challenge is not just to reactively regulate expansion of housing and infrastructure, as has been the conventional focus of planning, but also to proactively influence the future city to be more sustainable and resilient. The exposure aspect of the risk equation is largely driven by historical decisions and future projections, and of the three elements its management sits most comfortably within the remit of the spatial planner. The production and application of information can help forge a deeper relationship between risk and the city, providing the evidence base to adapt and facilitate resilience to water based threats. This isn't a matter of immediately and fundamentally changing cities, but adjusting the drivers for land use from being short term and economic, to longer term, and, as McHarg argued, allowing nature to have a larger input into the decision.

Conclusion

Aristotle described the city as: 'a place where men live a common life for a noble end' and although this view may be optimistic, it does reflect the enduring value of urban centres. Risk management isn't necessarily concerning the prevention of any catastrophic natural or human driven collapse, such as experienced in the distant past in Pompeii or more recently in Prypiat, an abandoned city near Chernobyl. Rather, it is about a logical adaptation to hydrometeorological conditions in the face of more weather extremes, rising urban living and a comprehensive reliance on the city as the sole overriding driver for prosperity. A more strategic consideration of land use and the local and regional water environment would help cities to adapt to changing environments, lessen exposure and be more naturally resilient to the impacts of climatic hazards.

Where urban areas were once seen as a place of safety, cities are now the hub of modern risks and there is a growing recognition that urban development patterns have profound implications for effectively managing exposure over the current period and, as the example of Tewkesbury Abbey outlined in chapter 1 demonstrates, into the far distant future. A longevity identified by Benedict and McMahon (2006: xiii) who argue: 'the protection of land is an expression of faith in the future; it is a pact between generations'. To facilitate this admirable vision in a modern context does however require the combined efforts of a wide spectrum of actors and agencies, all aiming towards improving the urban realm and its operation. Connectivity is not just needed between differing sectors, but also between generations, as it is clear that development and land use decisions can create a legacy of exposure to risk.

The information within this chapter has detailed a number of measures designed to positively influence exposure to water risks, whilst still having synergies with a growth agenda. The development of zero water buildings or the utilization of water efficient technology and metering can all reduce exposure to scarcity. A more sophisticated comprehension of water risks can help extend policies from a simple protection of floodplains to incorporate land use across the entire city; with, for example, greener spaces designed to absorb water as a matter of course and densification influenced by risk, not just by socio-economic factors. As both this and the previous chapter outlined, parts of the city have the potential to generate and receive risk in what may appear to be a disconnected manner. Yet, in reality the city can adopt a complementary land use strategy specifically designed to reduce overall exposure. When disasters do occur the impact of both flooding and scarcity events can vary widely however; the following chapter unpacks this notion in more depth by exploring vulnerability; the final aspect of the risk equation.

9 Vulnerability and resilience in the city

....

Now down the narrow streets it swiftly came,
And widely opening did on both sides prey:
This benefit we sadly owe the flame,
If only ruin must enlarge our way.

(John Dryden, *Annus Mirabilis*, 1666)

A few months after the Great Fire of London in 1666 the poet Dryden compiled the poem, *Annus Mirabilis*, which vividly described the effects and spread of the disaster. He drew attention to how the dense form of the urban environment both helped spread the flames and was altered in its wake. After the fire, an increased awareness of the vulnerability of the city to this particular hazard, such as the use of construction materials and the claustrophobic mesh of streets, resulted in the first bylaws introduced to regulate building design to inhibit the spread of fire. The event therefore served to highlight the links between urban form and risk and was an early example of planned intervention. The scale of devastation also provided a unique opportunity for some of the principal architects of the time to redesign London to become, as Dryden put it within the same historical poem: 'a city of more precious mould'.

Indeed, many of the great works of Sir Christopher Wren (1632–1723), foremost of which was St Paul's Cathedral, emerged in the aftermath of the event, their longevity providing empirical evidence of Wren's philosophy that: 'architecture aims at eternity'. He also received the chance to put his ideology into practice on a much wider scale by submitting plans to King Charles II to completely rebuild the city within days of the disaster. His redesign of London was intended to remove the medieval warren of interweaving alleys with a grander series of urban boulevards and squares, which would both help limit the spread of fire and enable access to extinguish any recurrences. The plan to reduce the ingrained vulnerability was never implemented, partly due to the autonomous adaptation of the populace in rebuilding on top of their existing foundations as soon as they were able to do so. The plan does however reveal an early example of the aim to embed resilience to natural hazards within the design of a city, with Wren's aspirational maxim also highlighting the value of planning buildings and land use for the long term to avoid future vulnerabilities. Figure 9.1 shows Wren's actual proposal for rebuilding London.

The difficulty in putting Wren's plan into practice reveals much about the inertia of the built environment, especially with regard to regeneration. Without significant intervention once areas have been developed they tend to stay that way, and whilst grand plans can provide a new vision, they rarely get the opportunity to be either drafted or implemented. In practice changes are organic, and, modern city building exercises aside, it is this process that planners have overwhelmingly focused on. This does not necessarily conflict with the need for a coherent response however; it just means that in reality the vision for a more resilient city will probably be implemented on an incremental scale.

An examination of the adaptive elements of resilience responses has a differing slant from that of mitigation. The management of hazard from a water context is essentially focused on the governance of precipitation, both with regard to the selected methodology and the managerial structures. The clear focus does provide an agenda for action, but in practice it may be problematic to solve from a city perspective. This is due to the drivers potentially being both internal and external, whilst the benefits of responses are incremental and possibly only realized over the longer term. Hazard management also encompasses a challenging strategic view where the risk may be generated from a source that may appear disconnected from the receptors. Moreover, although spatial planning can exert power over the hazard aspect, the agenda links with the provision of infrastructure and the supply of natural spaces, which may be covered within the remits of differing agencies. Conversely, the vulnerability element of adaption rests much more comfortably within the spatial planning remit, being related directly to the location of people and property, yet its scope can equally challenge intervention. The following sections unpack the issue of vulnerability in more depth before examining the outcome and contextual understandings of the concept, each of which can provide a differing focus for attention.

Managing vulnerability

Vulnerability essentially concerns sensitivity to external stresses and perturbations (Adger 2006) and may also be an ongoing state rather than being closely related to an event (Pelling 1997). The term has found resonance within natural disaster and climate change discourses as a means to understand why some individuals, communities or even regions may experience variable levels of negative effects, despite being exposed to the same hazard. This point is critical to understanding the difference between exposure and vulnerability, in that the latter may be best understood as directly related to the former. An aspect can be vulnerable but not exposed, and therefore this is not as critical an issue to address; but if you are both vulnerable *and* exposed then you may have a greatly limited ability to cope and recover. The idea of becoming more resilient

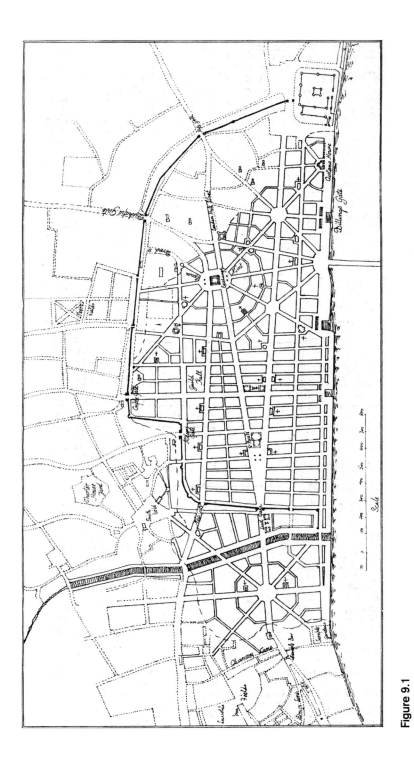

Figure 9.1

Sir Christopher Wren's 1666 plan for rebuilding a safer and improved London after the Great Fire

by lessening vulnerability is therefore concerned with reducing the sensitivity of a system to external forcing or shock.

Vulnerability can be further deconstructed into two understandings. The first is socially orientated and related to an inability to cope. The second is a top down perspective and is associated with a more mechanistic view that might be outlined, for example, by a process of scientific analysis designed to calculate vulnerability after any resilience policies have been considered. These notions have been termed 'contextual' and 'outcome' vulnerability respectively (O'Brien *et al.* 2007) and also serve to highlight the emerging differences in connotation between the social and natural sciences. Taken together, the terms can explain not just what is vulnerable, but why – and can help in understanding the wider processes embedding vulnerability within the city. The expressions also reflect the dual outcome and process orientated views of resilience outlined in chapter 5 and can be considered as mapping neatly onto the spatial planning remit, as they pertain to the built environment and societal inequalities.

Designing strategies to address vulnerability can be more difficult than that of exposure or hazard due to the strong social dimension, which presents challenges for a spatially orientated solution. Vulnerability is dynamic in that the existence and strength of the concept will change over time, and may alter in response to both macro- *and* micro-scale societal trends. For example, in addition to broad shifts in demographic change, social fragmentation or standards of living, the ability to access more local resources, such as community networks or family support can also affect vulnerability. This dimension also makes it difficult to measure; accurately quantifying the concept in a static spatial manner may be relevant for determining an outcome orientated view, but this may not be an effective approach to understand the contextual perspective.

To illustrate this point we can say with confidence that both Europe and Bangladesh will be exposed to climate change, and equally that their vulnerability to the threat is greatly different. This disparity may be due to a variety of factors, such as the existence and effectiveness of institutions, economic power and the ability to engender changes in behaviour. On the whole, in more advanced wealthy countries exposure is higher due to the concentration of economic assets, but vulnerability is lower perhaps as a result of the ability to use resources to provide defences or more effective emergency response strategies. Therefore, economic development has the potential to both increase exposure and decrease vulnerability; in quickly expanding cities however the former tends to rise more rapidly than the latter (UNISDR 2009). Consequently, the variance in vulnerability is also linked to an ability to adapt, both autonomously and planned. The difference in magnitude can be both scalar and temporal in that the impacts can be both more severe and last longer in particularly vulnerable areas; the concept is therefore connected with the potential to cope and recover.

The main focus for hazard and exposure, as outlined in the previous two chapters, is on those aspects most closely connected with the management of water and the location of people, from housing allocations, to the role of

GI, to the construction of new reservoirs. This chapter has a slightly different approach, shifting from the spatial perspective towards the operation of society as a whole. The divergence is due to a key difference between vulnerability and both hazard and exposure – as this chapter is essentially about *what* and *who* should be protected, whereas the previous are more concerned with the *where* and the *how*.

Resilience and outcome vulnerability

> While we cannot prevent natural phenomena such as earthquakes and cyclones, we can limit their impacts. The scale of any disaster is linked closely to past decisions taken by citizens and governments – or the absence of such decisions. Pre-emptive risk reduction is the key. Sound response mechanisms after the event, however effective, are never enough.
>
> (UNISDR 2009: iii)

The above statement is from the United Nations Secretary-General, Ban Ki Moon. The main message reflects the equally pragmatic tone of this book: naturally driven disasters will happen, but their effects can either be limited or exacerbated by decisions, some of which appear seemingly unrelated. Moreover, a heightened awareness of risk as a managing framework can help increase resilience in the city. Given the uncertain application of this modern concept, reducing vulnerability in the built environment has a surprisingly long history. The first Building Code was reputed to be in 1750 BC and was introduced by Hammurabi, the Babylonian King of Mesopotamia. The regulation was designed to ensure the structural integrity of housing as it ruled that if a dwelling collapses and kills its owner then the builder would be put to death. The scale of penalties may have lessened somewhat in the intervening years, but the intention is still the same: to develop a resilient response to a perceived threat. The current nature of urban form and function combined with socio-economic drivers can entrench or mitigate vulnerability. Consequently, a city that has pursued certain policies, or has limited access to financial measures to increase resilience, may have difficulties in managing vulnerability to water risks. Notwithstanding this impediment, a utilization of the data sources in chapter 6 does assist in addressing the outcome view of vulnerability.

The aspect of outcome vulnerability which provides the clearest, and most high profile, case is connected with the strategic protection of significant national assets. There is a strong view that those aspects of infrastructure that society holds most dear should be located by a more precautionary principle, not necessarily built then protected. A flood may affect a localized area, but if the water and sewerage network fails the effect is amplified and can result in a cessation of the water supply. All critical facilities should be identified and, where possible, relocated to an area not exposed to risk. Although sensible in theory, this may be difficult to achieve in practice. The operation of water treatment works has been designed in such a way that they need to be close to watercourses in order to discharge the cleansed water. Consequently, a significant amount of these plants are located in areas at risk from fluvial, estuarine or coastal flooding. For example, during the serious 2007 flood event in the UK a number of infrastructure assets were affected. Flooding at the Mythe water treatment plant in Tewkesbury resulted in around 140,000 homes without clean water for 17 days. Counter-intuitively therefore; flooding also resulted in water scarcity. Effectively the exposure of important assets results in a largely unrealized increase in society's vulnerability. In the aftermath of the 2007 inundation, the EA conducted research to establish the extent of the exposure and it discovered that more than 900 pumping stations and treatment works in England, over 55 per cent of the entire total, are in flood risk areas (EA 2009a).

In practice, it may take a flood event to drive a more accurate understanding of the nature of vulnerability. The extent of the risk also stretches way beyond water treatment works, and may include electricity infrastructure, hospitals, doctor's surgeries and care homes. For example, the same flood stopped the Castle Meads electricity substation in Gloucester from working, which left approximately 42,000 people without any power for 24 hours. The failure of communication networks such as roads, motorways and railways can also increase vulnerability, as the event affected parts of the M5 motorway, stranding an estimated 10,000 drivers, with thousands more hit by rail closures.

A final aspect of critical infrastructure worth highlighting is the location of emergency response stations. A positive aspect of the rise of any number of threats to cities has been the improvements in plans for operational reaction for both the immediate incident and its aftermath. In general urban areas are becoming better prepared, although the complexity and interconnectivity of society is proving a challenge. However, as could be seen in the case of Carlisle, improving emergency response procedures is irrelevant if the facility is under water. Figure 9.2 provides an insight into the nature and extent of infrastructure which may be at risk from flooding, displaying how a breakdown in basic services may amplify vulnerability and extend the impact of an event. It shows that in England embedded vulnerability is very significant, with the EA (2009a) estimating that infrastructure at risk from flooding includes: 2,358 schools and 2,363 doctors' surgeries; 4,000 km (10 per cent) of roads and 2,500 km (21 per cent) of railways; 55 per cent of water treatment works and pumping stations and around 7,000, or 14 per cent of all electricity infrastructure. Although there may be no comparable figures for other countries, it could be reasonably expected that other densely populated and advanced nations would also be similarly vulnerable.

The most desirable option for a flood resilient city would be to gradually shift the form of the city to avoid areas of high risk. Whilst over the longer term this may be a reasonable strategy in the short to medium term this may be unrealistic. Moreover, as with the case of the water infrastructure, there may be sound reasons why those assets are situated in their current position. The difficultly in

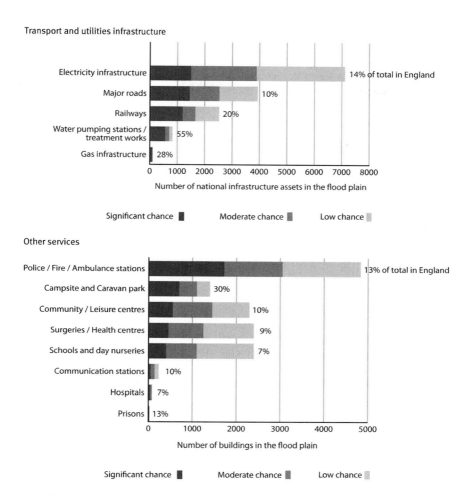

Transport and utilities infrastructure

Number of national infrastructure assets in the flood plain

Significant chance ■   Moderate chance ■   Low chance ▓

Other services

Number of buildings in the flood plain

Significant chance ■   Moderate chance ■   Low chance ▓

Figure 9.2

English infrastructure assets in flood risk areas
Source: EA 2009a

pursuing this aim, and of influencing the existing city, means that the planner should also engage with notions of *resistance, resilience* and *repairability*.

Resistance, resilience and repairability

Flood *resistance* is a strategy aiming to prevent flood waters from entering a property and can be effective in certain situations. Measures include artificial barriers, such as the wall surrounding the building, or even effective landscaping which can channel water away from the site. The onus may be on the homeowner to maintain these features however, and if temporary barriers are used, there is a requirement to receive adequate warning. The feasibility of such an approach also depends on the predicted flood level, as if flows are high then it may not be appropriate. Whilst resistance measures may appear to be effective, in reality, it can be difficult to prevent flood water from entering a building as the points of entry are numerous. Buildings are specifically designed not to be air tight, and so features such as vents, air bricks, or imperfect sealing can all provide a route, whilst water may even seep through the ground or from an internal wall with an adjoining property. Furthermore, in general building regulations have not yet engaged with the notion of flood proof materials, such as with regard to the utilization of low permeability products. This is where flood resilience and repairability strategies can also help reduce vulnerability.

New development in areas at risk could be subject to tighter building controls advocating design features, such as habitable spaces starting on the first floor above parking provision. If water does enter a building then the interior design of the house can be planned to minimize damage, from stone floors instead of carpets to the raising of appliance and electricity points to the use of differing material for floors and cupboards (Environment Agency and CIRIA 2001). Existing buildings could be altered either by the owner themselves as a preventative measure or by the insurer after any flood event. The general principle is to reduce the costs to the insurer/homeowner and to facilitate the restoration of the property. It is estimated that in the event of a 1-metre-deep flood if you compare a normal house with a 'flood resilient home', there would be a saving of £23,100 on repairs and the home would be habitable 42 days quicker (Norwich Union 2009). Therefore, spatial planning is amongst the agencies that can positively influence resilience by minimizing the impact and making the city less vulnerable and able to quickly recover.

The nature of development means that there are also clear windows available that facilitate the retrofitting of resilience into the city. Every building has periodic opportunities to integrate resilience, from ad hoc refurbishment, to more systematic short term refreshment, to significant longer term renewal. The onus here is not on the spatial planner, but on the owner to realize exposure to risks and design in resilient features. In addition, the aftermath of severe events also provides a window of opportunity to revisit the nature of the built environment. This is slightly more problematic than it sounds however, as in practice the authority here is the insurance industry. Cost therefore becomes a primary concern, as does the provision and content of insurance policies. One particular problem identified has been the traditional practice of the insurance sector in ensuring that they do not provide a much higher level of refurbishment than was previously the case; otherwise known as 'betterment'. In the UK there have been cases where householders have experienced flooding, but the insurer has refused to utilize resilient design features during refurbishment, as this may be more expensive. However, this is a short term policy that may cost the insurance company, as if the property floods again, as frequently happens, they may be presented with another huge bill (Douglas *et al.* 2010).

The discussion of outcome vulnerability thus far has been on the issue of flooding, but cities, industries and communities can also be particularly susceptible to a restriction in water resources. From a city perspective, water scarcity may occur due to the failure of the water supply infrastructure, whether from a flood or another unforeseen event. In addition to infrastructure breakdown, a simple lack of water supplies, storage capacity or an unsustainable balance of abstraction may also make an area more sensitive to systemic change. Further, an economic reliance on water intensive industries or agricultural output can increase city-wide vulnerability, as if a relative drought does occur then the impact may be harder than elsewhere. A strategy to increase resilience would therefore be aimed at economic restructuring and diversification, as has already happened in parts of the world suffering from over abstraction. A further measure could be improving the inputs into the network and reducing the sensitivity of water supply to external stresses.

With regard to water and vulnerability, resilience is also connected with an array of aspects such as how we act, the decisions we make and the way that we consume; these are however much more difficult to quantify and so have received less attention than the outcome or purely spatial aspects. Thus far the onus has been on making the built environment less vulnerable to risk, such as by examining the location of critical infrastructure. Although, there have also been advances in reducing vulnerability from a more social perspective, for example by improving flood warning systems and emergency response procedures. These aspects are however the most straightforward to address, perhaps due to the more manageable level of complexity and the clearest causal chain. In reality vulnerability stretches to a daunting scope and scale incorporating societal trends, such as demographic change and the availability of insurance, and personal aspects, such as supporting social networks, household financial assets and the ability to access resources. Resilience from this broad contextual view can therefore be pursued in a multiplicity of ways, a number of which are discussed within the following section.

Resilience and contextual vulnerability

> Planning to manage risk systems in their entirety further complicates land-use planning. Human settlements of all sizes are situated within larger socio-ecological systems that include environmental features (such as watersheds, regimes of coastal land erosion and sediment deposition, or earthquake zones), as well as social and cultural systems.
>
> (UN-Habitat 2007: 205)

There is an understandable tendency to associate resilience with the built environment. Whilst hazard and exposure are closely linked to the buildings and form of the city, vulnerability has a less obvious spatial dimension and has a focus on either the function of places, as outlined in the previous section, or as the opening quote delineates, on people and communities. The vast array of circumstances within which people live, from the national institutional capacity to their own individual outlook, can each play a huge role in exacerbating or limiting the effects of the same event. An appreciation of the factors influencing the variable capacity to cope with the impacts of natural hazards can assist in understanding just why some aspects of society may experience more severe and longer lasting outcomes from the same shock or stress.

The distinction between shock and stress to a system is important to delineate when unpacking contextual vulnerability. A shock arrives quickly whereas stress may be a continuous or slowly increasing pressure, such as on soil quality or water resources (Gallopin 2006). A factor exerting stress on a system may therefore be one of its usual components, for example consumer water demand, which is in itself experiencing pressure and changing as a result. The stressors are difficult to assign as an internal or external systemic force however as it depends entirely upon your scale of measurement. For example, any natural hazard is inside the global climatic system, but most likely external to its area of impact.

Although there has been progress on mapping vulnerability this is most relevant to analysis on large scales, such as the climatic vulnerability often attached to many developing countries. Adger (2006) draws attention to these countries being seen to be particularly vulnerable due to their lack of institutional capacity. Yet, he also highlights that they can be replete with citizens able to cope who may have a latent ability to adapt to changing circumstances. In simple terms, although they may be vulnerable, they do not view themselves as helpless. This aspect provides a further nuance, as in addition to governance factors, vulnerability can also relate to a feeling of insecurity within an individual. A sense of powerlessness may further discourage autonomous adaptation, whereby seemingly vulnerable people or communities can cope with different events in sometimes ingenious ways. This is an important distinction between 'vulnerability' used in a simplistic manner and understanding the various facets of contextual vulnerability. For example a region may have low resilience to outcome aspects, but high resilience to the contextual, and vice versa. The explicit identification of these two separate aspects of vulnerability allows more discrete targeting of action and an awareness of gaps in intervention.

This section is also linked to the discussion on the perception and communication of risks outlined in chapter 5, wherein certain groups or individuals may perceive themselves as being particularly vulnerable or powerless. This relative insecurity often also displays a huge disparity of impact – from a drought to a minor hosepipe ban, thus presenting a further challenge to intervention: if quantitative measures are imperfect, just how do you approach the problem from a qualitative approach? People may naturally feel more anxious about stresses to their well-being than others and think they may be less able to cope, whilst the availability of information about possible fears, such as pandemics to flooding may also influence opinion in either direction. Perceptions of vulnerability are therefore subjective, vary over space and time and be related to a host of factors, from the global credit crunch affecting their employment sector, to the location of a school in an area susceptible to flooding.

Adger (2006: 268) describes the concept of vulnerability as: 'a powerful analytical tool for describing states of susceptibility to harm, powerlessness, and marginality of both physical and social systems, and for guiding normative analysis of actions to enhance well-being through reduction of risk'. The second aspect of this statement is of particular relevance here. It is clear that addressing risk via a more sophisticated understanding of its constituent parts, which have been subsequently placed within the risk management framework detailed in chapter 6, can help the applicability of the notion within spatial planning. However, an investigation of contextual vulnerability moves the consideration from the more evident causal relationship displayed by a focus on outcomes, towards a multifaceted and challenging network of interrelated stressors. The ability to manage both shocks and stressors is the key to increasing resilience to water risks in the city, but the sheer complexity of its management combined with an uncertain spatial element has hindered strategic approaches.

Although vulnerability is a separate concept to exposure, the two issues are closely related. In this context they may be described as a measure of the sensitivity of a system *after* it has been exposed to water stress or shock, such as a scarcity or flooding episode. Contextual vulnerability is an ongoing and dynamic process, but with specific regard to water risks it only becomes active following a perturbation. Considering exposure in this way as a relational property to vulnerability is designed to assist in informing differing strategies to increase resilience, as there is an overlying spatial dimension to contextual vulnerability which can help design and target remedial policies.

A key difference between the two interrelated areas of water scarcity and flooding is the temporal dimension. Drought is commonly a large scale, macro-level event – a stressor, whereas flooding is a rapidly experienced risk – a shock. There is also a spatial aspect in that you can be subject to one and not the other, meaning that the integrated policies applicable with regard to hazard may not be analogous with respect to vulnerability. A normative intervention strategy is further inhibited as the underlying social causes of vulnerability and the general feeling of insecurity may be applicable regardless of location. The scale of intervention could therefore logically be focused on a multi-scalar level, from the nation to the household. A final point of note is the dynamic interaction between stressors clouding the cause and solutions to vulnerability. The linkages may encompass social groupings, sectors and spatial boundaries, all of which can inhibit an effective response. Although the subject is undeniably complex, engaging with the 'science of vulnerability' (O'Brien *et al.* 2009) can be a useful approach to increase the targeting and effectiveness of interventions.

Vulnerability therefore can operate on multiple scales and be subject to numerous stressors. All of which can complicate any assessment, perhaps explaining why the policy focus thus far may have been on the linear outcome perspective. The approach of quantitatively gathering and applying data designed to increase resilience to hazard, exposure and outcome vulnerability, is not readily applicable to this section. The interconnected nature of contextual vulnerability means that it cannot necessarily be looked at via its separate components as other aspects of risk can be. The need to consider complex and dynamic social contexts challenges measurement and simplification, especially when the ability to cope within individuals may also be in continuous motion. The differing aspects of stress also interact, ensuring that any intervention strategy is problematic. Addressing one stressor, such as a focus on increasing the wealth of a city or household, could increase vulnerability elsewhere. For example, increasing reliance on the economic success of an industry that is sensitive to changes in water resources.

Addressing contextual vulnerability

An unpacking of contextual vulnerability points towards a twofold strategy: one aspect targeting the broader social drivers for vulnerability and the second aimed at addressing the feeling of powerlessness. With regard to the former, tackling social inequalities is a core aim of planning and planners have expertise in applying policy interventions in a sophisticated and contested arena. To better prioritize interventions however requires an evidence base and system to appraise the level of vulnerability. Vulnerability assessments have been applied in a number of areas, most notably within the climate change field. The process may consider a wide variety of data to gain an insight into how an extreme natural hazard may impact upon an area, with a view to developing policies to increase resilience to shocks and stresses. Whilst the approach has value for decision making, the intricate nature of social and governance processes means that some factors may not be included, whether due to problems in scale, quantification or simply being hard to identify. It is incumbent therefore to recognize the uncertainty evident in this approach, and in particular the critical interaction between the stressors (O'Brien *et al.* 2009).

In practice, tackling social inequalities and allocating extra resources purely for the means of reducing contextual vulnerability to flooding or water scarcity may not hold enough weight when compared against more tangible poverty goals. Marginalized areas with a limited adaptive capacity may be hit hardest by any impacts, but in the absence of any catastrophic event would a process of renewal project be initiated on the strength of this possible threat alone? Although an improvement of the socio-economic prospects of an area, combined with more defences, better infrastructure or the retrofitting of resilience can all help reduce risk, the investment of capital to renew these areas is subject to wider, long established social agenda, such as housing provision and job creation. It may be that water risks need to add its voice to this contested arena and provide another strand to consider when allocating socially orientated investment.

Vulnerability to a changing water regime does not operate in isolation from the broader social context. It may be affected by the climatic and social drivers outlined in chapter 2, or inadvertently by a seemingly unrelated social interaction or shift in power. Effective intervention therefore needs to identify and focus on both inherent vulnerability and the driving forces. These can be further targeted by utilizing an understanding of exposure to these specific risks as outlined in the previous chapter. Areas which may be subject to significant deprivation *and* exposure to water risks could therefore be correlated and prioritized for renewal and the retrofitting of resilience.

As there is firm evidence that the impacts of many natural hazards are concentrated on marginalized groups the most vulnerable may also be amongst the most exposed. This is most easily identified within the climate change field as the developing world will both experience a significant amount of detriment and be the least able to pursue resilient strategies designed to limit vulnerability, such as strong sea walls, managed realignment policies, or the construction of new and improved infrastructure. In short, the vulnerable will have their ability to cope tested more frequently. These inequalities are further exacerbated due to vulnerable groups, regardless of their nation, usually having difficulty in accessing resources or influencing decision making.

Although comprehending the multiple stressors may be problematic, identifying the most vulnerable groupings of people is much more straightforward. A similar approach could be taken with those groups of society, which are deemed to be most vulnerable, such as the elderly or young. For example, a city more resilient to flood risks would aim to site schools, care homes or hospitals away from areas protected behind flood defences and adapt form and function to lessen the effect of any event. Similarly, cities subject to relative scarcity may wish to prioritize the improvement of the water supply infrastructure if their populations have a significant level of vulnerable citizens. However, the inability to access resources or to influence decision making by these groups means that spatial planners may have to intervene without any significant pressure from their needful populations.

The low level of engagement within sections of society has hindered their ability to influence the allocation of resources. For example, although flood defences may be allocated via a cost–benefit approach, vocal communities can help sway judgements. The representation of sections of society may also be a factor in determining the content of more general policies designed to lessen socio-economic drivers. One mechanism to address the inequality of influence would be policies designed to promote the inclusion of vulnerable groups within decisions concerning the management of water. This could help limit exposure and hazard generation with a view to gaining agreement on how vulnerability within an area should be addressed.

A clear synergy between the two areas of focus is that if any inequalities driving vulnerability in society are addressed, they almost automatically improve the feeling of powerlessness also inherent within these groups. A proactive measure specifically designed to mitigate this deficiency has been a more timely and accurate communication of risk, especially with regard to flooding, which can occur very swiftly. For example, there has been an emphasis on reducing contextual vulnerability by increasing the amount of people who are registered with flood risk warning systems, which can provide an automated telephone message, SMS or email when a threat may be imminent. In England over 430,000 people in flood risk areas have signed up to the Environment Agency's warning service (EA 2009a). The warning service helps people prepare for flooding by moving valuable possessions or documents to safety or perhaps to take measures to reduce exposure, such as the fitting of temporary flood barriers. A general increase in lay information, such as via risk mapping websites, also helps people to become aware of their exposure to flooding. The figures for England further estimate that 55 per cent of people living in at risk areas were aware of the threat, and of these 60 per cent had taken preparatory action. The improvements with regard to warning should also be considered alongside effective emergency response strategies designed to limit damage and decrease recovery time.

Conclusion

Disasters cannot be disassociated from the socio-economic context within which they occur; the impacts are directly related to the nature and vulnerability of our institutions, built infrastructure and lifestyles. Consequently, analysing them in an integrated manner can provide insights into how to develop effective policies and practices for shaping our cities. If we do not acknowledge the root causes of our risks, we adopt a short term, reactive approach, whereas the scope of impacts suggests we need to be reflexive, proactive and strategic. The content of this chapter highlights the difficultly in transforming these intentions into action however. Although, spatial planning is rare in that it can potentially address facets of both contextual and outcome vulnerability, there are real difficulties in application. Outcome vulnerability is the easiest aspect to target, reducing the level of critical infrastructure at risk is clearly achievable via a focus on the built environment, with the exception of operational constraints, such as with water treatment. Yet, in practice there may be limited ability to alter the location of buildings, which is where retrofitting becomes a key, and achievable, strand of the resilience discourse.

Conversely, the issue of contextual vulnerability is a much more thorny issue. If spatial planning is to contribute to increasing resilience to water risks via examining the vulnerability embedded within society, there are a series of challenges in targeting resilience. A focus on areas that are exposed to flooding and scarcity can provide a useful spatial dimension but to provide focus in a nebulous field an initial problem to addressing vulnerability is determining the specific risk in question. A further difficulty comes in unpacking the stressors driving the underlying vulnerability and ascertaining the nature of their interrelationship. Even if this can be approached there are inherent challenges in quantification, hampering the ability to gather a robust evidence base and influence decision making. Moreover, particularly vulnerable groups are commonly marginalized from policy formation and determination, compounding their problems. A policy of engagement with those aspects of society less able to cope with the impact of a hazard may be an effective way to increase resilience.

This chapter has argued that the city should not be seen purely from a structural standpoint, but should also encompass aspects such as the broad social context and the operation of our institutions and their ability to influence resilience within people and their supporting networks. Outside of outcome vulnerability, the broad disparities in national governance frameworks effectively preclude any specific, and detailed, recommendations. But one finding is clear: if risk research is to target all pathways to resilience it needs to engage with vulnerable groups and address the issues inhibiting the practical application of this science. An issue which risk managers have, perhaps understandably, struggled to acknowledge. In hindsight, it is understandable why the focus has been on tackling vulnerability by warning, emergency response and an assessment of critical infrastructure. The multiplicity of scales and stressors provides a daunting backdrop to a subject commonly managed via an overt and narrow engineering based approach. Yet, as the management of risk becomes more uncertain a complementary engagement with vulnerability also rises in importance. The final chapter attempts to draw the broad arguments within this book together and provide a strategic view of what a future city more resilient to water risks may look like.

10 Towards a more sustainable city

It is clear that the city-state is a natural growth, and that man is by nature a political animal, and a man that is by nature and not merely by fortune citiless is either low in the scale of humanity or above it.

(Aristotle, *Politics*)

The identification of the city as the natural habitat of humanity has long run parallel to its perceived importance as a locus for advancement. In more classical times, to live outside of the *polis* essentially represented a rejection of society and a poor status being deplored by Homer as: 'clanless and lawless and heartless'. Although thinking has since greatly evolved, it is undeniable that cities have always been great generators of capital, and, as a result, an understandable magnet for people. This relationship is never more apparent than in the present, where urban areas are almost universally identified as the key driver for economic growth on a global scale and frequently individual cities contribute a disproportionate amount of national economic income. For instance, London is widely acknowledged as the main engine room of the UK, whilst Mexico City accounts for approximately a third of Mexico's entire GDP (UN-Habitat 2007). These benefits should not just be measured in narrow economic terms however, as from a social perspective there is a rich variety of goods and services widely available. For example, the concentration of people has helped communication and collaboration, aiding the formation of agencies designed to provide a collective voice, improve standards, teach skills or facilitate mobility. Although the contrast between the rich and poor can be stark within urban areas, cities are also widely seen to be the best mechanism to help raise quality of life and alleviate poverty on both a local and global scale. An issue recognized by the United Nations Population Fund (2007: 1) who hold the opinion that:

> no country in the industrial age has ever achieved significant economic growth without urbanization. Cities concentrate poverty, but they also represent the best hope of escaping it.

In addition to economic growth, the city is also the unchallenged capital of education and culture, providing a wealth of opportunities for learning, leisure and recreation. Creativity, innovation and enterprise are commonplace within this volume of people and the generation of knowledge can drive advances across a number of fields. Furthermore, they are seats of administrative and legislative power, the influence of which can stretch far beyond their physical boundaries. The sheer concentration of people, goods and services also gives cities a whole host of advantages not experienced elsewhere, and assists the fostering of beneficial synergies across sectors. The multiplicity of benefits does mean that people intuitively perceive the advantages of city living and their continued migration to urban centres inevitably drives growth, especially in nations experiencing rural poverty. The dynamism, connectivity and complexity of current urban areas is clearly much greater than in the past, and presents a significant challenge to both an accurate identification of impacts and subsequent intervention by spatial planning.

Although cities do receive much unflattering attention, it is acknowledged by even their fiercest critics that they are absolutely vital for sustainability. Indeed, approximately half the world's population is clustered on just below 3 per cent of the land area, a demographic concentration that frees up land to be used for other activities, and in particular releases development pressure on non-urban ecosystems. The concentration of people and activities also provides opportunities for wider advantages, such as economies of scale, recycling, the efficient use of energy and sustainable transport. Concomitant with this issue is the dominating role of cities upon the planet, as both consumers of resources and producers of wastes, the importance of which suggests that there simply cannot be a serious goal of sustainable development without focusing upon the needs and functioning of the city. This process is hindered however by the current economically orientated governance framework, within which cities do not have to take account of their wider external environmental impacts.

Although cities can be influential, the relatively narrow city, regional or national administrative boundaries inhibit the ability to intervene, especially when the impacts may be externalized to the other side of the world. Addressing the *internal* effects of activity are however vitally important for cities; as negative impacts may mean that the need to compete and maximize economic growth could be severely compromised. Moreover, the need to protect cities is intensified by their overwhelming ability to concentrate resources and so magnify the potential risks. Given the huge growth in urban dwellers there is a need to take steps to ensure that future social, economic and environmental conditions are not detrimentally affected by present land use decisions and therefore move towards planning strategically for successful urban living. In short, given the extreme importance of cities we need to think more carefully about their extent, nature, operation and form, particularly in respect to emerging environmental threats.

Impacts and intervention

Mirroring a number of previous quotes regarding the persistent nature of land use problems, concern as to the way that these issues have actually been tackled in theory and practice is also a recurring theme. Patrick Geddes provided an early example that has lasting contemporary resonance as to perceived inadequate governance and managerial frameworks within his seminal book *Cities in Evolution* (1915: 1) stating:

> the problems of the city have come to the front, and are increasingly calling for interpretation and for treatment. Politicians of all parties have to confess their traditional party methods inadequate to cope with them.

As with the Unwin extract in chapter 7 the quote from Geddes is particularly interesting due to its lingering intergenerational relevance – you could make a strong argument that it would be topical and applicable to any era since its publication in the early twentieth century. For example, the quote could be interpreted as pertaining to the arch twenty-first-century issues of implementing sustainable development or climate change mitigation. The extract illustrates both the enduring difficulties in managing problems within urban areas and also that effective governance structures and policies are key tools in creating a framework for effective intervention. Consideration of habitual views such as this also provides an insight into the degree to which the problems of cities have actually been addressed by the managerialist approach of modern planning systems. More recently Hall (2002a: 424) reflects upon the changeable, but enduring, nature of problems in urban areas suggesting that:

> perhaps we came back full circle: at the end of nearly a century of modern planning, the problems of cities remained much as they had been at the start.

Although the drivers of the difficulties referred to by Peter Hall are not necessarily replicable to those experienced by Engels and others, a century on from formalized intervention via land use planning the onus only appears to have shifted from *standards* of living to *quality* of living. Cities still witness extreme poverty and whilst economies grow, new technology is developed and lifestyles change, there are still ageless concerns connected with seemingly wicked problems and a desire to improve our circumstances. Indeed, the gradual separation of the natural and built environments and the creation of a mechanism to structure and regulate development to avoid impacts are logically analogous. The remit and focus of the planning system, as the main strategy for intervention in the use of land, should therefore adapt, as the causes and scope of the impacts affecting both people and places gradually shift over time.

These two issues of *impacts* and *intervention* are therefore symbiotically related. The complexity and interconnectivity of the issues also means that there may be a number of unforeseen consequences of action in the built environment. In the same way that poverty and lack of equity can be correlated to a failure to effectively intervene, we should note that decisions are not always successful and within the relatively recent history of planning there are examples of a host of poor judgements resulting in long term undesirable consequences. With regard to water based hazards, the most high profile is the long history of floodplain development. But this is only part of the story, as building in areas with inadequate drainage infrastructure or water resources can increase the exposure to surface water flooding or scarcity respectively. There is a strong argument for more strategic planning of cities, but implementing resilience within existing urban areas may appear to be an intimidating proposition.

Where to begin

There is a famous punchline to an apocryphal joke concerning a city dweller lost whilst travelling in the countryside and asking a rural local for directions, upon which the response is: 'If I was you, I wouldn't start from here.' In recent times this advice arguably provides an appropriate analogy for the way that the historical development of many cities may appear to have almost been designed to maximize the risk of flooding and water scarcity. If that seems an unsuitable statement, take a moment to consider how, in the perverse situation of having to design a city to increase these risks, you would achieve the task.

As an initial measure, housing, industry and critical infrastructure would all be placed in areas at risk from flooding; both from natural and artificial sources. Strategies to increase the general risk of inundation would also be pursued by maximizing use of hard impermeable surfaces that generate runoff and the development of a drainage system centred on moving precipitation quickly into the nearest watercourse. More diligent readers would also want to minimize opportunities for infiltration, interception or evaporation, perhaps by increasing the density of the built environment and considering the value of urban greenspace via a narrow economic calculation. The intense nature of the city would also be designed to greatly limit groundwater recharge, whilst industries and agriculture would be allowed to abstract water for cheap export goods, almost regardless of the state of water supplies. Furthermore, a culture of water as a ubiquitous resource would be fostered and remain unchallenged, with the agency benefiting most from water consumption also being charged with reducing usage. The list goes on, and I'm sure you see the point. Although, this is a simplistic view, it is clearly illustrative – cities and citizens are starting from a position that may greatly inhibit future strategies to manage risk.

The main point to consider is that despite how inconvenient it may be for urban planners, cities are constrained by existing wide-reaching issues such as urban form, property rights, institutions, trade patterns and public attitudes. Moreover, any remedial strategies must be embedded within, and tailored to, the individual environment; in reality, cities are incredibly complex, interconnected and multiplex. The main overarching strategy of modern times to tackle these types of problems has been sustainable development, a concept that can theoretically connect seemingly disparate areas and provide a framework to link social, economic and environmental goals. However, the sectoral nature of politics and governance has an understandable tendency to shy away from this challenging remit towards a more simplistic and quantifiable pursuit of individual targets with integration added where easily achievable. With regard to managing natural hazards, consideration of principles of risk management as a central theme may provide more potential as a managerial framework.

A period of managerial shifts

From a flooding perspective, it is the recent paradigm challenging awareness that the majority of flood risk in some cities may not come from the readily identifiable and geographically fixed floodplains and coasts that presents the strongest argument for more water resilient cities. For example as outlined in box 3.1, in 2005 in England and Wales there were an estimated 80,000 homes at risk from surface water flooding, a figure that rose to an enormous 3.8 million in the space of five years. Just take a minute to consider the effect that this fundamental shift may have on those concerned with flood defence. Just how do you manage flooding when not only may your traditional hard defence engineered approaches be redundant, but there may be potentially hundreds of separate sources of risk which defy quantification? How can probability realistically be considered as a basis for decision making in this situation? How can the state even be seen to provide adequate protection against surface water flooding? This shift will be one of the emerging challenges on the early twenty-first century, particularly when considered in conjunction with the rise of more extreme climatic events and burgeoning urbanization. It may well be that the transition from defence to management, from probability to risk, and from the state to the individual, continues apace.

With regard to water scarcity, the rise in urban populations, changes in precipitation patterns and trends in usage will all challenge the traditional supply orientated predict-and-provide methodology to move towards more demand side approaches as the practical ubiquity of the resource becomes increasingly realized. The problems here may appear to be eminently more manageable than flooding in that cities can expect to require more water to function in the future and there are various options to cater for this need. But the solution may not be as simplistic in reality. The construction of new reservoirs, the provision of metering, influencing usage patterns or the wide scale introduction of new water efficient technology will all require time and resources to be implemented. Therefore, whilst water scarcity may present a gradually emerging threat, the ability to react may be equally slow and long term.

One logical way of reacting to this rise in uncertainty is to make our cities more aware of, and resilient to, water risks – and in this respect proactively and

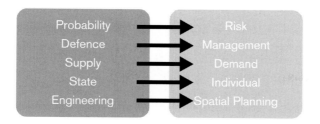

Figure 10.1

Recent and emerging shifts in water management

strategically influencing the use of land is key. Therefore, it may be that the most significant shift in the management of water will not be the one from probability to risk-based approaches, or from flood defence to flood risk management, or from water supply to water demand, but, rather, the impending transition in responsibility from engineering to spatial planning. This should also be seen in the context of an emerging shift in responsibility away from the state towards the individual as the ability to guarantee protection is seen to be unrealistic. People will be expected to consider the level of risk they are willing to accept. Whilst there will always be a role for providing hard structures to either defend against flooding or to supply fresh and wastewater services, there will clearly be a stronger role in linking water concerns with where, and how, we live. Figure 10.1 displays how a more sophisticated understanding of the ability to manage water in the city has led to a number of recent managerial shifts in a number of areas.

Envisioning a water resilient city

Although 'where to begin' may appear to be a difficult proposition, projecting 'where to end' is significantly more straightforward, especially when considered from a land use perspective. Whilst many aspects of risk management may challenge a purely spatial intervention, such as the role of social networks and engagement, figure 10.2 provides an insight into how a city more resilient to water risks may be structured and influenced by spatial planning. Using a spatial analysis of risk and the data provided in chapter 6 we can design a combination of local and strategic measures to proactively decrease hazard, exposure and vulnerability.

Within this notional representation of an urban area, a strategic long term approach to intervention can help envisage how a city could change to become more resilient to water risks. When considering an excess of water, the sheer uncertainty concerning the possible sources of flooding heightens the need to move towards multifunctional land use and to integrate water management within the urban area. For example, upstream storage areas can compensate

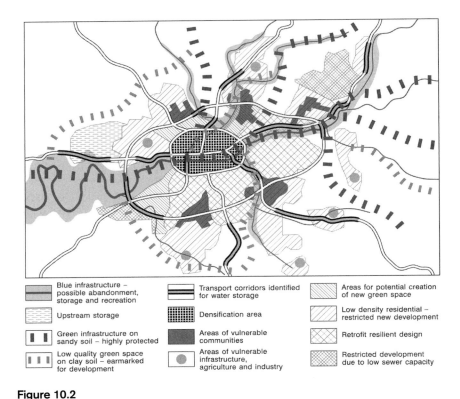

Blue infrastructure –
possible abandonment,
storage and recreation

Transport corridors identified
for water storage

Areas for potential creation
of new green space

Upstream storage

Densification area

Low density residential –
restricted new development

Green infrastructure on
sandy soil – highly protected

Areas of vulnerable
communities

Retrofit resilient design

Low quality green space
on clay soil – earmarked
for development

Areas of vulnerable
infrastructure,
agriculture and industry

Restricted development
due to low sewer capacity

Figure 10.2

A representation of a more water resilient city

for downstream densification, development in areas subject to surface water or pluvial flooding could be limited and urban infill can be more tightly controlled in areas with sandy soils. The focus isn't all on the restriction of the built environment however; to aid the multifunctionality of land use, poor quality greenspace could be released for development, particularly if it may not allow for effective water storage or infiltration. Further, areas at risk could provide the focus for retrofitting resilient design features, whilst new blue and green infrastructure locations can be created. An additional aspect would concentrate on influencing the resilience of vulnerable sectors both in terms of communities and infrastructure.

With regard to maximizing water resources, many of these measures also help to alleviate problems of scarcity. For example, allowing water to infiltrate into the ground will have a positive impact on resources, whilst pursuing resilient design options can help demand side issues. Employing more localized strategies to capture, retain and reuse water will also help to reduce overall demand. As a final illustration, the identification of those aspects of agriculture and industry particularly reliant upon the cheap availability of water would also enable a gradual shift in practices or increased security of supplies. Taken together these approaches would therefore include both people and places, and consider areas suitable for restriction, development or transition.

Implementing this vision may not be analogous with current administrative or managerial boundaries however. Why should autonomous urban areas on the fringe of the city forego additional investment, regeneration or housing growth in order to enable safer development in their affluent neighbouring authorities in the centre? Equally, should these already highly urbanized areas suffer a future lack of greenspace due to their underlying soil composition? The potential difficulty in applying this risk based approach emphasizes the possible tension between functional areas, for example a catchment, and artificially created administrative boundaries, a conflict that may inhibit the pursuit of resilience in the city. There are clearly balances to be made between social and environmental concerns within differing sectors of a city and although these measures can influence decision making other concerns should also contribute to the debate. The differing measures outlined in figure 10.2 can however assist in re-engaging the city with its local environment in order to manage its most precious and dangerous resource more effectively.

The past, present and future context

> Nature has provided against the absolute destruction of any of her elementary matter, the raw material of her works; the thunderbolt and the tornado, the most convulsive throes of even the volcano and the earthquake, being only phenomena of decomposition and recomposition. But she has left it within the power of man irreparably to derange the combinations of inorganic matter and of organic life.

The quote is from George Perkins Marsh's influential book *Man and Nature* (1864: 35), one of the first to explicitly identify humans as agents of change; challenging the commonly held opinion of the time that the Earth was solely the result of long term natural processes. Marsh also took the pragmatic view not that humanity should halt all intervention; rather, that this should be done with planning and an awareness of long term impacts. Although prescient, this approach will be increasingly difficult in a highly populated and interdependent world. Indeed, the rate of growth is such that if we continue at the same rate as we have done over the recent past, by 2600 we would by literally standing shoulder to shoulder (Hawking, 2001) – an evocative, but sobering illustration. The scope of the potential impacts on the environment and the extinction rate of species has led to bleak predictions, such as the view of E.O. Wilson (1998) who posits that humanity is leaving the Cenozoic, the age of mammals, and about to enter the Eremozoic, the age of loneliness. Although Hulme (2009) does caution against the use of catastrophic language as a tool to highlight risk based debates, such as frequently occurs within climate change, it is difficult to argue against the view posed by the English philosopher John Gray (2009: 397) who, after analysing the impact and behaviour of humankind, describes us as 'Homo rapiens' – an 'exceptionally rapacious primate'.

As chapter 1 argued, cities in the past may have been abandoned, but this is rare in the modern era. Urban areas are now durable in the sense that they usually continue to exist regardless of impact. Indeed, almost every traumatized city has been rebuilt, from the Chicago fire in 1871, to post-Second World War Berlin, to Kobe after the 1995 earthquake (Vale and Campanella 2005). Although cities may not become extinct in the aftermath of natural events, they do experience lingering social, economic and environmental penalties. This may include, for example, a loss of competitiveness in a global age or a significant reconstruction bill, all of which can take many decades, if ever, to recover from. Furthermore, there has been an emphasis on reactive resilience mainly in the post-disaster context. This is aptly illustrated by considering the provision of insurance, one of the main mechanisms developed by societies to enable individuals and companies to be more resilient. This remedial measure however can only be accessed *after* experiencing a tangible detriment, and has no real remit for the proactive avoidance of hazardous events.

The question of how 'natural' are natural hazards has been a central theme of this book. Although extremes of climate are natural occurrences, the ability of humanity both to force this via anthropogenic climate change and to take decisions that increase hazard, exposure and vulnerability, challenge a clear and uncontested natural culpability. Furthermore, those decisions on where, and how, we live provide a tangible link to spatial planning as a very significant, yet largely unknowing, gatekeeper of risk. All of which runs counter to a simplistic, and reassuring, Act of God interpretation to disasters. It is much more demanding to accept the key role society plays in magnifying its own risk, as embedded within this acknowledgement is a need, and duty, to engender change.

That is not to say that growth either economically or spatially is an unsustainable aim; it has after all been the most powerful driver for standards of living. It is however, important to recognize that tempered with these advances, industrialization and the unerring focus on growth and economic development also supplied enormous social and environmental impacts to the city. In 1840s Manchester, the city described as the cradle of the Industrial Revolution, the average life expectancy was a shocking 24, which coincidently was the same age as Engels when authoring his study on the condition of the working class. To provide context in 2008 these figures were 73 for men and 78 for women; slightly below the national average. The wide scale exploitation of energy sources in the form of fossil fuels, allied with scientific and technological advancement, has gradually helped bring benefits such as clean water, reliable energy and a regular supply of food. But as the value and populations of cities rise, so has the need for urban areas to continuously identify and adapt to potentially detrimental future influences. The existence of strong, long term drivers increasing urban risk to climatic hazards provides perhaps the most powerful argument for strategic intervention. Huge projected increases in urban global populations will inevitably drive risk, as will climate change predictions. Just as the importance of the city rises, so do the destructive forces; in reality, cities are the source of both our greatest assets and our highest risks.

Part I of the book also highlighted that civilization, and in particular urban living, has been in an undeviating, yet largely disconnected, discourse with the wider geo-climatic context. One of the most significant aspects of this relationship is the one between humanity and water. As a vital human need water has been absolutely critical to decisions as to where cities originate, how much they grow and the standard of living of the inhabitants. The connectivity is complex however; experiencing and managing the correct amount of the resource is absolutely critical: too little or too much can have catastrophic consequences. Given this importance you would expect that the relationship between cities and their water environment would be a sophisticated exchange characterized by a desire to simultaneously secure safe freshwater supplies and an urban environment protected from flooding. Cities can be planned to both minimize the exposure to flooding and water scarcity and to facilitate the existence of natural habitats, but the techno-economic dominance in determining city form and function has not only detrimentally affected this role, but may actually drive risk.

The problems of water in the city

> The Culture-man whom the land has spiritually formed is seized and possessed by his own creation, the City, and is made into its creature, its executive organ, and finally its victim.
>
> (Spengler 1923: 99)

The bleak title of Spengler's work, *The Decline of the West*, provides an insight into his fatalistic view of western civilization that depicts the city as a parasitical, homogenous expanse contradicting and denying the natural world. He further identifies the city as an organism with a discrete lifespan inevitably moving in an inexorable cycle of decline. Whilst undeniably evocative, this view does present an extreme perspective of the relationship between humanity and its prevailing mode of habitat. In reality, the citizen is both a victim and beneficiary, and although the city drives risk, it can also provide mitigation. The examination of water management provides an example of this notion in microcosm. Although problems are experienced, and are frequently anthropogenic in origin, solutions are mooted and new engineering constructions introduced. The overall message with regard to water is that this association, characterized by extremes of costs and benefits, can be re-examined to lessen the potential impacts.

Although counter-intuitive, the prevailing management methodology with regard to drainage, water supply and flood risk management in some cases may actually increase the hazard, exposure and vulnerability of cities to impacts from natural hazards. Whilst a process of urbanization, facilitated by a new defence or an increased drainage network, provides clear service to its immediate locality, the implications of this intervention for the city and its water environment as a whole may not be as clear cut. The rapid emergence of surface water flooding as the most widespread and difficult to manage source of flood risk provides evidence of this uncertainty. Risk therefore may not be removed, but instead transferred spatially and deferred temporally. In reality, a focus on a cycle of growth and the application of mainly technologically driven solutions may embed both direct utility and indirect jeopardy in the city.

This is not to argue that the city should be questioned as the most sustainable form of habitat, or that an alternative form of settlement should be pursued; rather, that cities should utilize more effective management principles to facilitate safer, more sustainable development. The sheer complexity of cities as a place where technological, natural and social components interact provides a daunting context for moving towards a city more resilient to water hazards. Although societal factors and current urban form and function can be a potential constraint, the sophisticated and potent nature of large urban systems does provide an inherent advantage to pursuing resilience as an aspirational aim. Cities can access enormous internal and external resources, such as finance, knowledge and networks, to better manage hazards in comparison to other scales of development (Allenby and Fink 2005). All of which increase the potential capacity to respond to threats and be more resilient.

A long term view would be a heightened awareness of risk in order to gradually adapt the city to be more sensitive to its geography and move towards a more sustainable pattern of development. Not one solely determined by socio-economic factors, but also its local geographical, climatic and environmental constraints. Thus far there has been a focus on both probability and structural resilience measures to protect against too much or too little water; this however repeats the technocratic mistakes of historic approaches to flood defence and essentially commits future generations to potentially unsustainable impacts and expenditure. Despite considerable advances within cities, there are still many significant problems, and the need to improve the relationship between people and places endures. Understanding and applying concepts such as risk, resilience and uncertainty does offer potential in informing appropriate action however, although these terms first have to be considered within a spatial planning and land use context.

Towards a conceptual framework

Risk, vulnerability and resilience are essentially natural science concepts that have been appropriated by social scientists and policy makers. Despite their emerging value within spatial planning, the way that these concepts have been articulated and applied has yet to reach maturity. Unpacking risk into component elements of hazard, vulnerability and exposure provides value by translating a broad concept into three separate, but interrelated agendas. A similar investigative process with regard to resilience reveals that there are also a number of separate understandings of the same term: in this case the notions concerning the ability to recover, adapt to changing normalities and the presence of social support networks; with each one offering a differing, but complementary, outlook to what is a deceptively complex topic.

In addition to a deeper understanding of the concepts individually, relating these ideas to each other creates the potential to design a framework for effective decision making. Although intended to manage water risks, the conceptual framework outlined in chapters 5 and 6 may also offer potential in addressing other problems, particularly when considered in conjunction with uncertainty. The collection and analysis of fresh data concerning causal processes helps to embed key risks in a spatial context, and can inform political priorities and facilitate collaborative approaches. Although this approach assists in the move towards evidence based planning, the information contained within chapters 7, 8 and 9 argue that some resilient approaches will not be included within a typical spatial assessment of risk, and instead relate to individual perceptions and the specific social framework of a city.

The potential utility of risk has risen alongside a recognition of the difficulties in managing natural hazards via the framing concept of sustainability. In practice there has been a lack of synergy between how sustainability has been pursued within spatial planning and the wider subject of risks. For example, urban containment polices, perhaps one of the most ubiquitous and influential sustainability approaches of the twentieth century, has also been identified as helping to drive exposure and losses from natural disasters (Burby *et al.* 2001). In the same way that risk is socially constructed, so are related concepts such as sustainability and resilience. Indeed, within spatial planning resilience has mainly been constructed around a narrow focus on post-disaster planning relating to the built environment. To better link with sustainability and risk management, resilience should be focused on the need to *avoid* the need to recover and cope with a disaster by developing a strategy to proactively reduce the impact of future threats on both people and places.

Intervention further requires an agency to implement resilience and weight a variety of data within the context of the city. Spatial planning is well positioned in this regard as it is an effective mechanism to influence the market, the built environment and instigate a more risk orientated approach. Guy and Marvin (1999) draw attention to the 'cacophony of voices' of the multiplicity of actors and agencies with the potential to shape city development. These range from utility companies to architects to environmental groups; each challenging the construction and interpretation of sustainability and pursuing varied urban futures. The agents who have the ability to act on behalf of cities in this area are numerous, but amongst the foremost are designers and planners as they hold the main power over future development within urban areas. Other key stakeholders include developers, water and sewerage providers, industry, the construction sector, government and, of course, the public.

An advantage in promoting a water resilient city as an aim for spatial planning is that resilience does not have any specific agenda beyond the pursuit of reduced hazard, vulnerability or exposure. Therefore, different patterns of urbanism or growth remain a viable option, provided they meet caveats related to risk or uncertainty. This provides a refreshing degree of flexibility and an onus on creative responses for differing settlement patterns, geographical constraints and development requirements. Although this elasticity is a clear advantage, it also provides a significant level of complexity and it is here that a concentration on the principles of risk can provide a much clearer focus. A continuation of the current strategy, and cities experiencing a rising level of detrimental water impacts, in effect, represents a market failure, with, for example, insurance unobtainable in many areas, constraints in water use and repeated state intervention necessary. In addition, the development of a different model of the city would not necessarily harm investment and growth; and an alternative exposure to risk may even enhance it. Although there is considerable inertia in the built environment, the success of any paradigm shift away from predominately engineered protection towards more strategic management needs to link an evidence base to an agency with power.

The uncertainties evident in this research suggest that the subject area is linked to post-normal science (Funtowicz and Ravetz 1985), having both potentially severe consequences and a degree of uncertainty. However, this model conflicts with the conventional science policy paradigm, whereby science would initially accurately quantify problems, thereby providing an evidence base to influence politicians and policy makers to act. In practice certainty may not be attainable, the facts required to act will not be forthcoming, and, consequently, risk exposure may be perpetuated. The rise of risks within urban areas presents a real challenge for achieving a high level of certainty, as in practice not only do we lack the required data, but the sheer complexity of the city also inhibits a convenient simplification of causal links. The failure to reach a consensus over international approaches to climate change provides perhaps the best example of uncertain post-normal science conflicting with long established policy making processes. Even though the science is more established and accepted, gaining agreement over international strategies is problematical.

Intervention in general may be linked with the moral concept of prudentialism, as opposed to the twentieth century ascent of neoliberalism, within which the market may determine the acceptable exposure to risk. As outlined previously, this can be a flawed process, as in practice there is a separation between the actors and agencies obtaining the profit and experiencing the costs. Recent policy shifts have emphasized that this inevitably places a responsibility on planners to act, to pursue sustainable risk management, and where evidence is uncertain, to take a precautionary approach to limit detrimental impacts. But what should those measures entail? The final section of the book was designed to delineate a few examples, to illustrate how the three aspects of risk; hazard, exposure and vulnerability, can each provide a separate, but complementary, agenda for a city more resilient to too much, or too little, water.

Planning for a sustainable future

The Spanish philosopher George Santayana stated that: 'those who cannot learn from history are condemned to repeat it'. The extensive relevance of the saying has given it a wide utility and it is now a well known axiom. This book frequently touches upon the past, especially where insight and endeavour have enabled significant advances with lasting intra-generational benefits. The heroic engineering achievements of the Romans or Victorians provide key examples of this process and the scale and impacts of the problems emerging in the twenty-first century may require similar, innovative approaches. It may be that we should revert to a more Victorian, foresighted approach – where we invest in the present, but with the knowledge that the measures will bring extended benefits over the long term, not just the short. There are times when governments do pursue this policy, but all too often society has to wait until suffering a single catastrophic event, or multiple insidious impacts, before any action occurs.

We are living in an age of more visible risk, where individuals and govern-ments have ever more knowledge about the possibility of a seemingly growing number of undesirable events, such as flu pandemics, terrorism, drought or flood risk (Cabinet Office 2008). The unpacking of urban hazards and drivers has helped reveal the subtleties regarding the risk of water based impacts. The threats are such that they cannot necessarily be viewed from either a narrow human rationality that seeks to command the natural world, or an equally restrictive view of environmental determinism: in reality risk management has links with both aspects. Indeed, after drawing attention to a number of flaws in the dominant culture of controlling nature, this book may have a surprising message by suggesting that we still need to intervene, and perhaps more so than ever before. To better manage the impacts we do however need to re-evaluate how we do this; in effect we need to do it better.

Moreover, the problem is not necessarily a classical environmental trade off between the welfare of present or future generations, as the climate change or sustainability arguments are frequently posited. Rather, the issue is about improving the well-being and success of people now, those relying on the success of the city in ten years time, and those in the more distant future. The argument is not extolling a reduction in consumption or other hairshirt sacrifice by current citizens; rather, that there are useful framing mechanisms connected with risk, adaptation and resilience that should influence decisions. These concepts should not obfuscate what should be a simple aim however: to have the right amount of water, in the right place, at the right time.

Although the overall effects of a change in planning policies and guidance may take decades to be seen, knowledge regarding the potential future impacts of water upon cites has been quantified on a much longer timescale and the possible social, economic and environmental damages for the long term are frighteningly large. We should also keep in mind that the most sustainable way to manage risk is simply to avoid it; therefore, the message here is a positive one, setting out the principles for a long term vision of the city based on the growing need to manage water. There is no intention to provide a definitive checklist of water resilience features; rather, to illustrate potential examples within the three elements of risk. Furthermore, if these measures are applied strategically; there is potential to make a larger system resilient; a precursor of moving from a resilient building towards a resilient city.

Bibliography

ABC News (2005) *Most Say God Not A Factor in Hurricanes*. Online: http://www.abc news.go.com/Politics/PollVault/story?id=1174220&page=1 (accessed 5 August 2009).

Abercrombie, P. (1933) *Town and Country Planning*, London: Butterworth.

Adams, J. (1995) *Risk*, London: University College London Press.

Adger, W.N. (2000) 'Social and ecological resilience: are they related?'. *Progress in Human Geography*, 24 (3), 347–64.

Adger, W.N. (2006) 'Vulnerability', *Global Environmental Change*, 16: 268–81.

Allan, J.A. (1998) 'Virtual water: a strategic resource – global solutions to regional deficits', *Ground Water*, 36 (4): 545–6.

Allenby, B. and Fink, J. (2005) 'Towards inherently secure and resilient societies', *Science*, 309: 1034–6.

Ashworth, G. (1987) *The Lost Rivers of Manchester*, Altrincham, Cheshire: Willow Publishing.

Ashworth, W. (1982) *Nor Any Drop to Drink*, New York: Summit.

Beck, U. (1992) *Risk Society: Towards a New Modernity*, London: Sage.

—— (1999) *Work Risk Society*, Cambridge: Polity Press.

Benedict, M.A. and McMahon, E. (2006) *Green Infrastructure: Linking Landscapes and Communities*, Washington, DC: Island Press.

Bernstein, P.L. (1998) *Against the Gods: The Remarkable Story of Risk*, New York: John Wiley and Sons.

Best, G. (1979) *Mid-Victorian Britain 1851–75*, London: Fontana Press.

Blaikie, P.M., Cannon, T., Davis, I. and Wisner, B. (1994) *At Risk: Natural Hazards, People's Vulnerability, and Disasters*, London: Routledge.

Bosher, L. (ed.) (2008) *Hazards and the Built Environment: Attaining Built In Resilience*, London: Routledge.

Britannia (2007) *Anglo Saxon Chronicles*. Online: http://www.britannia.com/history/docs/1014–17.html (accessed 12 October 2009).

Burby, R.J., Nelson, A.C., Parker, D. and Handmer, J. (2001) 'Urban containment policy and exposure to natural hazards: is there a connection?', *Journal of Environmental Planning and Management*, 44 (4): 475–90.

Cabinet Office (2008) *The National Security Strategy of the United Kingdom: Security in an Interdependent World*, London: Cabinet Office.

Carson, R. (1962) *Silent Spring*, London: Penguin.

Chandler, T. (1987) *Four Thousand Years of Urban Growth: An Historical Census*, New York: Edwin Mellen.

CLG (2007) *Improving the Flood Performance of New Buildings: Flood Resilient Construction*, London: RIBA Publishing.

Comprehensive Assessment of Water Management in Agriculture (2007) *Water for Food, Water for Life: A Comprehensive Assessment of Water Management in Agriculture*, London: Earthscan; and Colombo: International Water Management Institute.

Crichton, D. (1999) 'The risk triangle', 102–3, in Ingleton, J. (ed.), *Natural Disaster Management*, London: Tudor Rose.

Dale, T. and Carter V.G. (1955) *Topsoil and Civilization*, Norman, OK: University of Oklahoma Press.

Dawson, R. (2007) 'Re-engineering cities: a framework for adaptation to global change', *Philosophical Transactions of the Royal Society A*, 365: 3085–98.

Defra (2004) *Making Space for Water: Developing a New Government Strategy for Flood and Coastal Erosion Risk Management in England*, London: Defra.

—— (2008) *Future Water: The Government's Water Strategy for England*, London: Defra.

—— (2009a) *Surface Water Management Plan Technical Guidance*, London: Defra.

—— (2009b) *Honeybees in Crisis*. Online: http://www.defra.gov.uk/foodfarm/policy/farminglink/articles/0904/honeybees.htm (accessed 2 November 2009).

Department of Communities and Local Government (2006) *Planning Policy Statement 25: Development and Flood Risk*, December, London: DCLG.

Diamond, J. (2005) *Collapse: How Societies Choose to Fail or Survive*, London: Penguin.

Doe, R. (2006) *Extreme Floods: A History in a Changing Climate*, Stroud: Sutton Publishing.

Douglas, I., Garvin, S., Lawson, N., Richards, J., Tippett, J. and White, I. (2010) 'Urban pluvial flooding: a qualitative case study of cause, effect and non-structural mitigation', *Journal of Flood Risk Management* 3: 112–25.

Douglas, M. (1992) *Risk and Blame: Essays in Cultural Theory*, London: Routledge.

Douglas, M. and Wildavsky, A. (1983) *Risk and Culture: An Essay on the Selection of Technical and Environmental Dangers*, Berkeley, CA: University of California Press.

Dovers S.R. and Handmer, J.W. (1992) 'Uncertainty, sustainability and change', *Global Environmental Change*, 2 (4): 262–76.

Economist (1976a) 'How to save industry from the drought', August 21: 79.

—— (1976b) 'Why no rain gods?', August 21: 12.

Ehrlich, P. and Ehrlich, A. (1990) *The Population Explosion*, London: Hutchinson.

EM-DAT (2008) *EM-DAT: The OFDA/CRED International Disaster Database*, Université Catholique de Louvain, Brussels. Online: http://www.emdat.be/ (accessed 2 November 2009).

Engels, F. [1845] (1987) *The Condition of the Working Class in England*, London: Penguin.

Environment Agency (2005) *Living with the Risk: The Floods in Boscastle and North Cornwall, 16th August 2004*, Exeter: Environment Agency.

—— (2009a) *Flooding in England: A National Assessment of Flood Risk*, Bristol: Environment Agency.

—— (2009b) *Water for People and the Environment: Water Resources Strategy for England and Wales*, Bristol: Environment Agency.

—— (2009c) *Thames Estuary 2100: Managing Flood Risk through London and the*

Thames Estuary. TE2100 Plan Consultation Document, London: Environment Agency.

Environment Agency and CIRIA (2001) *Damage limitation: How to Make Your Home Flood Resistant*, Bristol: Environment Agency.

European Commission (2009) *White Paper: Adapting to Climate Change: Towards a European Framework for Action*, Brussels: European Union.

European Environment Agency (2003) *European Environment Agency Indicator Fact Sheet: Water Use Efficiency (in Cities): Leakage*. Online: http://themes.eea.eu.int/Specific_media/water/indicators/WQ06,2003.1001/ (accessed 7 July 2009).

—— (2004) *Impacts of Europe's Changing Climate: An Indicator Based Assessment*, Copenhagen: European Environment Agency.

—— (2006) *Urban Sprawl in Europe: The Ignored Challenge*, EEA Report 10/2006, Copenhagen: European Environment Agency.

—— (2009) *CSI 018: Use of Freshwater Resources – Assessment, Published January*. Online: http://themes.eea.europa.eu/IMS/ISpecs/ISpecification20041007131848/IAssessment1197887395187/view_content (accessed 7 July 2009).

European Union (2007) *Directive 2007/60/EC: On the Assessment and Management of Flood Risks*. Online: http://eur-lex.europa.eu/LexUriServ/LexUriServ.do?uri=OJ:L: 2007:288:0027:0034:EN:PDF (accessed 8 July 2009).

Evans, E., Ashley, R., Hall, J., Penning-Rowsell, E., Saul, A., Sayers, P., Thorne, C. and Watkinson, A. (2004) *Foresight. Future Flooding. Scientific Summary, Volume 1: Future Risks and Their Drivers*, London: Office of Science and Technology.

Fickling, D. (2004) 'Plunder Down Under', *Guardian*, 8 November. Online: http://www.guardian.co.uk/world/2004/nov/08/australia.worlddispatch (accessed 6 July 2009).

Foster, S.S.D. and Chilton, P.J. (2003) 'Groundwater: the processes and global significance of aquifer degradation', *Philosophical Transactions of the Royal Society*, 358: 1957–72.

Funtowicz, S.O. and Ravetz, J.R. (1985) 'Three types of risk assessment: a methodological analysis', 217–31, in Whipple, C. and Covello, V.T. (eds), *Risk Analysis in the Private Sector*, New York: Plenum.

Gallopin, G.C. (2006) 'Linkages between vulnerability, resilience, and adaptive capacity', *Global Environmental Change*, 16: 293–303.

Gandy, M. (2004) 'Rethinking urban metabolism: water, space and the modern city', *City*, 8 (3): 363–79.

Geddes, P. (1904) *City Development, a Study of Parks, Gardens and Culture-institutes: A Report to the Carnegie Dunfermline Trust*, Bournville, Birmingham: Saint George Press.

—— (1915) *Cities in Evolution*, London: Williams and Norgate.

Gentleman, A. (2007) 'Architects aren't ready for an urbanised planet', *International Herald Tribune*, 20 August, 11–29.

Gill, S. (2006) 'Climate change and urban greenspace', unpublished PhD thesis, University of Manchester. Online: http://www.ginw.co.uk/resources/Susannah_PhD_Thesis_full_final.pdf (accessed 9 November 2009).

Gill, S., Handley, J., Ennos, R. and Pauleit, S. (2007) 'Adapting cities for climate change: the role of the green infrastructure', *Built Environment*, 33 (1): 115–33.

Girardet, H. (1999) *Creating Sustainable Cities*, Totnes, Devon: Green Books.

Glacken, C.J. (1967) *Traces on the Rhodian Shore*, Berkeley, CA: University of California Press.

Gleick, P. (2008) *Environment and Security Water Conflict Chronology*. Online: http://www.worldwater.org/chronology.html (accessed 22 July 2009).

—— (2009) 'Wake up: here is what a real water crisis looks like', *San Francisco Chronicle*, 2 July. Online: http://www.sfgate.com/cgi-bin/blogs/gleick/detail?blogid=104&entry_id=42949 (accessed 21 July 2009).

Godschalk, D. (2003) 'Urban hazard mitigation: creating resilient cities', *Natural Hazards Review*, 4 (3): 136–43.

Government Office for the North West (2008) *The North West of England Plan: Regional Spatial Strategy to 2021*, Norwich: The Stationery Office.

Graves, H.M. and Phillipson, M.C. (2000) *Potential Implications of Climate Change in the Built Environment*, East Kilbride: Building Research Establishment (BRE), Centre for Environmental Engineering.

Gray, J. (2003) *Straw Dogs: Thoughts on Humans and Other Animals*, London: Granta Books.

—— (2009) *Gray's Anatomy: Selected Writings*, London: Allen Lane.

Green, R. (2008) 'Informal settlements and natural hazard vulnerability in rapid growth cities', 218–37, in Bosher, L. (ed.), *Hazards and the Built Environment: Attaining Built in Resilience*, London: Routledge.

Guha-Sapir, D., Hargitt, D. and Hoyois, P. (2004) *Thirty Years of Natural Disasters 1974–2003: The Numbers*, Louvain: Presses Universitaires de Louvain.

Guy, S. and Marvin, S. (1999) 'Understanding sustainable cities: competing urban futures', *European Urban and Regional Studies*, 6 (3): 268–75.

Hall, P. (2002a) *Cities of Tomorrow*, Oxford: Blackwell Publishing.

—— (2002b) *Urban and Regional Planning*, London: Routledge.

Halliday, S. (2004) *Water: A Turbulent History*, Stroud: Sutton Publishing.

Hansson, S.O. (2009) 'A Philosophical Perspective on Risk', 43–52, in Lofstedt, R.E. and Boholm, A. (eds), *The Earthscan Reader on Risk*, London: Earthscan.

Harvey, J. and Jowsey, E. (2004) *Urban Land Economics*, Basingstoke: Palgrave Macmillan.

Hawking, S. (2001) *The Universe in a Nutshell*, London: Bantam Press.

Hennayake, N. (2006) *Culture, Politics and Development in Post Colonial Sri Lanka*, Lanham, MD: Lexington Books.

Herrington, P. (2007) *Waste Not, Want Not? Water Tariffs for Sustainability*, Godalming: WWF-UK.

Hoekstra, A.Y. and Chapagain, A.K. (2007) 'Water footprint of nations: water use by people as a function of their consumption pattern', *Water Resource Management*, 21 (1): 35–48.

Holling, C.S. (1973) 'Resilience and stability of ecological systems', *Annual Review of Ecology and Systematics*, 4: 1–23.

Homer-Dixon, T. (2000) *The Ingenuity Gap*, London: Jonathan Cape.

Hough, M. (2006) *Cities and Natural Process*, Abingdon: Routledge.

House of Lords Science and Technology Committee (2006) *Water Management: Minutes of Evidence*, London: The Stationery Office.

Howard, E. (1902) *Garden Cities of To-morrow*, London: Swan Sonnenstein.

Hulme, M. (2009) *Why We Disagree about Climate Change*, Cambridge: Cambridge University Press.

Hulme, M., Turnpenny, J. and Jenkins, G. (2002) *Climate Change Scenarios for the United Kingdom: The UKCIP 02 Briefing Report*, Norwich: Tyndall Centre for Climate Change Research, University of East Anglia.

Huxley, A. (1932) *Brave New World*, London: Chatto and Windus.

Institution of Civil Engineers (2001) *Learning to Live with Rivers*, London: Institution of Civil Engineers.

IPCC (2001) *Climate Change 2001: The Scientific Basis. Contribution of Working Group I to the Third Assessment Report of the Intergovernmental Panel on Climate Change*, Cambridge: Cambridge University Press.

—— (2007a) *Climate Change 2007: Synthesis Report. Contribution of Working Groups I, II and III to the Fourth Assessment Report of the Intergovernmental Panel on Climate Change*, Geneva: IPCC.

—— (2007b) *Climate Change 2007: Impacts, Adaptation and Vulnerability*, Cambridge: Cambridge University Press.

James, H. [1888] (1989) *London Stories and Other Writings*, Padstow: Tabb House.

Jenks, M. and Dempsey, N. (2006) *Future Forms and Design for Sustainable Cities*, Oxford: Elsevier.

Jenks, M., Burton, K. and Williams, K. (eds) (1996) *The Compact City: A Sustainable Urban Form?* Oxford: E. & F.N. Spon.

JP Morgan (2008) *Watching water: A Guide to Evaluating Corporate Risks in a Thirsty world*. Online: http://pdf.wri.org/jpmorgan_watching_water.pdf (accessed 22 July 2009).

Jung, H.Y. and Jung, P. (1993) 'Francis Bacon's philosophy of nature: a postmodern critique', *The Trumpeter*, 10 (3): 86–9.

Kaplan, H.B. (1999) 'Toward an understanding of resilience: a critical review of definitions and models', 17–84, in Glantz, M.D. and Johnson, J.L. (eds), *Resilience and Development*, New York: Kluwer Academic.

Kenway, S.J., Turner, G.M., Cook, S. and Baynes, T. (2008) *Water-energy Futures for Melbourne: The Effect of Water Strategies, Water Use and Urban Form*, Canberra: CSIRO, Water for a Healthy Country National Research Flagship.

Kilvington, J. (2009) '900,000 tonnes of sewage spilled into Thames after heavy rain', *Kingston Guardian*, 14 July. Online: http://www.kingstonguardian.co.uk/news/4491460.900_000_tonnes_of_sewage_spilled_into_Thames_after_heavy_rain/ (accessed 14 July 2009).

Klein, R.J.T., Nicholls R.J. and Thomalla, F. (2004) 'Resilience to natural hazards: how useful is this concept?', *Environmental Hazards*, 5: 35–45.

Knight, F.H. (1921) *Risk, Uncertainty and Profit*, Chicago, IL: University of Chicago Press.

Laurence, C. (2004) 'Five years of drought force Las Vegas to tear up its grass', *Daily Telegraph*, 23 May. Online: http://www.telegraph.co.uk/news/world news/northamerica/usa/1462635/Five-years-of-drought-force-Las-Vegas-to-tear-up-its-grass.html (accessed 27 March 2009).

Lupton, D. (1999) *Risk*, London: Routledge.

Lynas, M. (2007) *Six Degrees*, London: Harper Perennial.

McEvoy, D., Lindley, S. and Handley, J. (2006) 'Adaptation and mitigation in urban areas: synergies and conflicts', *Municipal Engineer*, 159: 185–91.

McHarg, I.L. (1969) *Design with Nature*, New York: Natural History Press.

Manyena, S.B. (2006) 'The concept of resilience revisited', *Disasters*, 30 (4): 434–50.

Marsh, G.P. (1864) *Man and Nature; or, Physical Geography as Modified by Human Action*, New York: Charles Scribner.

Marvin, S., Graham, S. and Guy, S. (1998) 'Cities, regions and privatised utilities', *Progress in Planning*, 51: 91–169.

Meadows, D.H., Meadows D.L., Randers, J. and Behrens III, W.W. (1972) *The Limits to Growth: A Report for the Club of Rome's Project on the Predicament of Mankind*, New York: Universe Books.

Meteorological Office (2009) *UK 1971–2000 Rainfall Averages*. Online: http://www. metoffice.gov.uk/climate/uk/averages/19712000/areal/uk.html (accessed 6 July 2009).

Millennium Ecosystem Assessment (2005) *Ecosystems and Human Well-being: Current State and Trends*, Washington, DC: Island Press.

Ministry of Transport, Public Works and Water Management (2006) *Spatial Planning Key Decision: 'Room for the River'*. Online: http://www.ruimtevoorde rivier. nl/files/Files/brochures/EMAB%20PBK%20Engels.pdf (accessed 1 July 09).

Modelski, G. (2003) *World Cities: –3000 to 2000*, Washington, DC: Faros 2000.

Mumford, L. (1961) *The City in History: Its Origins, Its Transformations, and Its Prospects*, London: Secker and Warburg.

Munich Re (2008) *Natural Catastrophes 2007: Analyzes, Assessment, Positions*, Berlin: Münchener Rückversicherungs Gesellschaft. Online: http://www.munichre.com/ publications/302–05699_en.pdf (accessed 15 May 2009).

National Archives (2006) *The 1976 Drought: Appointment of Dennis Howell as Co-ordinating Minister; Legislative Proposal*. Online: http://www.nationalarchives.gov. uk/releases/2006/december/drought.htm (accessed 6 July).

National Audit Office (2001) *Inland Flood Defence*, London: The Stationery Office.

Norwich Union (2009) *Flood Resilient Project*. Online: http://www.flood resilienthome. com/index.htm (accessed 28 September 2009).

O'Brien, K., Quinlan, T. and Ziervogel, G. (2009) 'Vulnerability interventions in the context of multiple stressors: lessons from the Southern Africa Vulnerability Initiative (SAVI)', *Environmental Science and Policy*, 12: 23–32.

O'Brien, K., Eriksen, S., Nygaard, L. and Schjolden, A. (2007) 'Why different interpretations of vulnerability matter in climate change discourses', *Climate Policy*, 7 (1): 73–88.

ODPM (2002) *Land Use Change in England to 2001*, London: ODPM.

—— (2005) *Planning Policy Statement 1: Delivering Sustainable Development*, London: ODPM.

O'Keefe, P., Westgate K. and Wisner, B. (1976) 'Taking the naturalness out of natural disasters', *Nature*, 260: 566–7.

Parker, D. (1995) 'Floodplain development policy in England and Wales', *Applied Geography*, 15 (4): 341–63.

Pauleit, S. and Duhme, F. (2000) 'Assessing the environmental performance of land cover types for urban planning', *Landscape and Urban Planning*, 52 (1): 1–20.

Pearce, F. (2006a) *What Happens When the Rivers Run Dry?*, London: Transworld Publishers.

Pearce, J. (2006b) *Small Is Still Beautiful*, Wilmington, DE: ISI Books.

Pelling, M. (1997) 'What determines vulnerability to floods: a case study of Georgetown, Guyana', *Environment and Urbanization*, 9 (1): 203–26.

—— (2003) *The Vulnerability of Cities: Natural Hazards and Social Resilience*, London: Earthscan.

Pepper, D. (1996) *Modern Environmentalism*, London: Routledge.

Pickett, S.T.A., Cadenasso, M.L. and Grove, J.M. (2004) 'Resilient cities: meaning, models, and metaphor for integrating the ecological, socio-economic, and planning realms', *Landscape and Urban Planning*, 69: 369–84.

Pitt, M. (2007) *Learning Lessons from the 2007 Floods: An Independent Review by Sir Michael Pitt*, London: Cabinet Office.

Reader, J. (2005) *Cities*, London: Vintage.

Reith, G. (2009) 'Uncertain times: the notion of "risk" and the development of modernity', 53–68, in Lofstedt, R.E. and Boholm, A. (eds), *The Earthscan Reader on Risk*, London: Earthscan.

Rodriguez, J., Vos, F., Below, R. and Guha-Sapir, D. (2009) *Annual Disaster Statistical Review 2008: The Numbers and Trends*, Melin: Jacoffsett Printers.

Royal Horticultural Society (2006) *Gardening Matters. Front Gardens: Are We Parking on Our Gardens? Do Driveways Cause Flooding?*, Online: <http://www.rhs. org.uk/RHS Website/files/88/8855ec1d-444b-4caf-97a6–801ce421b460.pdf> (accessed 7 July 2009).

Rydin, Y. (2003) *Urban and Environmental Planning in the UK*, Basingstoke: Palgrave Macmillan.

—— (2004) *Planning, Sustainability and Environmental Risks*, LSE and ERM New Horizons Project for ODPM. Online: http://www.communities.gov.uk/publications /corporate/planningsustainability (accessed 17 August 2009).

Satterthwaite, D. (2004) *The Earthscan Reader in Sustainable Cities*, London: Earthscan.

Scheuren, J-M., Le Polain de Waroux, O., Below, R. and Guha-Sapir, D. (2008) *Annual Disaster Statistical Review: The Numbers and Trends 2007*, Melin: Jacoffset Printers.

Scott Wilson and AGMA (2008) *Strategic Flood Risk Assessment for Greater Manchester*, Manchester: Scott Wilson.

Shaw, R., Colley, M. and Connell, R. (2007) *Climate Change Adaptation by Design: A Guide for Sustainable Communities*, London: TCPA.

Shukman, D. (2008) *Flood Risk Fear over Key UK Sites*. Online: http://news.bbc. co.uk/1/hi/uk_politics/7386383.stm (accessed 14 July).

Smit, B., Burton, I., Klein, R.J.T. and Street, R. (1999) 'The science of adaptation: a framework for assessment', *Mitigation and Adaptation Strategies for Global Change*, 4: 199–213.

Spengler, O. (1923) *The Decline of the West, Volume Two: Perspectives of World History*, London: Charles Allen and Unwin Ltd.

Stern, N. (2006) *The Economics of Climate Change: The Stern Review*, Cambridge: Cambridge University Press.

Storey, G., Tillotson, K. and Easson, A. (1993) *The Letters of Charles Dickens, 1853–1855*, Oxford: Clarendon House.

Tibaijuka, A. (2007) 'Keynote Address by the Under-Secretary-General of the United Nations, Executive Director UN-HABITAT at the International Conference towards Sustainable Global Health', Bonn, Germany 9–11 May. Online: http:// www.unhabitat.org/content.asp?cid=4776&catid=14&typeid=8&subMenuId=0 (accessed 2 November 2009).

—— (2009) 'Statement of the Executive Director of UN-HABITAT, Mrs. Anna Tibaijuka, on the occasion of the 25th Meeting of the UNEP Governing Council', Nairobi, Kenya, 17 February. Online. Available HTTP: http://www.unhabitat.org/ content.asp?cid=6221&catid=14&typeid=8&subMenuId=0 (accessed 2 November 2009).

Timmerman, P. (1981) *Vulnerability, Resilience and the Collapse of Society*, Toronto: Institute of Environmental Studies, University of Toronto.

Tully, S. (2000) 'Water, water everywhere: today companies like France's Suez are rushing to privatize water, already a $400 bn global business. They are betting that H2O will be to the 21st century what oil was to the 20th', *Fortune Magazine*, 15 May. Online: http://money.cnn.com/magazines/fortune/fortune_archive/2000/05/15/279789/index.htm (accessed 3 July 09).

United Nations (2002) *General Comment No. 15: The Right to Water*, E/C.12/2002/11, Geneva: United Nations.

—— (2005) *World Urbanization Prospects: The 2005 Revision*. Online: http://www.un.org/esa/population/publications/WUP2005/2005WUPHighlights_Final_Report.pdf (accessed 30 November 2009).

—— (2007) *World Population Prospects: The 2006 Revision*, New York: United Nations.

United Nations Development Programme (2006) *Human Development Report 2006*, New York: United Nations Development Programme.

United Nations Environment Programme (2008) *Vital Water Graphics: An Overview of the State of the World's Fresh and Marine Waters*, 2nd edn, Nairobi: UNEP.

UNEP/GRID-Arendal (2005) *Number of Flood Events by Continent and Decade since 1950*, UNEP/GRID-Arendal Maps and Graphics Library. Online: http://maps.grida.no/go/graphic/number-of-flood-events-by-continent-and-decade-since-1950 (accessed 28 May 2009).

UN-Habitat (2006) 'A new start: the paradox of crisis', *Habitat Debate*, 12 (4): December.

—— (2007) *Enhancing Urban Safety and Security: Global Reports on Human Settlements 2007*, London: Earthscan.

—— (2008) *State of the World's Cities 2008/2009: Harmonious Cities*, London: Earthscan.

—— (2009) *Global Report on Human Settlements 2009: Planning Sustainable Cities*, London: Earthscan.

United Nations International Strategy for Disaster Reduction Secretariat (2009) *2009 Global Assessment Report on Risk Reduction; Risk and Poverty in a Changing Climate*, Geneva: United Nations.

United Nations Population Fund (1996) *The State of World Population 1996: Changing Places: Population, Development and the Urban Future*, New York: United Nations Population Fund.

—— (2007) *State of the World Population 2007: Unleashing the Potential of Urban Growth*. Online: http://www.unfpa.org/swp/2007/presskit/pdf/sowp2007_eng.pdf (accessed 2 November 2009).

United Nations University (2004) 'Two billion people vulnerable to floods by 2050', News Release, 13 June. Online: http://www.unu.edu/news/ehs/floods.doc (accessed 18 May 2009).

UN-Water (2006) *Coping with Water Scarcity: A Strategic Issue and Priority for System-wide Action*, Geneva: UN-Water.

Unwin, R. (1909) *Town Planning in Practice*, London: Ernest Benn Ltd.

Vale, L.J. and Campanella, T.J. (eds) (2005) *The Resilient City*, Oxford: Oxford University Press.

Villarreal, E.L., Semadeni-Davies, A. and Bengtsson, L. (2004) 'Inner city stormwater control using a combination of best management practices', *Ecological Engineering*, 22: 279–98.

Von Storch, H. and Stehr, N. (2006) 'Anthropogenic climate change: a reason for concern since the 18th century and earlier', *Geografiska Annalar*, 88A (2): 107–13.

Wamsler, C. (2008) 'Managing urban disaster risk: analysis and adaptation frameworks for integrated settlement sustainable development programming for the urban poor', unpublished PhD thesis, Lund University: Sweden.

Watson-Watt, R.A. (1935) *Through the Weather House, or the Wind, the Rain and Six Hundred Miles Above*, London: Peter Davies.

Webb, W.P. (1931) *The Great Plains*, Boston, MA: Ginn and Co.

—— (1957) 'The American West: perpetual mirage', *Harper's Magazine*, May, 214: 25–31.

Werritty, A. (2005) 'Sustainable flood management: oxymoron or new paradigm?', *Area*, 38 (1): 16–23.

Wescoat, J.L. (2006) 'Gilbert Fowler White (1911–2006), wisdom in environmental geography', *Geographical Review*, 96 (4): 700–10.

Whiston Spirn, A. (1984) 'The granite garden: urban nature and human design', 113–15, in Wheeler, S.M. and Beatly, T. (eds) (2004), *The Sustainable Urban Development Reader*, London: Routledge.

White, G.F. (1945) *Human Adjustment to Floods*, Department of Geography Research Paper no. 29, Chicago, IL: University of Chicago Press.

White, I. (2005) 'Barriers to effective environmental planning: the case of sustainable drainage utilization within the planning system in England', unpublished PhD thesis, University of Manchester.

—— (2008) 'The absorbent city: urban form and flood risk management', *Proceedings of the Institution of Civil Engineers: Urban Design and Planning*, December (DP4): 151–61.

White, I. and Alarcon, A. (2009) 'Planning policy, sustainable drainage and surface water management: a case study of Greater Manchester, UK', *Built Environment*, 35 (4): 516–30.

White, I. and Howe, J. (2005) 'Unpacking barriers to sustainable urban drainage use, *Journal of Environmental Policy and Planning*, 7 (1): 27–43.

White, I. and Richards, J. (2007) 'Planning policy and flood risk: the translation of national guidance into local policy', *Planning, Practice and Research*, 22 (4): 513–34.

White, I., Kingston, R. and Barker, A. (2010) 'Participatory GIS for developing flood risk management policy options', *Journal of Flood Risk Management*, 3 (2): (in press).

Wilderer, P.A. (2007) 'Sustainable water resource management: the science behind the scene', *Sustainability Science*, 2 (1): 1–4.

Wilson, E.O. (1993) *The Diversity of Life*, London: Allen Lane.

—— (1998) *Consilience: The Unity of Knowledge*, London: Little Brown.

Wisner, B., Blaikie, P., Cannon, T. and Davis, I. (2004) *At Risk: Natural Hazards, People's Vulnerability and Disasters*, London: Routledge.

Wittfogel, K. (1957) *Oriental Despotism: A Comparative Study of Total Power*, New Haven, CT: Yale University Press.

Wong, P. (2008) 'Water for the future': Speech to the 4th Annual Australian Water Summit, Sydney Convention and Exhibition Centre, 29–30 April. Online: http://www.environment.gov.au/minister/wong/2008/pubs/sp20080429.pdf (accessed 6 July 09).

World Commission on Environment and Development (1987) *Our Common Future*, Oxford: Oxford University Press.

World Economic Forum (2009) *The Bubble Is Close to Bursting: A Forecast of the Main Economic and Geopolitical Water Issues Likely to Arise in the World during the Next Two Decades*, Geneva: World Economic Forum.

World Water Assessment Programme (2003) *Water for People: Water for Life*, Paris: UNESCO; and New York: Berghahn Books.

—— (2009) *The United Nations World Water Development Report 3: Water in a Changing World*, Paris: UNESCO; and London: Earthscan.

WWF (Worldwide Fund for Nature) (2008) *UK Water Footprint: The Impact of the UK's Food and Fibre Consumption on Global Water Resources, Volume One*, Godalming: WWF-UK.

Wynne, B. (2009) 'Uncertainty and environmental learning: reconceiving science and policy in the preventative paradigm', 295–313, in Lofstedt, R.E. and Boholm, A. (eds), *The Earthscan Reader on Risk*, London: Earthscan.

Wynne-Jones, J. (2007) 'Floods are judgment on society, say bishops', *Daily Telegraph*, 1 July. Online: http://www.telegraph.co.uk/news/uknews/1556131/Floods-are-judgment-on-society-say-bishops.html (accessed 13 July 09).

Index

Page numbers in *italics* denote a table/figure

Pacioli Puzzle 91
Parakramabahu the Great, King 3–4
partnership approach 118, 143
Pascal, Blaise 91
peak oil 67
peak water 67
Pearce, J. 28
Pelling, M. 18
permeable paving 130
Phoenix (Arizona) 73
planning 11–12, 98; and control of
    water 43–4; key aims of 105; master
    11–12, 109, 120
Plato 25
Pliny the Elder 25, 65
pluvial flooding 54–5
population: growth of 20–1, *21*, 73,
    94; land use and growth of 22–4;
    relationship between resource use
    and 25–6, 28–9
poverty: and cities 172
precautionary principle 63, 89, 99,
    111, 150
precipitation 13–14; capturing and
    storing of 130, 136, 139, 150, 153;
    and climate change 23, 34, 90, 126;
    contribution to flooding 49, 54;
    interaction with surface of the city
    127, 128–9, 135; management of
    129; term 49; using records of to
    calculate flood-risk areas 87, 91
probability 91, 102
progress, and nature 9–11
Project Popeye 81

quality of life 4–5, 104

rainfall *see* precipitation
recurrence intervals: and flooding 45,
    62–3
reservoirs 136, 152, 176
resilience 17–18, 19, 88, 89, 93, 94,
    95, 97–100, 102, 106–10, 118,
    182, 183–4; deconstructing 96–7;
    dual connotations of 108–9; and
    exposure 144–56; and hazard
    125–43; holistic definition of
    99–100; and infrastructure 138–40;
    linking with cultural factors 120;
    reasons for importance of 102; and
    risk 96–7, 108–9, 118, 121; and
    spatial planning 97–100, 102; and
    sustainable development 99; and
    vulnerability 96, 97, 157–71

resource use: relationship between
    population and 25–6, 28–9
retention pond 130
retrofitting 170
Richardson, Lewis 13
Rio Grande 75
risk 90–4, 101–2, 106–8, 120, 182;
    adapting to urban 4–5; conceptual
    framework of 108–11; constituent
    aspects of 94–5, 102; definitions
    95; evolution of 90–2; framing
    concept of 88–9; generic equation
    of 95; influence of insurance
    and legal industries 92, 101; and
    mitigation and adaptation 108–11,
    110; perception of 100–1; and
    resilience 17–18, 96–7, 108–9, 118,
    121; scientization of 91; as socially
    and culturally constructed 92–3,
    101; and spatial planning 97–100,
    102; and uncertainty 111–12;
    using of as basis for intervention
    126
risk management 45, 94, 101–3, 109,
    148, 155, 176; addressing high levels
    of uncertainty in 111; development
    of within society 101; factors
    important to 47–8; flood *see* flood
    risk management; from land use
    perspective 117; inhibiting of 142–3;
    and resilience 17–18, 121, 183; shift
    in towards consumers 93–4
Romans 25, 65, 69
Royal Horticultural Society 55
Royal Society 89
Rumfeld, Donald 97–8
runoff 44, 50–1, 54, 55, 97, 99, 109,
    119, 129; effect of climate change on
    127, *127*; and green spaces 135; and
    SUDS 130–2
Rydin, Y. 111

Sale Water Park (Manchester) 135
Salt, Titus 11
sandy soils 114, 136, 150, 178
Santayana, George 185
science 10
Scotland 52
sea levels: rise in 34, 52–3
sewers 54–5, 61
Shelley, Percy Bysshe: *Ozymandias* 3
shipping 91
Sinclair, Upton 105
Sinhalese 3

Smart Growth 5
Smit, B. 109
social inequalities: tackling of 168
soft infrastructure 129–32
soil 54, 114, 128, 139, 166; clay 114,
    132, 150; sandy 114, 136, 150, 178
Soleri, Paulo 11
source-pathway-receptor model 49, 62,
    148
Spengler, O.: *The Decline of the West*
    181
Spirn, Whiston 10–11
sprawl 7, 12, 23, 72
Sri Lanka 3–4
Stern Review 34, 93, 142
Stern, Sir Nicholas 34
stormwater management 42, 43, 61,
    69
Strabo 69
strategic city planning 11–13
SUDS (sustainable urban drainage
    system) 129–33, *131*, 134, 138, 139,
    143; application of 132–3; barriers
    against implementation 132; main
    abilities 130–1; numbers of 132
Sumer 7
surface water 46, 113; flooding from
    54–8, 140, *141*, 182; and green
    spaces 135;
surface water management 62, 113,
    128–9, 138; information needed in
    113–14; problems associated with
    128–9; and SUDS *see* SUDS
sustainability 15, 26, 28, 88, 89, 183;
    and cities 12–13, 172–86
sustainable development 28, 88–9, 99,
    106, 176
sustainable urban drainage systems *see*
    SUDS
Swale 130
Symons, George James 14, 91
Syracuse 4

Tarmacadam 14
technology: controlling of nature by
    7–8, 9; limits of in controlling water
    43
Tewkesbury 7, *8*, 155, 162
Thames 7, 61
Thames Barrier 4, 43, 50, 53, 140
Thames Estuary 2100 Project 53
Thoreau, Henry David: *Walden* 29
Timmerman, P. 96
Tomasi, Guiseppi: *The Leopard* 36

torpor 8
transportation: of water 75
tropical modernism 11
Tulsa (Oklahoma) 149

UN-Habitat 44, 165
uncertainty 88, 91, 92, 100, 102, 103,
    110–12, 121, 182
Unilever 77
United Nations 23, 27, 59, 66, 118
United Nations Population Fund 172
United States: floodplain occupation 50
Unwin, Raymond: *Town Planning in
    Practice* 125
Ur 7
urban containment policies 183
urban creep: flooding due to 55
Urban Heat Island effect 15
urban water cycle 54
urbanization 8, 18, 34, 35, 36, 54, 55,
    70, 94, 125; growth of 21–2, 23–4;
    impact of on natural disasters 14, 17,
    18; impact of on streamflow levels
    after a precipitation event 50–1, *51*
utility companies 71, 119

Vale, L.J. 148
Vikings 3
virtual water 76–80, 81, 82, 114, 115
vulnerability 89, 94, 95, 97, 99, 102,
    110, *110*, 157–71, 182; contextual
    160, 165–71; and exposure 146, 158,
    167; and feelings of powerlessness
    168, 169–70; managing 158–61;
    mapping of 166; outcome 160,
    161–5, 170; and people and
    communities 166–7; and resilience
    96, 97; subject to numerous stressors
    167, 170; targeting broader social
    drivers for 168–9

Wamsler, C. 95
water: availability distribution *68*; as
    central driver in development of
    cities 6; constraints to availability
    66; domestic use of 73–5, *74*, 153;
    exploitation of 65–6; and growth
    71–3; and humanity 181; influence
    of access to on nature of cities 71;
    international tensions over 75; as
    key driver for economic growth
    76; leakage problems 75, 139;
    reducing demand of 74, 153–4; total
    consumption 73; transport of 75;

use of by agriculture 74; virtual 76–80, 81, 82, 114, 115

water management 42, 81, 118–19, 141, 142, 147, 181–2; key influences on 9; recent and emerging shifts in 176–7, *177*; and spatial planning 100; *see also* stormwater management; surface water management

water metering 74, 154, 156, 176

water quality 67

water resilient city 149–50, 176; envisioning 177–9, *178*; knowledge and foundation of 113–16, *116*

water resources 114–15; maximizing 178

water scarcity 23, 64–83, 165, 176, 178; and the city 80–2; definition 66; distinction from floods 64–5; exposure to and addressing of 152–5; figures 67; and green infrastructure 135; impacts 80; increasing supply and decreasing demand 153–4; in Las Vegas 72, 81; and metering 74, 154, 156, 176; in Murray-Darling basin 66, 77, 81; scope of 66–9; and SUDS 130; threat to well-being of global economic system 78; and virtual

water use 76–80; vulnerability to 165; and water supply infrastructure 69–71, 72; *see also* drought

water stress 67, 77, 80–1

water supply infrastructure 69–71, 72

water treatment works 162

watercourses: flooding from 49–51, 53; problem of diffuse pollution in 61

Watson-Watt, Robert: *Through the Weather House* 13

weather 13–14 *see also* climate change

Webb, Walter Prescott 71–2

wetlands 53, 130–1, 139

White, Gilbert 49, 99, 102

Wildavsky, A. 96

Wilson, E.O. 179

Wisner, B. 98

World Commission on Environment and Development (WCED) 27

World Economic Forum 66, 78, 82

Wren, Sir Christopher 157–8, *159*

Wright, Frank Lloyd 11

Wynne, B. 100

Yellow River 66

zero water buildings 153, 156